AF541279

Globalization and Educational Innovations

Globalization and Educational Innovations

Prof. Surinder Pal Singh

RANDOM PUBLICATIONS
NEW DELHI (INDIA)

Globalization and Educational Innovations

ISBN 978-93-5111-479-6

Published in 2015 in India by

RANDOM PUBLICATIONS

4376-A/4B, Gali Murari Lal, Ansari Road
New Delhi-110 002
Phone : +9111-43580356, 011-23289044, 011-43142548
e-mail: sales@randompublications.com,
info@randompublications.com, randomexports@gmail.com

Reprinted 2021

Type Setting by : Friends Media, Delhi-110089
Digitally Printed at : Replika Press Pvt. Ltd.

Preface

The word innovation means the introduction of novelties, the alteration of what is established, a novel practice and a change in established methods. Generally, in the field of education to innovate is to create something new which markedly deviates from traditional practices which have been followed since a long time to impart education at different levels. Innovation is necessary in education because we are now in the middle of a big change of a new era. The changes involve all of the life aspects towards a new era which called globalization era.

Globalization refers to the trend toward countries joining together economically, through education, society and politics, and viewing themselves not only through their national identity but also as part of the world as a whole. Globalization is said to bring people of all nations closer together, especially through a common medium like the economy or the Internet. Globalization is expected to generate intensified competition among nations, particularly in the fields of economics, science and technology. In addition, the massive and extensive globalization process affects the changes of economic, political and social conditions. The structural shift of the economy generates new trends and challenges which in turn affect the education system. Therefore, there are needs to adapt education to the industrial needs of the community, as well as improve science and technology to reach competitive excellence. Many countries are engaged in education reform in order to develop the human resources necessary to remain competitive in the international marketplace.

The present book explains the status, issues and trends of educational innovations in this era of globalization. It will be very useful for educational administrators, researchers and for training institutions to sharpen their programmes and to make them relevant to the needy.

Author

Contents

1

Education in the Age of Globalization

Historic changes are transforming the lives of people in the developed countries and most developing ones. National economies and even national cultures are globalizing. Globalization means more competition, not just with other companies in the same city or the same region. Globalization also means that national borders do not limit a nation's investment, production, and innovation.

Everything, including relations among family and friends, is rapidly becoming organized around a much more compressed view of space and time. Companies in Europe, the United States, and Japan can produce chips in Singapore, keypunch data in India or the Peoples' Republic of China, out source clerical work to Ireland or Mexico, and sell worldwide, barely concerned about the long distances or the variety of cultures involved. Swatch now sells a watch that tells "Internet time," a continuous time that is the same everywhere in the world. Even children watching television or listening to radio are re-conceptualizing their "world," in terms of the meanings that they attach to music, the environment, sports, or race and ethnicity.

A global economy is not a world economy. That has existed since at least the sixteenth century. Rather, a global economy is one where strategic, core activities, including innovation, finance and corporate management, function on a planetary scale on real time. And this globality became possible only recently because of the technological infrastructure provided by improved telecommunication networks, information systems, including the Internet, microelectronics machinery, and computerized transportation systems. Today, as distinct from even a generation ago, capital, technology, management, information, and core markets are globalized.

Globalization together with new information technology and the innovative processes they foment are driving a revolution in the organization of work, the production of goods and services, relations among nations, and even local culture. No community is immune from the effects of this revolution. It is changing the very fundamentals of human relations and social life.

Two of the main bases of globalization are information and innovation, and they, in turn, are highly knowledge intensive. Internationalized and fast-growing information industries produce knowledge goods and services. Today's massive movements of capital depend on information, communication, and *knowledge* in global markets. And because knowledge is highly portable, it lends itself easily to globalization.

If knowledge is fundamental to globalization, globalization should also have a profound impact on the transmission of knowledge.. The effects are of two kinds. The first is that globalization increases the demand for education, especially university education, and this increases pressure on the whole system for higher quality schooling, often producing perverse educational consequences, particularly from the standpoint of equity. An important question for democratic societies and societies transitioning to democracy is whether higher quality education for all is necessarily consistent with individual-centric democracy, particularly in societies marked by deeply-rooted ethnic conflicts and weak states.

The second effect is that globalization produces a reaction. This reaction takes many forms, but it seems in the current historical conjuncture to be increasingly focused on ethnic-religious nationalism/regionalism. The implications of the reaction for the transmission of knowledge are also important. Ethnic-religious nationalism represents a search for an identity that is often the antithesis of globalism/internationalism and even individualism. In some cases (religious-based nationalism) it confronts the concept of globalized knowledge as interpreted by the West with a different form of globalized (universal) knowledge, namely religious fundamentalism. In other cases, it confronts globalized knowledge with localized notions of knowledge/identity.

Why does globalization increase the demand for education and for educational quality? The answer lies in two parts. The first is economic: rising payoffs to higher education in a global, science based, knowledge intensive economy make university training more of a "necessity" to get "good" jobs. This, in turn, changes the stakes at lower levels of schooling, and drastically changes the function of secondary school. The second part is socio-political: demographics (the changing family) and democratic ideals increase pressure on universities to provide access to groups that traditionally have not attended university.

Globalized Markets and the Globalization of Skills

Governments in a global economy need to stimulate investment, including, in most countries, foreign capital and increasingly knowledge intensive capital, which means providing a ready supply of skilled labor. This translates into pressure to increase the average level of education in the labor force. The payoff to higher levels of education is rising worldwide as a result of the shifts of economic production to knowledge-intensive products and processes, as well as because governments implement policies that increase income inequality. Rising relative incomes for higher educated labor increases the demand for university education, pushing governments to expand their higher education systems, and, correspondingly, to increase the number of secondary school graduates ready to attend post-secondary. In countries, such as those in North Africa and the Middle East, that were previously resistant to providing equal access to education for young women, increased competition in product markets and the need for more highly educated labor (including the expansion of the education system itself) tends to expand women's educational opportunities.

In the past fifty years, most countries have undergone rapid expansion of their primary and secondary education systems. This is not universally true. But thanks to a generalized ideology that basic education should be available to children as a right, even financial constraints in many debt-ridden countries, such as those in Latin America, did not prevent them from increasing access to basic and even secondary education.

The Soviet Union and the nations it controlled, as well as China, Cuba, and Vietnam, all organized economically and politically under Communist regimes, made especially large investments in education and produced highly schooled populations even in previously illiterate regions, such as Central

Asia. The Communists not only expanded educational systems, but also increased the quality of the education in terms of teaching math and language skills. Whatever the reasons for this educational expansion, when these societies opened up to establish market economies and, in some cases, became politically democratic, they entered the new era with relatively highly skilled labor forces and highly literate populations.

University education has also expanded in most of the world's societies but, given the bias of global demand for the higher educated, the tendency is to push up rates of return to investment in higher education relative to the payoffs to investing in primary and secondary schooling. Rates of return to higher levels of education are also pushed up by structural adjustment policies. These tend to favor those with higher skill levels hooked into the export sector and the multinational companies. Estimated rates of return in countries such as Hong Kong, the Republic of Korea, and Argentina, as well as in a number of the OECD countries, show that rates of return to university education are often as high or higher than to either secondary or primary. Furthermore, some of these same studies were able to measure rates of return for several different years in the 1970s, 1980s, and 1990s. They suggest that rates of return to university have risen *relative* to primary and secondary rates. This is certainly the case in the former Communist countries, where university education was not highly rewarded before the 1990s, and now increasingly unequal incomes favor university graduates. Rising rates of return to higher education relative to lower levels of schooling also characterize many countries where measured rates to investment in university remain lower than to investment in primary and secondary.

Rates of return to higher levels of schooling increase not necessarily because the real incomes of university graduates are rising in *absolute* terms. Real incomes of university graduates could stay constant or even fall but, if the incomes of secondary and primary graduates fall more than those of workers with higher education, the rate of return to higher education rises and pressure on the higher education system increases. Many years ago, Mark Blaug, Richard Layard and Maureen Woodhall studied the paradox of Indian universities. Graduates seemed to suffer high rates of unemployment, yet the demand for university education continued unabated. They found that although the rate of unemployment was, indeed, high among university graduates, it was even higher among secondary school graduates. This helped push secondary school graduates to go on to university. In the past 25 years in the United States, the real incomes of male college graduates have risen very slowly, but the real incomes of male high school graduates have fallen sharply, again raising the college income premium and increasing enrollment in higher education.

Globalization may therefore benefit university graduates only in *relative* terms, but the implications for general educational investment strategies are the same as if university graduates' incomes were rising more rapidly than incomes of those young people with less schooling. By increasing the *relative* demand for university graduates more rapidly than universities can expand their supply, globalization puts continuous pressure on the educational system to expand.

Yet, there is another side to this coin. Many analysts focus on the fact that globalization is *reducing* demand for unskilled and semi-skilled labor, that the new technology may be reducing demand for labor as a whole, and that countries have to compete for this shrinking demand by keeping wages low. These analysts claim that this is the reason that real wages are falling (or growing very slowly) in most countries.

This is an incorrect analysis of both the effects of globalization and of the new technology. New information technology displaces many workers, just as all new technologies have done in the past, and this may influence short-term education and training investments. But this aspect of labor markets does not negate the more important issue for educational strategies: globalization and the new technology are knowledge intensive, and the new labor markets are increasingly information-intensive, flexible, and *disaggregative*, or individualizing, of labor, separating workers from traditional communities. The increasing individualization of workers and the increasing importance of education in defining individuals' social roles tends to make institutions that transmit and create knowledge, such as schools and universities, new centers of *knowledge communities*. Individualized families organize their activities around their children's and their own knowledge acquisition.

Increased Income and Educational Inequality

Higher rates of return (both private and social) to higher education have important effects on the rest of the educational system and on income inequality. Rising rates to higher levels of schooling mean that those who get that education are benefited relatively more for their investment in education than those who stop at lower levels of schooling. In most countries, those who get to higher levels of schooling are also those from higher social class backgrounds. So not only do those families with higher social class background have more capital to start with, under these circumstances, they get a higher return to their investments. This is a sure formula for increased inequality in already highly unequal societies. It is also a sure formula for increased inequality in previously Communist societies, which were characterized by very equal incomes.

In addition, higher socio-economic status (SES) students are those who get access to "better" schools in regions that are more likely to spend more per pupil for education, particularly in those schools attended by higher socio-economic class pupils. Competition for such higher-payoff education also increases as the payoff to higher education increases, because the stakes get higher. Higher SES parents become increasingly conscious of where their children attend school, what those schools are like, and whether they provide access to higher levels of education. The total result is therefore that schooling becomes more stratified at lower levels rather than less stratified, especially under conditions of scarce public resources. National economic competition on a global scale gets translated into sub-national competition in social class access to educational resources.

If rates of return to university are pushed up by globalization, intensifying the competition for access to higher education, higher-educated, higher income parents tend to step up the amount they spend on primary and secondary school to assure their children's university enrollment. This means that if promoting private education at the primary and secondary levels through vouchers is part of the strategy to expand access, parents who can afford it are likely to send their children to selective private schools. Even in the public system, wherever possible, parents with more motivation and resources will seek "selective" public schools that serve higher social class clientele. These same parents, willing to spend on the "best" (often private) primary and secondary schools for their children, then end up fighting for high quality, essentially free, public universities.

Similarly, the countries of the former Soviet Bloc, now democratic or transitioning to democracy, are also transitioning from purely state schooling and university systems that focused heavily on vocational education to a system with increasing numbers of private schools and a shift to general education. Further, under Communism, teachers and students were distributed among schools by a centralized state bureaucracy. Since the Soviet economic system was self-contained, the educational systems were insulated from the influence of international competition and increasingly unequal distribution of earning in the rest of the world. In the new democracies, the educational system is no longer insulated, and "quality" teachers and students are increasingly distributed among schools according to the social class of students (the ability of families to pay).

At the same time, globally rising rates of return to university pressure on universities to accommodate more students. But financial constraints on increased public spending for education have pushed countries throughout the world to generate such higher education expansions by allowing for the rapid growth of *private* universities, often financed at least partly by Ministry subsidies to students. These private universities compete for students but, in fact, the number of students wanting a degree is so great that competition hardly has to be fierce to attract students. Even so, private universities in some countries, such as Malaysia, "twin" with European and Australian universities to draw students. Most of these students are not "good enough" to get into the top public universities, so a private one, high fees and all, is their best hope for a professional career. In Brazil, Chile, and Colombia, and many other countries, commercial, private universities tend to be "diploma mills," serving students from lower rather than higher-income families. The payoff to private university students is generally lower than the return to those who attend the more prestigious public universities.

Globalization and Women's Education

In addition to raising the payoff to higher levels of education, globalization appears to have raised the rate of return to women's education. In many countries rates of return to education for women are higher than for men. The reasons for the increased participation of women in labor markets are complex, but two main factors have been the spread of feminist ideas and values and the increased demand for low-cost semi-skilled labor in developing countries' electronics manufacturing and other assembly industries. The world-wide movement for women's rights has had the effect of legitimizing equal education for women, women's control over their fertility rates, women's increased participation in wage labor markets, and women's right to vote. The increased demand for low-cost labor and greater sense by women that they have the same rights as men has brought enormous numbers of married women into wage employment world-wide. This, in turn has created increased demand for education by women at higher and higher education levels. So globalization is accentuating an already growing trend by women to take as much or more education than men.

This does not mean that women receive wages equal to men's. That is hardly the case. Nor does it mean that women are taking higher education in fields that are most lucrative, such as engineering, business, or computer science. That is also far from true. Women are still vastly under-represented in the most lucrative professions even in the most "feminized" countries, such as Sweden or the United States. But globalization seems gradually to be changing that, for both positive and negative reasons. The positive reasons are that flexible organization in business enterprise requires flexible labor, and women are as or more flexible than men, and that information technology and telecommunications are spreading democratic ideas worldwide. The negative reason is that women are paid much less than men almost everywhere in the world, and it is profitable for firms to hire women and pay them lower wages than men. Yet, both sets of reasons gradually seem to be driving both the education and the price of women's labor up relative to men's. For example, the percent of women in science and engineering university faculties is increasing worldwide. Although such increased "professionalization" of women may contribute to the transformation of family life, it does serve to democratize societies and raise greatly the average level of schooling.

Changing Demographics and the Impact on Education

Except in a few places such as Sweden in the late 1980s and early 1990s, where fertility rates rose on the effect of postponed bearing of a third child among older women, stimulated by a generous paid parental leave system, and extensive, high quality, subsidized child care, and the United States, with a bulge in the female population of child-bearing age and a large immigrant population, women in OECD countries are averaging far fewer children than a generation ago. This trend is also spreading to developing countries. It has long been the norm in the Communist bloc and characterizes the transition democracies of Eastern Europe and Central Asia. One of the many reasons for the drop in fertility may be that women's average education is much higher now than ever and, at least in the OECD countries and former Communist countries, higher-educated women are more likely to engage in "career" work and to postpone marriage and having children. Since they start bearing children when they are older, they end up having fewer children than less-educated women who marry at a younger age. In the developed countries, this appears to be the dominant pattern. In the developing countries, the pattern may be more complicated, especially because infant mortality rates may be considerably higher in low-income families.

Added to the low fertility rates among higher educated women in Western Europe, the United States, Australia and New Zealand, these countries/regions are hosts to increasing less-educated immigrants from "South" countries. The Latin American and African immigrants to Europe and the U.S. are especially likely to have high fertility rates.

Greater fertility among less-educated, lower-income families affects societies, especially in the current global environment. It means that most children may be growing up in families that cannot prepare them adequately for the ever-higher educational requirements needed to succeed in labor markets. This is not to say that higher educated men and women make better parents than those with less education. But being a parent in the global economy requires much more information than in the past, and the stakes in children's educational success are much higher. *On average*, less-educated parents are increasingly at a disadvantage in supplying what it takes for young children to be prepared to do well in school. Children living in families with less-educated parents are significantly behind middle-class children when they enter school, and there is no evidence that they catch up as they move through the grades.

This potential problem is accentuated by three other factors. First, income distribution in many countries has become more unequal in the past generation, with the real incomes of less-educated families stagnating or even declining. The second is that a high fraction of females heading households are not only poor because they are women, but are doubly poor because they have low levels of schooling. The third factor is public investment in the early care and education of children worldwide is low. Under these three conditions, the ability of children of less-educated families to escape poverty is the exception rather than the rule. Even in a rich country such as the United States, in the mid-1980s, an unusually high 37 percent of children were growing up in poverty or near poverty. Although that proportion declined in the 1990s, it remains the highest in the OECD. At the other end of the spectrum, less than 10 percent of children in Sweden fell into this category, thanks to a well-developed system of social welfare, including generous unemployment compensation, subsidized childcare and other forms of family support. Since the family is still the entity responsible for child rearing, differences in access to information and networks extant among social groups are likely to be reproduced from this generation into the next. The State can and should play an important role in offsetting differences in access to resources and information. This may be the only way to raise achievement for lower income children.

Changing labor markets and demographics combine to create major changes in universities as well. In the past twenty years, "new" demand for higher education in both developed and developing countries has come mainly from two groups that traditionally did not attend universities: a "rising" lower-middle social class and women. These sources will continue to fuel higher educational expansion and will be fighting for more places in elite institutions. But a major source of growth in population in developed and developing countries is now and will continue to be very low-educated families, many of them disadvantaged majorities in the developing countries and disadvantaged minorities in the developed countries. The increasing proportion of such children in secondary school is already posing a serious dilemma for educational policy. As secondary education becomes increasingly less valuable in labor markets, this growing part of the school population becomes the next "wave" of potential college graduates, yet in the traditional sense, they may not be "prepared" for college education.

Poverty rates in developing countries are much higher, and this means that universities will face similar or even greater problems as they expand than those in developed countries. Even though most of the children raised in poor families today, especially in developing countries, are unlikely to get access to universities, as universities in developing countries expand more rapidly than incomes rise, they will take increasing numbers of young people from such "disadvantaged" backgrounds. The paradox is explained by the relatively low fraction of young people in developing countries who live in high or even middle-income families. If the university system expands from admitting 10 percent of the age cohort to 25 percent, and 80 percent of young people live in low-income, less-educated families, at least 5 percent of university entrants (assuming that not all middle-class young people end up at university) would have to come from "disadvantaged" families. This would represent 20 percent of university students. In addition, the "disadvantaged" would not be distributed evenly through the university system. Most would be concentrated in less endowed institutions known for their poor quality or in night courses at major universities, or in specialties that are "easier" and are not defined as full-time programs. These are usually associated with low completion rates and low economic returns.

Income Inequality and Declining Educational Quality

One of the major impacts of globalization on education is increased pressure to improve the quality of schooling. This is the result of the increased pressure on economies to be more productive in the face of greater competition. Part of the formula for increasing educational quality pushed by international organizations has been the decentralization of educational administration, including promoting competition in the educational sector from private education and through parent choice of schooling for their children. The notion of dismantling centralized educational bureaucracies in favor of school autonomy and school competition is based on the notion of greater efficiency associated with markets and local control. There are important political reasons for local control of educational decision-making, as we shall discuss below, but unless there exists an even distribution of capacity to manage and deliver education at the local level or among schools, there is a high probability that decentralization would contribute to greater inequality in the quality of schooling. Parent choice and increased competition among schools is supposed to increase educational quality, but this also assumes that the management and teaching capacity exists across schools to respond to increased competition. Again, it is likely that in lower-income areas, there is less capacity to increase quality in response to competition, hence schools in those areas will tend to lose better students to schools with higher social class student bodies, and quality might decrease further.

There are other factors associated with democratization of centralized, authoritarian societies that may also reduce the quality of schooling during this process. Centralized, authoritarian societies tend to be more economically equal and more socially ordered societies. Democratization and marketization is associated with increased income and social inequality, greater choice, and less order. This often means greater violence, more child labor, and greater spatial mobility, all factors that have a negative impact on student achievement, especially among lower-income students. Unless there is a strong civil society (community) to replace central authoritarian institutions, state-driven social capital is not replaced by family and community social capital, and schools become less effective because it becomes more costly to produce student achievement than before the democratic transition.

When school decentralization is added to these other factors, we would expect not only a decline of student achievement, but much greater disparity of student achievement among social classes than under centralized authoritarianism.

This is one of the great contradictions of the transition to democracy in the formerly Communist societies. It is also one of the great contradictions of globalization. On the one hand, globalization represents the next stage of democratization—this time on a world scale; on the other hand, globalization threatens democratization with increased social inequality and increased inequality in access to the high quality of education needed to develop democracy to that next level. Globalization may also weaken the power of the national state or regional governments to control economic development and the demand for education to the degree that they could in the past. As we have argued here, globalization may even pose a threat to decreasing the quality of education in many societies, or at least posing major barriers to increasing educational quality.

Globalization and Struggles of Educational Community

Education does much more than to impart skills needed for work. Schools are transmitters of modern culture. The meaning of modern culture as interpreted by the state is a crucial issue for educators and is contested in every society. Globalization redefines culture because it stretches boundaries of time and space and individuals' relationship to them. It reduces the legitimacy of national political institutions' to define modernity.

So globalization necessarily changes the conditions of identity formation. Individuals in any society have multiple identities. Today, their *globalized identity* is defined in terms of the way that global markets value individuals traits and behavior. It is knowledge-centered, but global markets value certain kinds of knowledge much more than others. As noted in the discussion of the changing market for skills, one major feature of global markets is that they place high value on scientific and technical knowledge and less on the kinds of local, artisan skills which serve more basic needs.

The global market does not work well as a source of identity for everyone. Markets also increase material differences among individuals. So that even if the market creates a sense of community among those who share the same professional networks, it also continuously destroys communities, isolating individuals until they are able to find new networks and new sources of social worth. With the individualization of workers and their separation from "permanent" jobs, even the identity individuals have with work places becomes more tenuous and subject to more frequent change.

Globalization is not the only force changing modern culture. Important social movements have challenged globalization in favor of cultural singularity and local control over people's lives and their environment. Caught in between are the traditional mainstays of culture: religion, nationalism, gender relations, and the power relations that have developed historically in local regions, for example because of landowning pattern. In Manuel Castells' words,

> They include pro-active movements, aiming at transforming human relationships at their most fundamental level, such as feminism and environmentalism. But they also include a whole array of reactive movements that build trenches of resistance on behalf of God, nation, ethnicity, family, locality, that is, the fundamental categories of millennial existence now threatened under the combined, contradictory forces assault of techno-economic forces and transformative social movements.

For those less successful in the global marketplace, the search for identity *turns in other directions, and does so more intensely than in the past.* When the search for other identities does not coincide with existing national territories, they also seek to redefine nationality. Ethnic identity is certainly one option. In sociologist Göran Therborn's words,

> "Affirming an ethnic identity amounts to discounting the present and the future for the past, to thinking and saying that the past is more important than the present... Who your parents were is more important than what you do, think, or might become...So, the less value the present appears to provide, the more important ethnicity, other things being equal".

Religious identity is another direction to which the less globally successful turn. Religious fundamentalism is on the rise worldwide. It rejects the market as authority, and although fundamentalist groups have targeted the nation-state as a power base, there is an inherent contradiction between religious fundamentalism and a territorially defined nation. The same contradiction does not exist when it comes to local communities or to globalized movements for religious identity. But religious localism necessarily means communities based on exclusion. Even ethnic movements move away from their inclusionary focus. Rather than centering on nation-state legislative and financial intervention that *includes* the particular ethnic or race group in the *national* project, they now focus on cultural identities independent from the national project or seek recognition in global terms, *above* nationality. The fastest growing self-identity group among the world's economically marginalized peoples is Muslim fundamentalists. Christian fundamentalism is an increasingly important movement, not only in the United States, where it appeals to working class whites, but also in Latin America, particularly among the rural poor. Hindu fundamentalism is also mobilizing similar groups in South Asia. Such fundamentalism provides a new "self-knowledge" that stands above market success. All the information you need to lead a fulfilling life is in the Koran or the Bible or the Torah. Fundamentalist beliefs do not exclude being successful in the market. But the appeal to fundamentalism is strongest for those who feel simultaneously threatened by the "inclusiveness" of a multiculturalist version of welfare democracy (or even the authoritarianism of a single party state) that offers a bureaucratic vision of nationality, and the "inclusiveness" of the global market that serves the power of money and complex information systems.

Cultural identity, whether religious, ethnic, racial, or gender, and whether local, regional or more global, is an antidote to the complexity and harshness of the global market as the judge of a person's worth. For nationalists, cultural identity is also an antidote to the globalized bureaucratic state. But such a trend could mean increased social conflict. If some localities/ethnicities/religious groupings feel increasingly excluded from the high end of the market, a weakened nation-state incapable of reincorporating them socially could mean less stability. Even though the political positions of various nationalist movements may differ considerably, they all tend to play to the sense for many of exclusion from participating in the fruits of globalizing national economies.

The market in itself has never been sufficiently inclusive. Strong undemocratic, non-egalitarian nation-states existed before the free market dominated economic systems, so many believe that states are no guarantee of inclusion. But the modern capitalist state developed into a successful market "softener." The decline of that role in the face of powerful global marketization of national economies pushes the "dispossessed" to seek refuge in new and more *exclusive* collectives. These collectives generally do not have the power or the funds to help the dispossessed financially nor to develop the skills and knowledge valued by global markets. They can help develop self-knowledge and therefore self-confidence. They can provide community and therefore a sense of belonging. They often do so by defining others as "outsiders" without the "true" self-knowledge or the "right" ancestors. At the extreme end, the communities are often highly undemocratic. If the nation-state does not have the financial capability or the political legitimacy to dissipate such movements by incorporating its members into much broader notions of community and values, societies unable to maintain market success may face serious, irresolvable divisions.

The conflicts in identity formation necessarily affect education. The distribution of access to schools and universities, as well as educational reforms aimed at improving its quality, are all headed toward forming labor for a market conditioned by globalization. But education can become more inequitable rather then more inclusive. Thus, in any strategy, central governments must still assume responsibility for leveling the playing field for all groups. This is particularly true because left-out groups see the educational system as both crucial to knowledge acquisition yet not serving the needs of their "community." Schools and the educational system become primary targets for social movements organized around "self-knowledge," such as religious or ethnic identity. The educational system has enormous resources devoted to knowledge formation for dominant groups. Why should not education in a democratic society serve all groups, even those that differ markedly from the ideal of the new, competitive, globally sensitive worker? It is no accident that much of the struggle, for example, between religious fundamentalists and the secular, rational state, is over state education. The public sector has the funds to place children in an educational institution, but not the commitment to create a moral community. Instead, the state has succumbed to crass materialism on a global scale. Fundamentalists want to attract those who are not happy with their value in a world economy, and to educate them and their children in a way that will strengthen religious affiliation, not economic productivity. The more they succeed, the less the educational system will be able to develop global economy workers. Yet, at the same time that schools and universities are the site of intense struggles over the definition of culture, they represent to those who are not included in the global economy the single most important route to access global culture. Minority groups may try to control the cultural norms purveyed by schools and universities, but they often engage in such battles believing that their children should have a chance to learn skills valued by the global economy.

Decentralization of educational management to meet the goal of empowering regional and local social movements makes eminent sense when it is these movements that seek to gain control of the educational institutions that affect their children Educational democratization movements have pushed for more power for parents and teachers at the educational site. Again, decentralization of control could promote greater educational productivity and greater sense of community when it is communities themselves that want that control. It might also effectively assuage groups seeking greater self-identity through influencing the production of knowledge in schools. Whether or not this contributes to a multicultural alternative to globalized individualism remains to be seen.

In addition, pro-active movements, such as feminism and environmentalism, postmodern in their outlook and in direct conflict with globalization, are attempting to redefine the conception of "global" in the education system. For example, feminism is gradually shaping global culture to include gender equality and equity, first in education, then in labor markets. Environmentalism has had an enormous impact on global culture through environmental programs in schools worldwide. These pro-active movements are having a major impact on how schools define new global culture, and in that sense, are most closely associated with challenges to the techno-economic definition of globalized culture. Education plays and will continue to play a fundamental role in this struggle.

The women's movement has made significant inroads into the educational system even in traditional Muslim countries. This reflects the movement's power over the past generation to shape knowledge institutions at the heart of the globalization process. Even so, as the continued subordination of women in societies such as Pakistan and Afghanistan suggest, other anti-global movements rooted in male-dominated traditional culture see women's equality as a *global* notion, and oppose it as part of their resistance to globalization.

Educational Policy in Newly Opened Societies

Globalization is having significant impact on knowledge formation because it revalues different types of knowledge, particularly the knowledge associated with higher levels of education. As it does so, it increases the pressure to expand higher education and it increases the competition at lower levels of schooling among families trying to "game" the education system for their children's social mobility. This increases the potential for greater inequality of access to quality education, even as globalization brings new kinds of people into universities and other types of post-secondary schooling.

For societies in the transition to democracy from state socialism—those in Eastern Europe to those in Central Asia—the transition in the context of this economic globalization poses great challenges for educational policies. The transition societies have generally inherited well-developed, high quality educational systems, in which teachers used to be paid wages little different from wages paid to other professionals.

With the disintegration of their command economies and their insertion into global markets, these societies' social services, including education, have suffered severe budget constraints. Teaching has become a relatively low-paid profession, and private funding of schooling has increasingly supplemented public funding, with predictable increases in inequality of access to quality education and ensuing declines in average student academic performance. Correspondingly, increasing institutional diversity has also marked universities.

Ethnic and Class Competition

The former Soviet Union was built on the Russian Empire, which included many regions that were, strictly speaking, Russian colonies. Eastern European and Baltic countries also fell under Soviet control after World War II. Russian emigration to regions that were ethnically and culturally very different and the "colonial" relation between Russia and local ethnic groups has created another level of issues for education in post-Soviet democracy. Namely, in some countries local ethnic groups are making access to higher education for Russian-origin young people more difficult. The opening of these societies has therefore not been able to overcome the prejudices and conflicts inherent in nineteenth and twentieth century history. Rather than being a path to resolving such prejudices and conflicts, the educational system in the new democracies is often at the forefront of the conflict.

The difficulty of maintaining relatively high levels of K-12 schooling quality for young people in the opening societies is part of the overall problems created by increasing economic and social inequality. The increase in inequality poses a potential threat to the deepening of democratic institutions. Thus, educational privatization, while an important source of new funding for resource-starved schools, simultaneously threatens conceptions of fairness and equity that are key to the deepening of civil society and democratic institutions.

Put another way, families cannot be faulted for trying to use private resources to give their children the best chance possible at social mobility in the new market economy. As a stopgap measure to assure that at least some fraction of the school-age population gets high quality schooling, greater inequality of access to quality education may a necessary, if not entirely satisfactory, way to provide social services. Similarly, in higher education, students and their families want to do what is necessary for the university to make them valuable in the global economic system.

At the same time, educational institutions, as the main sites of knowledge transmission in a knowledge economy, are the new loci of community formation. Higher education institutions are not only sites of community formation but, as in the past, also continue to act as centers of cultural leadership. Schools and universities are therefore under new kinds of pressures because global market culture is highly exclusive and destructive of local culture and, furthermore, also stresses individuality, competition, and unequal outcomes—factors that are not very consistent with building democratic institutions, particularly in societies that have long been accustomed to considerable emphasis on equity, at least in education, income, and employment. The new and contradictory pressures from greater competition and inequality will be played out in expanding educational systems over the next generation.

Multicultural Education in a Global Environment

Schools and universities do not just serve to add market worth to students hoping for a place in the globalized economy. Universities are definers of culture for national and diverse regional and local communities. In many ways schools and universities are also cultural centers as such. For example, the school or university may represent for a community a center of particular culture in a multicultural society, or, may represent a new definitions of multiculturalism. Thus, the school or university becomes an important site of conflict between global culture *qua* preparing students to be economically successful in a global economic environment (scientific, global, economically-valued knowledge) and local cultural forms that build self-identity (self-knowledge). Often, this self-identity is an antidote to a global identity that fails to include even many university graduates in the developing countries. It may be also be consistent with a new kind of globalism that creates incorporative multicultural forms. The newly open societies face additional problems of ethnic conflicts and increasing social class inequality. If states in the opening societies contribute to the cultural conflict by using education to exacerbate cultural divisions, new social identities consistent with democracy on a global environment will be impossible to achieve. All this complicates further the incorporation of all these groups equitably into the global knowledge society.

Today's more globalized notion of national identity in a period of declining state power makes it less logical to impose a narrow sense of national, regional or local culture. Since markets are increasingly global, an individual's economic value is determined by broader criteria than his or her local "acceptability." Further, declining state capacity to impose norms creates political space for counter-dominant concepts of self-knowledge. In practice, groups that do not do assimilate well into the global market knowledge culture have greater political options today than even a generation ago of forming relatively autonomous cultural groups with their own knowledge institutions. This is true for fundamentalist religious groups as well as particular immigrant groups wanting to preserve language and native culture.

In terms of how school systems and universities may react to globalization, this suggests approaches to a self-knowledge community very different from those of the past. Two models come to mind. The first is one where the state allows any community group to create a knowledge institution with public funds as long as it met minimum legal criteria. Each community in a society could therefore socialize its children and transmit knowledge in the way it chose. This implies a vision of society where groups with widely different beliefs are held together by market relations but not necessarily other common bonds. Those who support educational vouchers, charter schools, and ethnic or religious schools and universities catering toward very different groups tend toward this approach.

The second model is one where the state uses a multi-cultural self-knowledge approach to socialize all young people in the public system. This multi-cultural approach differs from totally autonomous definitions of self-knowledge by each group. It also abandons the imposition of a single dominant culture, but does make all children attending *publicly funded* institutions learn about the variety of cultures in the community (and their points of view). In that sense, the state (national, regional, or local community) continues to impose an ideological perspective, but one that reflects the diversity of today's post-industrial societies.

The first model assumes that market relations (the profit motive) are enough to keep increasingly diverse societies working together successfully. In knowledge-based society, a common school and university experience with young people having at least some diversity in background and values serves this function. A multicultural approach to socialization does more: it allows children of various groups to gain an understanding of their own history and culture but also allows them to think critically about it. This makes it consistent with the higher-order problem-solving skills needed for an innovative, democratic society. It is also consistent with a *positive, constructive* vision of what post-industrial societies are becoming—a vision distinctly opposed to the parochial, defensive, anti-globalism of the nationalist right.

REFERENCES

Braudel, F.(1979). *The Wheels of Commerce, Volume II of Civilization and Capitalism.* New York: Harper and Row.

Carnoy, M. (2000). *Sustaining Flexibility: Work, Family, and Community in the Information Age.* Cambridge, MA: Harvard University Press and New York: Russell Sage.

Carnoy, M., Castells, M., Cohen, S., and Cardoso, F.H. (1993). *The New Global Economy in the Information Age.* University Park. PA: Pennsylvania State University Press.

Castells, M.(1996). *The Rise of the Network Society.* London: Blackwell.

Psacharopoulos, G. (1989). Time trends of the returns to education: Cross-national evidence, *Economics of Education Review,* vol. 8, no. 3:225-39.

2

Global Education Reform Movement

Globalization has not only increased competition in world economies but also within and between the education systems. Policies and strategies that drive educational reforms have been adjusted to the new realities by creating structures in education systems that allow assessing, comparing and rank-ordering national and regional education performances. Education reforms in different countries today share similar assumptions, values and characteristics due to the endless flow of information and harmonization of education policies through increased global educational borrowing and lending.

Research literature confirms the value of investing in education. More precisely, evidence shows that both primary and secondary education significantly contributes to economic development and growth. This research recognizes people as human capital and demonstrates how increased investment in knowledge, skills and health provides future returns to the economy through increases in labor productivity. Moreover, better quality education increases average earnings and productivity and reduces the likelihood of social problems that, in turn, are harmful for economic development.

The body of educational change knowledge that forms the technical foundation of education reforms underway in practically all education systems has significantly expanded during the last three decades. According to Hargreaves and Goodson, education reform has gone through three consecutive phases. The first was the age of optimism and innovation. This was the era of growing student populations and economic growth that promoted optimism about individual emancipation and technological enhancement through education. Education reforms were based on large-scale curriculum reforms, increased professional autonomy of teachers and school-driven improvement through innovations. The fact that student populations were relatively homogenous and students with special needs were taught in specific institutions increased the high expectations for implementing innovations. The second phase was the age of complexity and contradiction. Education reforms focused on increasing external control of schools, teachers and students through inspections, evaluations and assessments that led to an increase of regulations in schools and decreased autonomy of teachers. At the same time, however, the neo-liberal movement increased the freedom of choice in education. Student populations became more diverse creating a need for inclusive approaches and shifting the emphasis to learning for all. The third phase is the age of standardization and marketization. Education reforms have been designed based on centrally prescribed curricular, learning and assessment standards monitored through intensive assessment and testing and on increased competition between schools. Therefore, teachers are losing their professional autonomy and learning is being focused on successful performance in standardized tests.

Many countries are reforming their education systems to provide their citizens with knowledge and skills that enable them to engage actively in democratic societies and dynamic knowledge-based economies. The fundamental requirement for this is that everyone has sufficient knowledge and skills in literacy, numeracy and information and communication technologies (ICTs). Rather than shifting emphasis onto standardized knowledge of content and mastery of routine skills, many of the advanced education systems are focusing on flexibility, creativity and problem solving through modern methods of teaching, such as co-operative learning, and using multilateral clusters, community networks and ICT in teaching. According to the existing body of educational change knowledge, it seems that many of the ongoing education development efforts are not likely to bring the improvements expected. For example, the widespread approach of increasing external pressure on teachers and students in order to improve the quality and effectiveness of education has not been proved to be sustainable. As a reaction to the overemphasis on knowledge-based teaching and learning, ministries in China, Japan, Singapore and in the European

Union are developing more flexible forms of curriculum, introducing authentic forms of assessment and accountability, and supporting teachers to work together to find alternative instructional approaches that promote learning of essential knowledge and skills required in knowledge economies. Instead of focusing on single institutions, education reforms are beginning to encourage clustering of schools and communities. At the core of this idea is complementarity and co-operation between the members of the cluster. Clustering and networking appear to be the core factors in economic competitiveness.

Economic competitiveness is the key attribute of economic development and growth. In the knowledge-based economies in the last two decades expectations of education, especially the qualities desired in educated and trained people have dramatically changed. For example, Microsoft CEO Bill Gates argues that ''training the workforce of tomorrow with the high schools of today is like trying to teach kids about today's computers on a 50-year-old mainframe. It is the wrong tool for the times.'' Therefore, business leaders, politicians and educators are looking for solutions for improving economic competitiveness and thereby economic growth. Market values like productivity, effectiveness, accountability and competitiveness are increasingly being embedded in global education reforms. This is based on the assumption that education will improve according to the logic of enhancing performance of market economies: opening doors to competition and choice. As a result, standardization and consequential accountability have been commonly proposed as solutions to improve the quality and effectiveness of teaching and learning in many school systems. The idea of market-ization of education has been at the core of global education reforms since the early 1990s. Then argument is that the educational requirements of building democratic societies and enhancing economic competitiveness often contradict the changes introduced in these global education reforms.

Globalization and Improvement of Education Systems

Globalization is a cultural paradox: it simultaneously unifies and diversifies people and cultures. It unifies national education policies by integrating them with the broader global trends. Because problems and challenges are similar from one education system to another, solutions and education reform agendas also are becoming similar. Due to international benchmarking of education systems by using common indicators and the international comparisons of student achievement, the distinguishing features of different education systems are becoming more visible. For example, the OECD's Program for International Student Assessment (PISA) has mobilized scores of education experts to visit other countries in order to learn how to redefine their own education policies.

Globalization has also accelerated international collaboration, exchange of ideas and transfer of education policies between the education systems. Analyzing global policy developments and education reforms has become a common practice in many ministries of education, development agencies and regional administrations. Therefore, the world's education systems inevitably share some core values, functions and structures. The question arises whether increased global interaction among policy-makers and educators, especially benchmarking of education systems through agreed indicators and borrowing and lending educational policies, has promoted common approaches to education reform throughout the world.

Although improvement of education systems is a global phenomenon, there is no reliable recent comparative analysis of how education reforms in different countries have been designed and implemented. However, the professional literature indicates that the focus on educational development has shifted from structural reforms to improving of quality and relevance of education. At the same time, primarily due to global declarations such as Millennium Development Goals and Education for All, increased efforts have been made to provide basic school education to all children and to expand access and relevance of secondary education. As a consequence, curriculum development, student assessment and teacher evaluation, integration of information and communication technologies into teaching and learning and proficiency of basic competences, i.e. reading and writing skills, and mathematical and scientific literacy have become common priorities in education reforms around the world

Today's education reform policies have been influenced by research and development in Anglo-Saxon countries. Through intellectual exchange and technical assistance that are often provided by the experts from these countries, educational change knowledge has been widely exported to transition countries and increasingly also to the developing parts of the world. Hargreaves et al. and his research team have presented a useful synthesis of global education reform efforts that they call ''a new education reform orthodoxy.'' They outline the logic and evolution of education development as most countries adjust their education systems to respond to fit new economic realities and social challenges.

The inspiration for the emergence of the global education reform movement comes from three sources. The first source of inspiration is the new paradigm of learning that became dominant in 1980s. The breakthrough of cognitive and constructivist approaches to learning gradually shifted the focus of education reforms from teaching to learning. According to this paradigm, intended outcomes of schooling emphasize greater conceptual understanding, problem-solving, emotional and multiple intelligences and interpersonal skills rather than the memorizing of facts or mastering irrelevant skills. At the same time, however, the need for proficiency in literacy and numeracy has also become a prime target of education reforms. The second inspiration is the public demand to guarantee effective learning for all pupils. Inclusive education arrangements and the introduction of common learning standards for all have been offered as means to promote the ideal of education for all. The third inspiration is the accountability movement in education that has accompanied the global wave of decentralization of public services. Making schools and teachers accountable for their work has led to introduction of education standards, indicators and benchmarks for teaching and learning, aligned assessments and testing and prescribed curricula. As a result, various forms of consequential accountability have emerged where school performance and raising the quality of education are closely tied to the process of accreditation, promotion and financing.

The global education reform movement has had significant consequences for teachers' work and students' learning in schools. Because this agenda promises significant gains in efficiency and quality of education, it has been widely accepted as a basic ideology of change, both politically and professionally.

The global education reform movement emphasizes some fundamental new orientations to learning and to education administration. It suggests three strong directions to improve quality, equity and effectiveness of education: putting priority on learning, aiming at good learning achievement for all students and making assessment as an integral part of the teaching and learning process. Firstly and most importantly, the global education reform movement shifts the focus in education from what teachers should teach to what students should do and learn. It thus addresses the need to understand learning as a process of making meanings and building understanding rather than as recitation of facts and isolated knowledge It puts a strong accent on mastering the basic skills of reading, writing, mathematical and scientific literacy for almost all students by defining explicit learning targets for students and teachers. Second, through a common curriculum it also tries to ensure that irrespective of school or teacher, each student will be provided with appropriate learning environments. Such environments feature problem-solving, critical thinking and co-operative learning. These types of ''deep learning'' are more compatible with the needs of the knowledge-based economy and the development of the network society than are conventional models of learning. Third, new and alternative forms of assessment that are linked to learning objectives help both teachers and students to adjust their efforts to achieve the intended goals in school. Assessment becomes an integral part of the learning process using a variety of approaches, such as performance assessment, portfolio and self-assessments.

The impact of the global education reform movement in education systems becomes particularly interesting when analyzed in light of the expectations of economic development and growth. For example, the European Union has acknowledged that the region has been confronted with a quantum shift resulting from globalization and knowledge-driven economy. As a response to this challenge the EU has agreed that by 2010 it will ''become the most competitive and dynamic knowledge-based economy in the world, capable of sustainable economic growth with more and better jobs and with greater social cohesion''. These targets require radical transformation of the European economy and a challenging program for the modernization of education systems. Similar demands for enhancing economic competitiveness and growth have been made on education authorities in the United States, Asia and in several transition economies.

Economic Competitiveness and Education

Education for the knowledge-based economy has become a buzz phrase in education policy discourse throughout the developed world and the transition economies but also increasingly in developing countries. However, it has rarely been transformed into operational strategies or reform programs for education systems or educators.

Typically, education reform that is targeted on serving knowledge-based economies emphasizes mathematics and science, information and communication technologies, basic knowledge and skills in literacy and development of interpersonal skills. Moreover, a successful knowledge economy also requires advanced secondary and tertiary education provision able to boost labor productivity, research and innovation. Many of the education reforms aimed at promoting economic competitiveness in the knowledge economies take the form of centrally steered structural and programmatic directives. Only rarely are these changes directly related to what teachers and students are doing in schools and classrooms.

Successful economies compete on the basis of high value, not only low cost. High value is best guaranteed by well-trained and educated personnel and flexible lifelong learning opportunities for all citizens. The most frequently presented general idea for increasing economic competitiveness is to equip people with the skills and attitudes for economic and civic success in an increasingly knowledge-based economy. This is rhetoric typically written into the strategies or policies that address the relation between economic competitiveness and development of education. In the midst of global education reforms it is difficult to answer the question that many teachers ask: ''What should we do differently in schools in order to contribute effectively to economic competitiveness and growth?'' Before exploring this question further, we need to examine what economic competitiveness means in order to understand better what schools should do differently.

Competitiveness is based on the determinants of the complex process of economic growth and development. When the competitiveness of economies is compared, a set of institutions, policies and structures is constructed using sub-indices that try to grasp the heterogeneity of different countries. The Economic Growth Competitiveness Index is built on three central ideas :

- Economic growth can be analyzed within the macro-economic environment, the quality of public institutions and technology.
- Technological advance is the ultimate source of growth but its origins may be different across countries.
- The importance of the determinants of economic competitiveness varies for core and non-core innovators.

Based on these commonly used determinants of economic competitiveness and various indicators of knowledge economy, three core domains have been utilized to explain economic growth:

- education and training (human capital),
- use of information and communication technologies,
- innovations and technological adaptation.

Education reforms have been classified in various ways. Using the three pillars above and combining them with the structural, qualitative and financing dimensions of education reforms to convert them to more concrete principles and actions for schools and teachers.

Governments have an essential role to play by offering and guaranteeing good education that adequately emphasizes the core determinants of economic competitiveness. However, it has been difficult to translate this central role of education into concrete actions and programs that lead to improved human capital and therefore contribute to the social and economic progress. There are several aspects of economic competitiveness that have a direct relation to teaching and learning in schools. They are: rethinking innovation, revisiting the conception of knowledge, focusing on interpersonal skills and enhancing the will and skill to learn.

Rethinking Educational Innovations

Living in and working for a world of innovations requires fundamentally different attitudes, knowledge and skills from the citizens. Technological adaptation and innovation have been the main drivers of economic growth in developed countries since the WWII and are proving to be important factors also in many developing countries. Therefore teachers and students need to work with and learn from innovations in order to be able to contribute successfully to the development of innovation in the knowledge economy. Innovations linked to economic development have three characteristics that are also relevant to education reforms. First, the process of innovation is non-linear rather than linear. This implies that in order to work in an innovation-rich environment one has to develop mindsets able to identify and understand nonlinear, systemic processes. Teaching and learning have traditionally been conceptualized as linear, deterministic procedures. Therefore, shifting the focus of education to address the needs of working with innovations requires rethinking teaching and learning as non-linear, non-deterministic and complex processes. In professional development of teachers and in school improvement this means exploring and expanding the existing pedagogic conceptions and beliefs and upgrading the current knowledge base related to teaching and learning. Education policies and curricula should pay more attention to learning how to learn and how to understand the process, i.e. meta-cognition. Second, innovation is most often a collective process created and maintained by a group of people rather than by one inventor. In this sense innovation requires shared knowledge and complementary skills from more than one person. In order to promote these collective and creative qualities, education at all levels needs to focus on learning to learn together and work productively with other people, for instance through co-operative learning. Third, innovation is an organic entity that should be viewed from the systemic point of view. The process of innovation can be characterized as complex or even chaotic process of self-organization. This means that knowledge and skills that are related to innovation are attained through active construction rather than direct instruction and accommodation. Therefore, teaching and learning in schools should be viewed as systemic processes that rely on principles of active participation, social interaction and reflection (social constructivism).

New Conception of Knowledge

Human capital can be understood as a stock of educated and skilled citizens. Knowledge plays a key role in increasing human capital. Human capital is one of the main drivers of economic competitiveness. It is not primarily what individuals know or do not know, but more what are their skills in acquiring, utilizing, diffusing and creating knowledge that are important for economic progress and social change. Formal education, especially at pre-tertiary levels, has been criticized for outdated conceptions of knowledge. Traditionally the foundation of knowledge has been based on positivist scientific method. Conventionally knowledge has been viewed as objective and knowledge-formation as a linear, cumulative process. In other words, the ideal of knowledge has been understood as static, eternal and free from subjective values and interpretations. Due to the breakthrough of new scientific paradigms in economics, mathematics, natural sciences, neuroscience, cognitive sciences and information technologies, knowledge is now understood in a new way. It is seen as relativistic and diverse in terms of its interpretations. It is created through multiple processes, including hermeneutic and subjective 'scientific' methods. This shift in the paradigm of knowledge has created a challenge for education. Teaching and learning in schools should focus not only on transmission of information but also on construction and transformation of knowledge that are fundamental processes in knowledge-intensive and innovation-rich societies. However, due to participation in the global education reform movement many countries are moving to opposite direction: what seems to be valued is conventional knowledge in selected core subjects that can be reproduced in tests using lower level intellectual processes.

Focusing on Soft Skills

Success in the world of work requires different knowledge and skills from employees and managers than before. Operating in an innovation-rich environment and coping with increasing amounts of knowledge is changing the ways we think about education and schools. Individual performance and inventions created by one person only have given a way to collective intelligence, shared knowledge and team-based problem-solving. Interestingly, successful economies are based on the idea of strategic alliances rather than raw competition for markets and clients. Indeed, economic competitiveness requires a stronger focus on the development of interpersonal skills throughout the cycle of education. More specifically, habits of mind and social skills that are necessary in productive group processes, whether in work or school, are becoming more important in the schools of those countries that are genuinely concerned about their economic competitiveness and sustainable development. Initiating and managing productive teamwork, problem-solving and continuous learning in schools and workplaces alike requires what is known as emotional intelligence. According to Goleman emotional intelligence adds value to cognitive intelligence and significantly improves labor productivity and personal relations.

Soft skills is a sociological term relating to a person's "EQ" (Emotional Intelligence Quotient), the cluster of personality traits, social graces, communication, language, personal habits, friendliness, and optimism that characterize relationships with other people. Soft skills complement hard skills (part of a person's IQ), which are the occupational requirements of a job and many other activities.

Soft skills are personal attributes that enhance an individual's interactions, job performance and career prospects. Unlike hard skills, which are about a person's skill set and ability to perform a certain type of task or activity, soft skills relate to a person's ability to interact effectively with coworkers and customers and are broadly applicable both in and outside the workplace.

A person's soft skill EQ is an important part of their individual contribution to the success of an organization. Particularly those organizations dealing with customers face-to-face are generally more successful, if they train their staff to use these skills. Screening or training for personal habits or traits such as dependability and conscientiousness can yield significant return on investment for an organization. For this reason, soft skills are increasingly sought out by employers in addition to standard qualifications.

It has been suggested that in a number of professions soft skills may be more important over the long term than occupational skills. The legal profession is one example where the ability to deal with people effectively and politely, more than their mere occupational skills, can determine the professional success of a lawyer.

Soft Skills are behavioral competencies. Also known as Interpersonal Skills, or people skills, they include proficiencies such as communication skills, conflict resolution and negotiation, personal effectiveness, creative problem solving, strategic thinking, team building, influencing skills and selling skills, to name a few.

One of the typical features of almost any school system is that as pupils move from elementary to middle school and from middle school to secondary school, their interest in studying and learning in school tends to decline. Lifelong learning requires students to leave school with the desire to learn more about themselves, other people and the world around them. The knowledge society is a learning society in which economic development and competitiveness depend on the will and skill of workers to keep on learning alone and from one another. Increased emphasis on standards and accountability has led in many countries to micro-management of teaching and thereby also of learning that, in turn, has eroded teachers' autonomy of judgment and conditions of work and decreased the meaningfulness of learning among students.

Because macro-economics, the quality of public institutions and the advance of technology vary greatly from one country to another, it is difficult to establish one universal approach to education reform that would benefit economic growth and competitiveness in particular. It has become clear that country-specific strategies addressing the country-specific constraints to growth are most likely to be successful. Indeed, policy-makers should be cautious in drawing conclusions too hastily from how education reforms have been designed in other countries, when planning reforms to strengthen economic competitiveness and support continuous growth of their own countries. For example, if the country is so called non-core country in terms of innovation, it would make more sense first to try to make the education system ready to utilize and benefit from the innovations created in the core countries. On the other hand, especially in the countries of advanced innovation and technological cultures, it is important to give teachers in schools and universities sufficient autonomy to maintain creative and open cultures of learning for their students. Competitive businesses need first and foremost individuals who are creative, who are capable and willing to take risks and who can use these skills both working independently and together in teams.

Implications for Schools

Teaching in schools is influenced by two change forces that often are more contradictory than complementary. The first force is the global education reform movement. It is shifting the focus of improving education towards basic knowledge and skills in some core subjects, common standards for teaching and learning, measurable knowledge and stronger accountability for results, especially at school level. The other force is the increasing external expectation that schools should do more to help the countries' economies to develop and become more competitive. Caught in the middle of these change forces are the teachers and students who often find it difficult and meaningless to react to these contradictory external pressures.

An analysis of the concrete consequences that each of these changes have fostered can clarify the contradiction. For the sake of simplicity, we can take one example from each level of education: the system level, school level and classroom level. This not only means providing flexible education and training opportunities for all in the society, young and old. It also refers to flexibility in the curriculum, in the organization of work in schools, in using various teaching and learning arrangements and in reporting on progress and achievements. Creativity becomes an important principle at the school level. Teachers who are catalysts of learning in the knowledge society must therefore be provided with incentives and encouraged to make their work place and classrooms creative learning organizations where openness to new ideas and approaches flourish. Finally, risk-taking needs to be encouraged in daily life and learning in schools. There is no creativity in schools without flexibility in the education system and no creativity without risk – the risk of trying a new idea, experimenting with an unfamiliar practice, being prepared to fail or look silly when trying something new, not taking setbacks to heart, being responsive rather than overly sensitive to critical feedback and so on.

The global education reform movement is also fostering standardization in education, stronger accountability for results in schools and teaching for measurable results. Standardization has become a common change strategy at the education system level.

Standards for learning, teaching, curriculum and assessment have been introduced in many education systems as a means of securing unified 'delivery' of education services to all citizens. The prevalence of standardized tests and other forms of assessment has gradually made schools and teachers more accountable than before for their students' learning. At the classroom level teachers are increasingly teaching for predetermined results and targets that are often described in centralized curriculum and national education standards documents.

Steering education systems towards producing intended outcomes requires congruence between teaching for the knowledge economy and what education reforms are expecting from teachers and students. In some cases, however, what schools are explicitly or implicitly assumed to do to improve their performance within ongoing education reforms contradicts what is needed from schools to support economic competitiveness. Comparison of these two change forces at the level of education systems, schools and classroom indicates some difficult incompatibilities and controversies. At the macro level, economic competitiveness demands an education system flexible enough to be able to react to weak signals and to produce a coordinated and collaborative response. Such a reaction and response is made possible by sustainable leadership. An education system's flexibility is promoted by freedom of choice, decentralized management and a culture of trust in professional communities, i.e. teachers and educational leaders. At the same time education reforms are equipping education systems with standards and regulations that set the criteria and targets for success and measurement. These education standards aim at raising the expectations of teaching and learning by specifying what every student should know and be able to do. At school level economic competitiveness needs the organization of work to enable alternative scheduling, integration of subjects and increased teacher collaboration. Creativity is promoted by using a wide spectrum of teaching methods, such as co-operative learning, and building bridges between the school and the community. Due to global education reforms, however, work in schools is influenced by prescribed curricula that are often used to determine the performance level and even, mistakenly, the quality of schools. Teachers tend to rely on traditional teaching arrangements and methods in order to minimize the risk of failure. Finally, teaching and learning for more competitive economies requires teachers and students to work together in safe and stimulating learning environments that focus on broad learning objectives, encourage everyone to participate and use alternative approaches to achieve goals. Risk-taking in teaching and learning is promoted by co-operative cultures, mutual trust and feedback that recognize students' efforts as well as attainment.

As a result of typical education reforms, however, teaching and learning are often characterized by stress and fear as the focus is on being successful in achieving the predetermined learning outcomes. Therefore students primarily learn alone rather than co-operatively in small groups in order to minimize personal risks. Open and alternative teaching methods and task designs are not favored.

Standards-based curriculum reforms have become increasingly common in many parts of the world recently (England, Germany, many Central and Eastern Europe countries and most states in the United States, for example). In practice, as Hargreaves and his colleagues claim ''the common, standards-based curriculum is often [...] a clinical and conventional curriculum in which literacy, numeracy and science are accorded supreme importance.'' In the 1988 national curriculum reform in England and Wales the so-called core subjects were mathematics, science and English. Similarly these same subjects have increased their status in many other countries due to the strengthened political significance of the international student learning comparisons and benchmarking. As a consequence, curriculum standards in many countries place too strong an emphasis on what Habermas has called systemworld of knowledge, i.e. structural knowledge of system, technical skills and cognition. Instead, successful and competitive knowledge economies draw upon the lifeworld of culture – especially beliefs, values, morality, meaning and social experiences. Both are important and both must be in balance for schools to be able to produce expected outcomes. Changing societies and complex knowledge economies require that students are educated equally for the artistic, social and critical lifeworld as much as for the rational systemworld of numeracy, literacy, scientific and technological competences. However, the situation in many countries is opposite: the importance of aesthetic and moral education and social sciences in school curricula, for example, has been reduced due to the need to strengthen the teaching of what some call fundamental or core subjects, i.e. mother tongue, mathematics and natural sciences. Although there is no evidence globally of any significant quantitative shifts within curricula, international comparisons of student achievement and national high-stakes external evaluations are increasing the imbalance between systemworld and lifeworld knowledge that students learn in school. These comparisons and evaluations usually judge the quality of individual schools and education systems using test scores gained only in the core subjects. At best this represents a rationalistic, partial and extremely reductionist judgment of the subtle and complex process of education for the knowledge economy and democratic society.

Education Reform and Economic Competitiveness

Is there a correlation between the quality of education and economic competitiveness? Using available international studies and surveys the answer is simply: 'No.' Countries like the United States (2nd) and Norway (6th) rank high in the 2004 global competitiveness ratings but only modestly or poorly in the assessments of their students' learning achievement, such as the OECD PISA study that is commonly seen as a forward-looking and relevant measure of educational quality. On the other hand, Korea, Canada and the Netherlands are high in the student learning comparisons but not at the top in economic competitiveness rankings (29th, 15th and 12th, respectively). Many countries seem to reach similar opposite positions in these two ratings, simultaneously at the high and low ends of the scales, therefore the assumption that these two measures correlation has to be avoided. Nevertheless, some countries seem to do consistently well in both rankings.

The Case of Finland

Finland has been ranked as the most competitive economy three times out of four in this decade. This is significant given that Finland experienced a severe economic crisis in early 1990s with 17 percent unemployment and more than a 10 percent drop in Gross Domestic Product (GDP). Becoming a global economic leader and one of the most advanced societies in terms of adopting information technologies required major restructuring of economy. Good governance, strong social cohesiveness and an extensive social safety net provided by the welfare state made an exceptionally rapid economic recovery possible. Interestingly, at the beginning of the 1990s Finland did not have a particularly good reputation in education, except in literacy. Finnish students' success in mathematics and science assessments was average if not below. In this decade, however, according to the PISA ratings, Finland has ranked top in both PISA cycles in mathematics, science and literacy.

Attempts to understand and explain the differences between education systems in terms of students' learning outcomes and variation of the quality of schools has raised some questions of the role of country-specific characteristics. For example, authorities in countries that have not performed well in PISA have claimed that the tests used do not adequately measure what is taught in schools.

Some of them also argue that winners in mathematics and science Olympiads are better proof of high quality education systems. It is true that standardized international tests are never able to completely match with teaching and learning practices and hence please all participating countries.

Some international observers have argued that Finland has been able to develop high performing education system because of its peculiar characteristics. It is important to realize that indeed education systems are operating as interconnected part of wider social and political systems. However, one has to be careful in establishing credible causal relationships between education system performance and national characteristics. The following four beliefs are myths often heard around the world regarding the Finnish educational success.

It has been argued that good results in education are easier to achieve in a small country than in a large one. Although the size may matter in this case, it is hardly a significant explaining factor. Countries of similar size are performing differently, for example Norway, Denmark, Ireland or Luxemburg. Therefore, it is difficult to argue that the size of population would have significant affect on the results in the sample-based assessments.

Finland is Socially and Culturally Homogeneous

While this may have some impact on the learning results, it is difficult to make the link when other countries with similarly homogeneous populations do not do as well in international assessments as Finland. For example, Denmark, Norway, Hungary and Poland that all are in many ways similar to Finland in terms of their social and cultural structures have very different PISA results compared to Finland. Some countries have removed their immigrant pupils from the PISA sample in order to determine the affect of that sub-population on the gross sample. In Germany, for example, the overall rank in 2003 mathematics scale increased by two places In case of Finland it should be noted that Finland is a trilingual country with two official national languages, Finnish and Swedish, and growing number of ethnic minorities.

PISA Tests Match the Finnish Curriculum

Some observers have argued that the test items that are used in PISA cycles especially favor Finnish students because they are more aligned with the current curriculum in Finland than in many other countries. This belief may well be true and if it is, then the curriculum should deserve more attention in understanding the educational success. However, it should be noted that each and every country has to accept all test items used in PISA and that way confirm that they are conform with what should be taught in schools.

Finland is a Country with Severe Climate

The most extreme statements expressed by some educational commentators claim that being a cold and dark arctic country the youth in Finland have less outdoor attractions and hence they spend more time with educational activities. This is simply nonsense. According to the international surveys Finnish pupils spend less time on homework than their international peers. Secondly, the climate in the parts of Finland where most people live does not significantly differ from the climate or amount of the daylight in other Nordic countries, Canada or the northern states of the US.

Education system performance has to be seen in the context of other systems in the society, e.g. health, environment, rule of law, governance, economy and technology. It is not only that education functions well Finland but it is a part of well-functioning democratic welfare state. Attempts to explain the success of the education system in Finland should be put in the wider context and seen as a part of overall function of democratic civil society. Economists have been interested in finding out why Finland has been able to become the most competitive economy in the world since 1990. The quality of a society is rarely a result of any single factor. The entire society needs to perform satisfactorily.

There are some interesting parallels between education and economic development policies in Finland during the period of transformation and related rapid growth in 1990s. Four common features are often mentioned as contributory factors towards positive educational and economic progress. First, policy development has been based on integration rather than exclusive sub-sector policies.

Education sector development is driven by medium-term policy decisions that rely on sustainable basic values, such as equal opportunities to good education for all, inclusion of all students in mainstream publicly financed education and strong trust in public education as a civil right rather than an obligation. These medium-term policies integrate education and training and involve the private sector and industry in the creation and monitoring of their results. Similarly, economic and industrial policies have integrated science and technology policies and innovation system with industrial clusters. Integrated policies have enhanced systemic development and interconnectedness of these sectors and have thus promoted more sustainable and coherent political leadership for their successful implementation.

Second, strategic framework development and change have been built upon longer-term vision. National development strategies, for example Information Society Program, National Lifelong Learning Strategy and Ministry of Education Strategy 2015 have served as overarching frameworks for the sector strategies. These and other strategies have emphasized increasing flexibility, coherence between various sectors and development of local and regional responsiveness and creativity in institutions.

Third, the roles of governance and public institutions have been central in policy developments and implementation of both education and economic reforms. Good governance, high quality public institutions and rule of law play important roles in policy development and implementation of planned changes. Evaluation approaches in both sectors are development-oriented and various players in the system are held accountable for process and outcomes. Specific institutions, such as the Committee of the Future and Vocational Education and Training Committees are shared by private and public representatives as well as the key stakeholders of the society for consensus-making purposes.

Fourth, a highly educated labor force and broad participation in education at all levels guarantee the stock of human capital that is necessary for both good education service delivery and economic growth. For instance, all teachers are required to hold a Masters degree and most workers are encouraged to participate in continuous professional development as part of their work. Teachers are professionals in their schools and therefore actively involved in planning and implementing changes in their work.

Flexibility is one of the key denominators of education and economic development in Finland. The education system went through a major transformation in early 1990s when most State regulations were abolished and pathways to education opportunities were dramatically increased.

Similarly, private sector regulations were loosened and more flexible standards were introduced, especially to foster networking between firms, universities, public research and development institutions.

Strong integrated policy frameworks and longer-term strategic visions have enhanced sustainable leadership in education and private sector developments. Due to this sustainability factor the education system has been quite passive in adopting the market-oriented principles of the global education reform movement. For example, learning and teaching standards, high-stakes tests or consequential accountability, have never been favored in Finnish education policies.

Frequent and open dialogue between private and public education sectors has increased the mutual understanding of what is important in achieving the common good and promoting the development of knowledge economy. Indeed, active co-operation between education and industry has encourage schools to experiment with creative teaching and learning practices, especially in nurturing entrepre-neurship and building positive attitudes towards work. Most importantly, the main principle in development of Finnish society has been encouraging intellectual growth and learning. Developing cultures of growth and learning in education institutions as well as in work places has proved to be one of the key success factors.

There are many attempts to explain Finland's educational success. The OECD's PISA compares cognitive competences that students have developed in literacy, mathematics and science in school. In other words, it is a forward-looking evaluation of how well students can use their knowledge and skills to solve real world problems rather than a test of whether they remember specific points of grammar or a formula to solve a physics problem.

During the "educational pilgrimage" to Finland since 2001, visitors hear a variety of possible reasons for the success of country's education system. Teachers and resources certainly contribute. However, the key difference between Finland and most of the world is that Finnish schools are almost totally test-free. The only compulsory standardized test is the high school exit examination, taken at age 18. The learning environment is therefore safe and free from fear and anxiety often caused by failing in tests. Thus, as most Finnish teachers will tell you, they are free to focus on developing understanding, fostering an interest in learning and cultivating open trust-based relationships between teachers and students. Since stu- dents are rarely coached for tests they can focus on the knowledge and skills they deem important. Creativity and risk-taking are common in Finnish classrooms. Parents trust teachers to tell them how well or poorly their children are learning in school.

Emerging Issues

There has been a great temptation in many countries to imitate the education reform efforts designed and implemented in other countries. Part of the problem is that the actual results of education reforms are rarely analyzed simply because the most important outcomes are only visible in the longer-term, later than most administrators or politicians can wait. Another part of the problem is that it is common to complete a strategic development plan and then allocate mechanisms of accountability and support to implement the plan. What is often missing is the ability to modify change strategies by continuously shaping and reshaping intentions, ideas and actions.

The emergence of the network society and knowledge-based economies appears to be a powerful justification for education reforms in developed countries. Schools and teachers are being asked to do more than they have done before but also in a different way. At the same time, globalization has generated education reform that also requires teachers to do more and differently.

Education reforms currently planned or implemented throughout the world need to include deeper and more comprehensive analysis of what and how schools and teachers should do in order to contribute to the development of economic competitiveness of their countries. This requires at least three actions. First, education reforms at the outset should provide a stronger pool of educational change knowledge to those who are involved in planning and implementing the education reforms. Fullan sees change knowledge as understanding and insight about the process of change and the key factors that lead to success in practice.

The possession of educational change knowledge does not necessarily lead to success, but its absence ensures failure. Second, analytical work on the knowledge economy and learning society should focus on moral purpose and on the processes of teaching and learning, not only on the structure and the content of education. Third, the sustainability and spread of educational change can only be understood by analyzing change efforts in a wider range of settings over a longer period of time. Most education reform literature, however, focuses on specific aspects of early implementation rather than the long term persistence of change.

Education reforms – if they are to make any significant impact on economic competitiveness – should address more clearly the aspects of teaching and learning that have been found in recent research to be related to economic competitiveness. In general, co-operation rather than competition or isolation is the key principle of change. Economic competitiveness can therefore be promoted and enhanced by fostering co-operation and interaction at three levels in education: schools, teachers and students.

Three other conclusions can be drawn from available knowledge base on educational change. First, supporting networking of schools has to be given a high priority in education reforms. Almost in any education system necessary innovations and ideas for improvement already exist in the system. The challenge is to share them between schools. Therefore, developing the education system in a way that encourages and enables schools to create partnerships and information exchange networks is likely to spread existing good practices. Second, helping teachers to work as professional communities should be emphasized in combating the isolation that is common to many teaching cultures. Learning to teach in new way is not easy. A safe and supportive professional climate in schools is a necessary condition for professional improvement of teachers. Designing education reforms in a way that will provide teachers with opportunities and incentives to collaborate more will increase the likelihood of sustainable implementation of intended changes. Third, making learning interesting for students is the imperative for sustainable development and change in schools. Economic competitiveness is above all about learning. When individuals or societies have severe learning difficulties the economic forecasts will not look good. If students do not learn in their schools and universities to love learning, they will not find learning and change attractive afterwards. Therefore, education reforms should first and foremost try to make learning in schools interesting for all students without sacrificing the other important goals of education.

Improving economic competitiveness requires well educated and trained people, technological and network readiness and knowledge and skills to work in an innovation-rich world. Co-operation and networking rather than competition and disconnectedness should therefore lead the education policies and development of education systems. Schools and other educational institutions should cultivate attitudes, cultures and skills that are necessary in creative and collaborative learning environments. Creativity will not flourish and be sustained in schools unless people feel secure to take risks and explore the unknown. Moreover, working with and understanding innovations require creative and risk-intensive contexts. In brief, economic competitiveness can be best promoted by developing fear-free learning and professional development environments in schools. The fear-free school is a place where students are not afraid to try new ideas and ways of thinking. Equally importantly, in the fear-free school teachers and principals will step beyond their conventional territories of thinking and doing that are often conditions for making a difference in students' learning and schools' performance.

References

Aho, E., Pitkanen, K. & Sahlberg, P. *Policy Development and Reform Principles in Finland since 1968.* Washington, DC: World Bank.

Anon,. 55 *Policy Recommendations for Raising Croatia's Competitiveness*. Zagreb, Croatia: National Competitiveness Council.

Brooks, J. & Brooks, M.. *In Search of Understanding: The Case for Constructivist Classrooms.* Alexandria, VA: Association for Supervision and Curriculum Development.

Carnoy, M.. *Globalization and Educational Reform. What planners need to know?*. Paris: Unesco and IIEP.

Sarason, S.. *The Unpredictable Failure of Educational Reform. Can we Change the Course Before it's Too Late?*. San Francisco, CA: Jossey-Bass.

Steiner-Khamsi, G. (ed.). *The Global Politics of Educational Borrowing and Lending.* New York, NY: Teachers College Press.

World Bank. *Expanding Opportunities and Building Competences of Young People*. A New Agenda for Secondary Education. World Bank, DC: Washington.

3

Educational Innovations in the Knowledge Economy

The most significant political and policy development over the past decade is the emergence, globally, of a new, very powerful, discursive imaginary; the assertion that we now live in, or are moving toward, a knowledge-based economy, and that the recalibration of institutions, and their desirable geographies, are crucial to enable this to be realized. This focus on knowledge, as the key motor for the economy, on how to create, distribute and manage it, has placed education at the centre of policy and politics. Among policymakers, there is now intense interest in:

- nurturing 'creativity' and 'entrepreneurship' as a basis for innovation and invention;
- the idea that new, more active, learner-centered pedagogies are desirable;
- that learning spaces can be architecturally manipulated to generate ideas that in turn generate inventions;
- that digital technologies can transform learning; and
- that we can 'hothouse talent' and 'incubate' ideas to generate value.

Earlier versions of human capital theory have been invigorated by new growth theorists who argue that it is not just more education that matters, but the kinds of education experiences that foster active learning and innovative aptitudes, whilst popular intellectuals, such as Richard Florida, have promoted concepts like the 'creative class' as the basis for producing competitive economies. We have also seen intense focus on research and evidence, and how this might inform evidence-based, or evidence-informed, policymaking.

It is against this backdrop that the ideas: 'education', 'knowledge' and 'innovation', are being promoted as central to the development of a globally-competitive knowledge-based economy.

The knowledge-based economy rests on four interconnected, interdependent pillars:

- Innovation
- Economic and institutional infrastructure
- Information infrastructure, and
- Education.

Today, new "frontier" technologies are transforming and expanding many economies in the same way that earlier industrial and technological revolutions changed the course of history. Just as the steam age and the information technology age, for example, went through various stages of development, so too will the technologies considered to be at the frontiers of knowledge today. Countries must seize the opportunities now available in areas such as biotechnology, nanotechnology and the "hydrogen economy" to establish capabilities that will provide long-term, sustainable solutions in national priority areas such as health and energy, while boosting economic growth. Today, a growing percentage of wealth in the world's largest economies is created by knowledge-based industries that rely heavily on human capital and technological innovation.

Emergence of a Knowledge-based Economy

The idea of a knowledge-based economy has its roots in work developed by a group of 1960s intellectuals, futurologists and information economists, including Fritz Machlup, Peter Drucker and Daniel Bell. These writers argued that societies were in transition to becoming knowledge-based; in other words, that 'muscle-based' work was being replaced by 'mind-based' work. Their thesis at the time was regarded as highly speculative. Two decades later, it was added to by urban sociologist, Manuel Castells, and his theory of the emergence of a network society. A core argument too in this body of work is that information/knowledge is now a new factor in production, and that digital technologies offer, for the first time, the potential to annihilate the barriers of time and space because of the ways in which we can generate feedback in real time, making our capacity to respond to this feedback significantly different and potentially effective for product and service development.

International organisations, like the OECD, have been heavily influenced by these arguments. During the 1970s, they took on board the idea of an 'information society', enlisting the expertise of a range of economists concerned with mapping and measuring information. By the 1990s, the concept of a *knowledge-based* economy was eventually reflecting the contribution of economists such Foray, Lundvall, and Romer.

At the heart of the OECD's version of the 'knowledge economy' is the idea that knowledge has *value*. As Bell put it:

> Knowledge is that which is objectively known, an *intellectual property*, attached to a name or group of names and certified by copyright, or some other form of social recognition (e.g. publication). ...It is subject to a judgment by the market, by administrative or political decisions of superiors, or by the peers as the worth of the result, and as to its claim on social resources, where such claims are made. In this sense, knowledge is part of the social overhead investment of society, it is a coherent statement, presented in a book, article, or even a computer program, written down or recorded at some point for transmission, and subject to some rough count.

The OECD then moved toward developing sets of indicators to both measure and guide national state's development toward a knowledge-based economy. The effect of producing statistics to measure a KBE in turn stabilized the idea of a knowledge-based economy around four pillars: 'innovation', 'new technologies', 'human capital' and 'enterprise dynamics'.

The World Bank's foray into the 'knowledge' arena began in the early 1990s. The World Bank was the first cooperation agency to explore the implications of 'knowledge' both for its own activities as an organisation, and also for its clients. This ambitious work began in 1996 under the leadership of World Bank President, James Wolfensohn, where it reinvented itself as 'the Knowledge Bank'. Its 1998 World Development Report (WDR), *Knowledge for Development*, laid the foundations for much of the Bank's work over the next decade. The WDR placed knowledge at the centre of the work of the Bank's activities – so that in the education sector the focus was now shifted to include higher education.

There was, nevertheless, a very particular set of 'knowledges' being privileged in this K4D programme: Western science and technology, enabled by ICTs and the institutional structures that supported a liberal market economy based on value realized from intellectual property. As King argues, this was pretty much business as usual for the Bank.

Like the OECD, the World Bank's K4D programme is based on four pillars:

1. An *economic and institutional regime* that provides incentives for the efficient use of existing and new knowledge and the flourishing of entrepreneurship.
2. An *educated and skilled population* that can create, share, and use knowledge well.
3. An *efficient innovation system* of firms, research centres, universities, think-tanks, consultants, and other organizations who can tap into the growing stock of global knowledge, assimilate and adapt it to local needs, and create new technology.
4. *Information and Communication Technologies (ICT)* that can facilitate the effective communication, dissemination, and processing of information.

We can get a good sense of the World Bank's strategic framing of what it means to be a knowledge economy, as well as the tools used by the Bank to help shape a country's strategies, by looking at the content of the *Knowledge Assessment Methodology* (KAM).

The KAM is the centrepiece and underpinning architecture of the Bank's K4D programme. It is an interactive, diagnostic and benchmarking tool that provides a preliminary assessment of countries and regions 'readiness for the knowledge economy'. The KAM enables countries from around the world to benchmark themselves with neighbours, competitors, or other countries they wish to learn from on the four pillars of the knowledge economy. It is therefore a tool aimed at promoting 'learning' amongst both developing and developed countries about the elements that constitute the Bank's version of a knowledge economy.

Since its launch, the KAM has undergone a series of refinements. In 2004, 121 countries were included in its KAM database and 76 structural and qualitative variables were available as measures of knowledge-based economies. In 2006 the KAM was relaunched, this time with 128 countries and 80 variables. By 2007, four further countries were added. The KAM currently consists of 81 structural and qualitative variables for 132 countries to measure their performance on the four Knowledge Economy (KE) pillars: Economic Incentive and Institutional Regime, Education, Innovation, and Information and Communications Technologies. Variables are normalized on a scale of zero to ten relative to other countries in the comparison group. The KAM also derives a country's overall *Knowledge Economy Index* (KEI) and *Knowledge Index* (KI) based on an aggregation of the 14 key variables.

The European Commission offers a similar way of looking at knowledge and innovation—the basis for stimulating the realisation of the Lisbon Agenda—to be the most competitive, knowledge-based economy in the world. And whilst a social cohesion agenda has been a hallmark of what marks out the European strategy as different from those such as the USA or the UK, it is fair to say that this agenda plays second fiddle to the more powerful narrative of jobs, growth and innovation.

Through the 1990s, with steerage from dominant nations, regions and agencies, such as the US, EC, WTO, OECD and World Bank, the idea of a 'knowledge-based economy' was promoted so that it eventually emerged as a powerful master economic narrative in economic development strategies around the world. This project has been significantly buoyed by the idea that the services sectors could be developed and be the basis for generating a competitive advantage for the developed economies. Both Europe and the USA claim for themselves a competitive edge at the high value-added end of the commodity chain. This has prompted a concerted effort to widen and deepen the services sectors (eg education, health, finance, transport, and so on), to extend intellectual property rights (e.g. on pharmaceutical products, cultural products and put into place the means to protect those rights internationally so as to return value across borders. These ideas have contributed to the formation of the *World Trade Organisation* (WTO), and the creation of new agreements, such as the *Trade Related Intellectual Property Services Agreement* (TRIPS) and *General Agreement on Trade in Services* (GATS) which materialised in 1995.

The GATS Agreement, bilateral agreements between third world countries and EU Member States (e.g. Erasmus Mundus), the extension of the Bologna Process to include not only the official 46 Member States but its global take-up, are all directed toward opening up education as a services sector so that it can contribute directly to the economy. Movements of students are seen, not in cosmopolitan, but commodity terms, raising important issues around the movement of knowledge and brain drain, and the trade-offs between aid for development and trade for development. These initiatives have been highly controversial in those countries around the world where there has been a history of state-subsidy and a generous view about global mobility and global community.

Importance of Re/Framings

It is important we now address how innovation is framed within the KBE discourse, and from there what this framing means for how we think about knowledge, research and development. Whilst recognizing that innovation, and invention are vital to all societies and their economies, and that higher education institutions have historically, and indeed more crucially now, been asked to play an important role in this regard, what is clear is that we continue to work with the narrow framing of innovation coming from the KBE narrative outlined above. In other words, innovation is viewed in high tech science and technology terms. Hidden in this framing are all kinds of social and other innovations – often referred to as 'soft' and 'process'. For instance, larger sectors, such as the cultural and creative industries, the public sector, the professions such as education, health, law, the retail sector, the medical world, and so on are largely absent. Yet all offer remarkable insights into innovations, and indeed innovation in these sectors is critical if they are to not only engage with the possibilities of new technologies, but to offer better quality services. Missing, too, are ways of talking about innovation in those services that will become more and more important over the next decade, such as recycling, aging, transport and so on. These are hidden, but they are innovations none-the-less.

There are other problems here too. Typical indexes of innovation, such as the Innovation Scoreboard, measure outputs, or start-ups, spin-out companies, and patents, the latter of course chiefly relevant to high and medium high technology areas. In other words, the measures of what constitutes innovation, and what motivates innovative behaviour (such as commercial success), are also very narrow. This is important because it limits institutions access to funding for highly relevant knowledge transfer funding activity. Institutions might also put into place the wrong, or at best a limited, set of incentives and rewards for innovative research activity.

A major challenge, then, for knowledge/research centres whose research activities operate predominantly in this 'hidden innovation' zone is to enter into a debate about the importance of reframing innovative activity so that it is sufficiently broad-based and broad-minded to take our current real (and local) economies into account, and value and reward them, rather than some imagined one.

One effect of a broader conception of innovation is that we may then be better placed to think in new ways about how innovation occurs. For researchers like Lundvall, this includes openness to the role of 'learning' in innovation, such as the contribution of interactions with clients as partners, along with the importance of imagination, analysis, problem-solving, and so on. Being more open and broad-minded may end up being more challenging for traditional higher education institutions, many (though not all) of whom have often worked at a distance from their local communities, their private and public sectors.

Knowledge and Innovation in City/Regions

Higher education institutions embedded in close local and regional networks are particularly well placed to participate in the development of 'knowledge regions'— currently the preferred model for economic development for governments, largely because of knowledge transfer reasons. Several lines of research feed into this model of best practice for how education, knowledge and innovation might contribute to economic and social development (where the city-region is regarded as the most efficient and effective because of access to local political decision-making, the value of proximity for generating spillovers, the activation of networks for trust, and so on). Key influences have been Etzkowitz and Leydersdorff's 'triple helix' (state-university-industry), Porter's work on clusters as a means of realizing a 'competitive', 'comparative' and 'constructed' advantage, and Richard Florida's work on what he refers to as the 'creative class'.

At the same time, there is also a pull outward, toward the global, in part through:

(i) the way discourses around global cities, globally-competitive regions, and world class higher education institutions work;

(ii) student populations, who rightly see their own credentials in terms of the value/return it has in a wider labour market (hence seek knowledge and skills that have some wider cache); and

(iii) the concerns of teaching faculty who seek promotion, and increasingly importantly, need to play the publication game.

This sets up a tension between the centripetal (*inward* oriented nature of knowledge regions) and the centrifugal (*outward* nature of academic economy) dynamics of the higher education/city-region relation which, in combination, are likely to create uneven networks of cooperation. The 'Out-There-Globally-Competitive' might well work against the 'In-Here-Community-Cohesion' in important ways, for instance, what is viewed as valued research and research-based knowledge, how this knowledge circulates, and to whom? How do local and globalising dynamics talk with each other in ways that are additive rather than canceling each other out? It is important not only that institutions understand the causes and effects of these dynamics, but also work toward working with them in new and innovative ways.

Here, it would seem, it is important research centres generate spaces that enable them to think in more innovative ways; of how to produce knowledge and activate networks where the local and the global, the insider and the outsider, the newcomer and the old-timer – to use Jean Lave's terms with regard to 'communities of practice'—come together so that social relations can be re/negotiated despite the inevitable barriers of time, space and culturally-mediated socialities.

A challenge here is also thinking in innovative ways about how to build epistemic communities, for instance by drawing upon new digital tools, such as social networking, blogging, wikis and so on. In other words, how might we work with individuals and communities across time-space, and across cultural barriers? How might we set up new learning relationships?

Transformation of Higher Education

To say that the university is in crisis is to echo the thoughts and sentiments of a generation of post-war commentators. The word 'crisis', accordingly, has almost lost the theoretical purchase it once had and slipped into a kind of rhetoric that is now consistently invoked by writers and scholars of all political persuasions. The term crisis was used to refer to the crisis of governance of the university following the student unrest and resistance of the late 1960s. Analysis of the demands made by the student movement pointed to the need for a greater democratisation of the university. It revealed the elitist functions of the university based upon the myths of 'pure inquiry' and 'objective knowledge' which operated, ideologically, to screen out different cultural and gender values that determine both what counts as knowledge and legitimate ways of pursuing it.

The term was used again during the 1970s to refer to the decline of the humanities. This was a period when increasing numbers of students in western universities opted for science and technology and the first real pressures for universities to become more vocationally oriented began to be felt. The general shift to the Right that took place in global politics during the 1980s and the emergence of a set of policies based upon neo-liberal principles expressing both the failure of 'big' government and a commitment to free-market solutions, became associated with a double notion of 'crisis'. The first was linked to the university's survival: it was linked to problems of funding and was seen, above all, as a fiscal crisis — one of external legitimation and principally a crisis focusing upon the continued financial viability of the institution. The second centred on the curriculum and the crisis of the humanities. In the American academy especially, this notion of crisis had been manufactured by those dedicated to a conservative cultural project.

The transformation of higher education in Anglophone countries from a universal welfare entitlement into a private investment in 'human capital' established a similar pattern shared by a number of OECD countries. First, a transparent alignment of the university system to reflect the needs of an emerging 'post-industrial' economy, with increasing demands for highly trained, multi-skilled, tertiary-educated workers. Second, the introduction of new forms of corporate managerialism and the emulation of private sector management styles; the coporatization of the university system — an emphasis on so-called 'clear accountability structures' including the attempted simplification of goals or purposes, and the institution of new forms of delegated authority. Third, the introduction of corporate or strategic planning and the move to institute a form of 'ownership monitoring' in order, allegedly, to reduce the financial risk of the State. Fourth, under neo-liberalism, there was an attack on faculty representation in university governance and the general attempt to discredit democratic forms of university governance on 'efficiency' grounds. Finally, the introduction of user-charges, student loans, and the creeping privatisation of the system as a whole took place to varying degrees in countries like New Zealand, Australia, Canada and the United Kingdom.

The writing was on the wall in the 1980s when calls were made for a reappraisal of the university institution. Thus, for instance, the OECD Intergovernmental Conference on 'Policies for Higher Education' in 1983 referred not only to 'the crisis of performance' but, more fundamentally, pointed to 'an internal crisis of purpose'. The OCED publication, *Universities Under Scrutiny* began by questioning 'the very purposes and functions of higher education in post-industrialised societies'.

The OECD Secretariat emphasised the mismatch between the university's self-definition and external expectations and suggested a set of policies that, at one and the same time, promoted a greater vocationalism and sense of 'appliedness', and a greater focus on efficiency, productivity and accountability. The 'massification' of higher education within OECD countries also involved the implementation of new financial models, which determine the manner and amount of institutional funding. This policy move was predicated on the basis of an official recognition that there is an alleged need to reduce the burden on governments to act as sole providers and that private sector had an increasing role to play either directly or in partnership with public institutions. In some countries it also indicated that arguments that education constitutes a private good had found favour with politicians who often believed that competition for funds increase institutional efficiency and responsiveness.

Experimentation with alternative institutional funding mechanisms in OECD countries over the past couple of decades appear to follow a similar pattern: adoption and increased sophistication of institutional formulae-founding; greater financial autonomy and market freedom for institutions; an increasing proportion of income from student fees; sharper distinction between funding of research and of teaching; an increased proportion of public funding to be 'bid for' by the institutions; and the encouragement of a diversification of funding sources with the promotion of partnerships with business. Even with the diversification of funding sources, universities have struggled to cope financially and many have kept student fees relatively low only by drawing upon their reserves. The 1990s became an era of managerial restructuring and closure for some departments, faculties and institutions especially as the spectacular growth in participation experienced in the last few decades forced institutions not only to compete with each other in the market for student places but also absorb the cost of providing extra, unfunded, student places, at declining levels of State funding.

The result has been, as the UK White Paper, *The Future of Higher Education* acknowledges, serious under-funding. While there is a positive recognition of the under-funding crisis and a promised increase in spending on research of 1.25 billion it is delayed to 2005-06, there is also a greater pragmatic emphasis on creating and encouraging a greater 'knowledge exchange' with business and regional development agencies. The discourse of 'excellence' characterises the document, a kind of empty signifier. The dis-ease, the diagnosis and the remedy are now part of an on-going policy mantra in higher education designed to come to terms with the impact of globalization.

In *The University in Ruins* Bill Readings suggests that there is a general uncertainty as to the role of the university: university teaching staff are being proletarianized; the number of part-term contracts have increased; the production of knowledge is uncertain. The crisis of the humanities would not in itself be significant, he maintains, were it not accompanied by an external legitimation crisis. His analysis is that the role of the university has shifted as the forces of globalization have become more evident:

> the University is becoming a different institution, one that is no longer linked to the destiny of the nation-state by virtue of its role as producer, protector, and inculcator of an idea of national culture. The process of economic globalization brings with it the relative decline of the nation-state as the prime instance of the reproduction of capital around the world. For its part, the University is becoming a transnational bureaucratic corporation, either tied to transnational instances of government such as the European Union or functioning independently, by analogy with a transnational corporation.

The emergence of the concept of culture, he suggests, should be understood as a particular way of dealing with the tensions that arose between the University and the State, as essentially *modern* institutions. When he writes of the University he is referring to the German model that Humboldt instituted at the University of Berlin. The notion of culture as the central legitimating idea of the modern University has come to the end of its usefulness and, accordingly, 'the story of liberal education has lost its organizing center'. The overall nature of the University has become corporate rather than cultural. University administrators, government officials and policy experts increasingly talk of the University's mission in terms of 'excellence' rather than 'culture', yet 'excellence' is non-ideological, Readings argues, in the sense that 'what gets taught or researched is less important than the fact that it be excellently taught or researched'.

Taking lead from Bill Readings shall argue that three ideas of the university dominate the modern era: the Kantian idea of reason; the Humboldtian idea of culture, and; the techno-bureaucratic idea of excellence.

Readings summarises the history of the modern University in terms of three overarching ideas:

> The history of the modern University can be crudely summarised by saying that the modern University has had three Ideas, the Kantian idea of reason, the Humboldtian notion of culture, and now the technological idea of excellence. The distinguishing feature of the last... is that it lacks all referentiality — it is the *simulacrum* of the Idea of a University
>
> ... in the Kantian University [the president's] function is the purely disciplinary one of making decisive judgements in inter-faculty conflicts on the grounds of reason alone. In the University founded on culture, the president incarnates a pandisciplinary ideal of a general cultural orientation... In the contemporary University, however, a president is a bureaucratic administrator... From judge to synthesiser to executive.

One might argue that the founding discourses of the modern university have been permanently fractured and that under the combined pressures of globalization, managerialism and marketization, it is no longer possible to talk of the idea of modern university, of an institution both regulated and unified through the force of a single idea. The idea of the modern university based on Kant, Humboldt or Newman has become historical in the sense that the techno-bureaucratic idea of excellence has instituted an historical break or rupture with the modern. In other words, the university has become 'post-historical'.Use of the term 'post-historical' is not meant to suggest an 'end of history' or 'the end of ideology' thesis: these are the melodramatic tropes of Hegelians who believe that history is motored by a dialectical struggle of opposing forces that ends when one side prevails over the other. Thus, right Hegelians like Francis Fukuyama, believe that the collapse of communism after 1989 and the end of the Cold War signals the triumph of capitalism, and, therefore, the 'end of history', in much the same way that Marxists, of at least one persuasion, believed that history ended with establishment of the 'classless' society and the rule of the proletariat.

The Modern University

In his book *The University in Ruins* Readings suggests that with the advent of globalization and the decline of the nation state as one of the major organizing principles of economic and cultural development both the Kantian and Humboldtian ideas have become problematic. Universities now function as one more bureaucratic subsystem among others harnessed in the service of national competitiveness in the global economy. In the age of global capitalism universities have been reduced to a technical ideal of performance within a contemporary discourse of 'excellence'.

The university becomes modern when all of its activities are organized in terms of a single regulatory and unifying idea: the 'uni' of the 'versity', so to speak. As Timothy Bahti argues:

> Bahti indicates that whereas the seventeenth century had been heyday for the European academies of sciences, the eighteenth had been the low point for German universities: student rioting and drunkenness, dropping enrolments and little relationship between subjects taught and vocations. In the last decade of the eighteenth century there was talk of abolishing the university altogether, allowing the academies of sciences and the new practical vocational schools to take its place. And then in 1810, the University of Berlin was founded. In the intervening years were the reorganization of the Prussian bureaucracy following the defeat of Prussia by Napoleon and, as Bahti points out, 'the philosophical writings on and for the university, from Kant and Schelling and then from Fichte, Schleiermacher, and Humboldt'.

For Kant it was the idea of reason, which provided an organizing principle for the disciplines, with 'philosophy' as its home. Reason is the founding principle of the Kantian university: it confers universality upon the institution and, thereby, ushers in modernity. Reason, as the immanent unifying principle of the Kantian university, displaces the Aristotelian order of disciplines of the medieval university based on the seven liberal arts, (divided into the trivium [grammar, rhetoric and knowledge] and the quadrivium [arithmetic, geometry, astronomy, and music]), to substitute a quasi-industrial arrangement of the faculties. The three higher faculties —theology, law, and medicine, have a content, whereas the lower faculty, philosophy, does not. It has no content apart from the free exercise of reason and the self-critical and self-legislating exercise of reason, embodied in the philosophy faculty, controls the higher faculties, checking their credentials and credibility, and thereby establishing autonomy for the university as a whole. In *The Conflict of the Faculties* Kant writes:

> It was not a bad idea, whoever first conceived and proposed a public means for treating the sum of knowledge (and properly the heads who devote

> themselves to it), in a quasi *industrial* manner, with a division of labour where, for so many fields as there may be of knowledge, so many public teachers would be allotted, professors being trustees, forming together a kind of common scientific entity, called a university (or high school) and having autonomy (for only scholars can pass judgement on scholars as such); and, thanks to its faculties (various small societies where university teachers are ranged, in keeping with the variety of the main branches of knowledge), the university would be authorised to admit, on the one hand, student-apprentices from the lower schools aspiring to its level, and to grant, on the other hand — after prior examination, and on its own authority — to teachers who are 'free' (not drawn from the members themselves) and called 'Doctors', a universally recognised rank (conferring upon them a degree) — in short, *creating* them.

Reading argues that there is, in Kant, a problem or paradox that haunts the constitution of the modern university: how to institutionalise reason's autonomy, how to unify reason and the state, institution and autonomy? Kant attempts to reconcile the conflict through the *republican subject*, the universal subject of humanity, who incarnates this conflict. Thus, while it is one of the functions of the university to produce technicians or men of affairs for the state, the state must protect the university to ensure the rule of reason in public life. Philosophy, as the tribunal of reason, must protect the university from the abuse of power from the state and must act to distinguish legitimate from illegitimate conflict, that is, from the arbitrary exercise of authority.

The legitimacy of the state in Germany derives from the notion of ethnicity, as opposed to the French focus on the idea of humanity, more generally. On this basis, once the idea of reason is replaced with the idea of a national culture, the university is pressed into service of the state. Culture, like reason, serves as a unifying idea for the university, tying it to the nation-state. Readings argues that Humboldt's project for the foundation of the University of Berlin is decisive for the modern university up until the present day. For the German idealists, from Schiller through Schleiermacher to Fichte and Humboldt, the unity of knowledge and culture, exemplified best in the organicity of ancient Greek culture, has been splintered and lost. It can be reintegrated into a unified cultural science through *Bildung*, the formation and cultivation of moral subjects. Readings argues:

> Under the rubric of culture, the University is assigned the dual task of research and teaching, respectively the production and inculcation of national

> self-knowledge. As such, it becomes the institution charged with watching over the spiritual life of the people of the rational state, reconciling ethnic tradition and statist rationality.

The German idealist's notion of culture is given a literary turn by the British and Americans. In particular, the English, under John Newman and Matthew Arnold, continue the efforts of Humboldt by substituting literature for philosophy as the central discipline of the university, and, therefore, also of national culture. The possibility of a unified national culture is defined explicitly in terms of the study of a tradition of national literature.

Literature and the function of criticism is entrusted with a social mission in the Anglo-American university. In England, the idea of culture gets its purchase in opposition to science and technology, partly as a result of the threat posed by industrialisation and mass civilisation. Newman gives a 'liberal education' as the proper function of the university, which educates its charges to be gentlemen, not through the study of philosophy, but through the study of literature. In 'Literature: A Lecture in the School of Philosophy and Letters' delivered in 1858, Newman 'explicitly positions as the site of the development of both an idea of the nation and the study of literature as the means of training national subjects'. Newman suggests that 'A literature, when it is formed, is a national and historical fact; it is a matter of the past and present, and can be as little ignored as the present, as little undone as the past'. National language and literature defines the character of 'every great people', and Newman speaks of the classics of a national literature by which he means 'those authors who have had the foremost place in exemplifying the powers and conducting the development of its language'.

Readings argues that 'For Arnold, as for Eliot and Leavis after him, Shakespeare occupies the position that the German Idealists ascribed to the Greeks: that of immediately representing an organic community to itself in a living language'. In 'The Idea of a University' F. R. Leavis proposes that all study should be centred in the study of literature, centred in the seventeenth century and based on Shakespeare as the natural origin of culture. Leavis believes that the University of Culture can provide the lost centre and heal the split between the organic culture and mass civilization.

The grand narrative of the university, centred on the cultural production of a liberal, reasoning, citizen subject, in the wake of globalization, is no longer credible. 'The University ... no longer participates in the historical project for humanity that was the legacy of the Enlightenment: the historical project of culture'. The movement from cultural élite formation to the post-war massification of higher education has subjected the universalism of liberal education to criticism of its privilege based on the lines of class, gender and ethnicity. It is precisely at this point that the link between the university and the nation-state breaks down and the discourse of excellence gains a purchase. The University of Excellence replaces the University of Culture. As Readings argues:

> The economics of globalization mean that the University is no longer called upon to train citizen subjects, while the politics of the end of the cold war mean that the university is no longer called upon to uphold national prestige by producing and legitimating national culture.

Readings suggests that excellence has become the last unifying principle of the modern university. When Ministry policy analysts or university administrators talked about excellence, unwittingly they bracket the question of value in favor of measurement and substitute accounting solutions for questions of accountability. As an integrating principle excellence has the advantage of being entirely meaningless: it is non-referential. It signifies the corporate bureaucratization of the university. Universities have become sites for the development of 'human resources'. Guided by mission statements and strategic plans, performance output is measured TQM assures quality outcomes. Readings remarks:

> University mission statements, like their publicity brochures, share two distinctive features nowadays. On the one hand, they all claim that theirs is a unique educational institution. On the other hand, they all go on to describe this uniqueness in exactly the same way.

The 'Post-historical' University

Anyone with a passing familiarity with Readings' thesis as have presented it must recognize the traces of Jean-François Lyotard's influence. His *The Postmodern Condition: A Report on Knowledge* originally published in Paris in 1979, became an instant *cause célèbre* because Lyotard analysed the status of knowledge, science and the university in way that many critics believed signalled an epochal break not only with the so-called 'modern era' but also with various traditionally 'modern' ways of viewing the world. It was written, Lyotard asserts, 'at this very Postmodern moment that finds the University nearing what may be its end.'

In *The Postmodern Condition* Jean-François Lyotard was concerned with grand narratives which had grown out of the Enlightenment and had come to mark modernity. In *The Postmodern Explained to Children* Lyotard mentions: 'the progressive emancipation of reason and freedom, the progressive or catastrophic emancipation of labour..., the enrichment of all through the progress of capitalist techno-science, and even... the salvation of creatures through the conversion of souls to the Christian narrative of martyred love.' Grand narratives are the stories that cultures tell themselves about their own practices and beliefs in order to legitimate them. They function as a unified single story that purports to legitimate or found a set of practices, a cultural self-image, a discourse or an institution.

Lyotard holds that capitalist renewal after the 1930s and the post-war upsurge of technology has led to a 'crisis' of scientific knowledge and to an internal erosion of the very prospect of legitimation. He locates the seeds of such 'delegitimation' in the decline of the legitimating power of the grand narratives of the nineteenth century. In particular, the process of European cultural disintegration is symbolised most clearly by the end of philosophy as the universal meta-language able to underwrite all claims to knowledge and, thereby, to unify the rest of culture.

Since the late 1970s neo-liberalism has become the dominant grand narrative. A particular variant revitalises the master discourse of neo-classical economic liberalism and advances it as a basis for a global reconstruction of society. A form of economic reason encapsulated in the notion of *homo economicus*, with its abstract and universalist assumptions of individuality, rationality and self-interest, has captured the policy agendas of Western countries. Part of its innovation has been the way in which the neo-liberal grand narrative has successfully extended the principle of self-interest into the status of a paradigm for understanding politics itself, and, purportedly, *all* behaviour and human action. In the realm of higher education policy at every opportunity the market has been substituted for the state: students are now 'customers' or 'clients' and teachers are 'providers'. The notion of vouchers is suggested as a universal panacea to problems of funding and quality. The teaching/learning relation has been reduced to an implicit contract between buyer and seller. As Lyotard argued prophetically in *The Postmodern Condition* not only has knowledge and research become commodified but also so have the relations of the production of knowledge in a new logic of *performativity*.

University in The Knowledge Economy

The crisis of the idea of the modern university has been brought about largely by changes in the nature of the capitalist system, through attempts by governments to structurally adjust their national economies to the new conditions, and by consequent shifts in the production of knowledge that leads to the de-territorialization of knowledge and intensified knowledge flows. The new global knowledge economy is not just a universalisation of capitalism after the collapse of actually existing communism, it also involves the rise of finance capitalism, supported by the emergence of new information and communications technologies, and a series of international agreements concerning the liberalisation of world trade. The Dearing report recognized globalization as the major influence upon the UK economy and the labor market with strong implications for higher education. Analyzing the Dearing report it is possible to talk of the *globalization of tertiary or higher education*, according to three interrelated functions: the *knowledge* function, the *labor* function, and the *institutional* function. Knowledge is valued for its strict utility rather than as an end in itself or for its emancipatory or enlightenment effects. The globalization of the labor function is formulated in terms of both the production of technically skilled people to meet the needs of global corporations and the ideology of lifelong learning, where individuals can 're-equip themselves for a succession of jobs over a working lifetime'. The institutional function is summed up in the phrase 'higher education will become a global international service and tradable commodity'. The competitive survival of institutions is tied to the globalization of its organizational form (emulating private sector enterprises) and the globalization of its 'services'. With this function already a strong and closer alliance between global corporations and universities has developed, especially in terms of the funding of research and development, and, in some cases, the university as a global corporation with international sites for teaching and research. The latter is a trend likely to develop further with the world integration and convergence of media, telecommunications and publishing industries. The institutional form of the university depicted by Dearing, then, is one form of the post-historical university – the university as a global service corporation.

The GAL report proclaims both the end of 'the era of homogeneity' under state planning and the beginning of another era, which will be consumer-oriented, more diversified and exposed to international competition. The remnants of an era of state planning show that while costs of production are world competitive, productivity incentives are poor and capital management requires reform. The existing providers are protected in the Australian domestic market but not for too much longer.

The report identifies the following forces for change: the reducing Government fee structure, the associated shift of power to the consumer, increasing international competitive exposure and changes in the technology of production and consumption. Computers will lower costs of marketing and the provision of customer services while at the same time as promoting greater access to learning and enhancing the quality of the learning experience. Back-end systems will be automated and learning systems will increasingly apply computers so that courses can be delivered over the Web. The effects of these forces will lead to 'the hollowing out of the university'. The report is worth quoting at some length here:

> The vertically integrated university is a product of brand image, government policy, history and historical economies of scale in support services. If government policy is no longer biased in favor of this form, and technology liberates providers from one location, then would expect to see new forms arising such as multiple outlet vertically integrate specialist schools and web based universities ... Specialist service providers, such as testing companies and courseware developers will arise, as will superstar teachers who are not tied to any one university. Many universities will become marketing and production coordinators or systems integrators. They will no longer all be vertically integrated education version of the 1929 Ford assembly plant in Detroit.

The overall result of the effects of these combined forces of changes are an increased segmentation of markets, an increased specialization and customization of supply of courses and an increased specialization of providers. The new university business system will take the form of one of a series of possible business models: low cost producer university; Asia middle class web university; Harvard in Australia university; world specialist school university.

Clearly, the economic importance of education has been rediscovered as fundamental to understanding the global economy and its expression in its latest phase as the knowledge economy. The OECD and the World Bank have emphasised the significance of education and training for the development of 'human resources', for upskilling and increasing the competencies of workers, and for the production of research and scientific knowledge, as keys to participation in the new global economy. Both Peter Drucker and Michael Porter emphasise the importance of knowledge — its economics and productivity — as the basis for national competition within the international marketplace. Lester Thurow suggests 'a technological shift to an era dominated by man-made brainpower industries' is one of five economic tectonic plates that constitute a new game with new rules: 'Today knowledge and skills now stand alone as the only source of comparative advantage. They have become the key ingredient in the late twentieth century's location of economic activity.' Equipped with this central understanding and guided by neo-liberal theories of human capital, public choice, and new public management, Western governments have begun the process of restructuring universities, obliterating the distinction between education and training in the development of a massified system of higher education designed for the twenty-first century.

Knowledge Capitalism

Among the variety of discourses of the knowledge economy, those might characterise as third generation Chicago school economics (the economics of information, of knowledge and of education) have had perhaps the greatest impact, shaping national policy constructions of the 'knowledge economy' not only in the West —USA, United Kingdom, Ireland, Australia, Canada and New Zealand – but also in the developing world, most notably, China and S. E. Asia, especially through the influence of world policy agencies. Often the link is made between technology, innovation and knowledge focusing on policies designed to assimilate the university more fully into the mode of production. The United Kingdom's White Paper *Our Competitive Future*, for example, begins by acknowledging the fact that the World Bank's 1998 *World Development Report* took knowledge as its theme, citing the report as follows:

> For countries in the vanguard of the world economy, the balance between know ledge and resources has shifted so far towards the former that knowledge has become perhaps the most important factor determining the standard of living... Today's most technologically advanced economies are truly knowledge-based.

The report suggests that already other countries including, US, Canada, Denmark and Finland, have identified the growing importance of knowledge and reflected it in their approach to economic policy.

The report emphasises so-called 'new growth theory', charting the ways in which education and technology are now viewed as central to economic growth. Neo-classical economics does not specify how knowledge accumulation occurs and, therefore, cannot acknowledge externalities. By contrast, new growth theory has highlighted the role of higher education in the creation of human capital and in the production of new knowledge. On this basis it has explored the possibilities of education-related externalities. In short, while the evidence is far from conclusive there is a consensus emerging in economic theory that education is important for successful research activities (e.g., by producing scientists and engineers), which is, in turn, important for productivity growth, and; education creates human capital, which directly affects knowledge accumulation and therefore productivity growth. The report emphasises not only R&D expenditures provide a positive contribution to productivity growth but also that education is important in explaining the growth of national income.

The White Paper emphasises that 'knowledge economy' does not mean a return to interventionist strategies of the past but neither does it mean a naïve reliance on markets. As Tony Blair expresses the role of government in the *Foreword* to the White Paper:

> The Government must promote competition, stimulating enterprise, flexibility and innovation by opening markets. But must also invest in British capabilities when companies alone cannot: in education, in science and in the creation of a culture of enterprise. And must promote creative partnerships which help companies: to collaborate for competitive advantage; to promote a long term vision in a world of short term pressures; to benchmark their performance against the best in the world; and to forge alliances with other businesses and with employees.

In education at all levels there is a strong emphasis on the culture of enterprise and building skills of entrepreneurship which is not very different, if at all, from the policy emphases initiating by Lord Young under the Thatcher Government. There is an equal emphasis on the promotion of university-based research, on industry-education relationships especially in higher education, on workplace learning, and on building a culture of learning (including the establishment of individual learning accounts).

The United Kingdom's White Paper *Our Competitive Future: Building the Knowledge Driven Economy* defines a knowledge-based economy in the following terms:

> A knowledge driven economy is one in which the generation and the exploitation of knowledge has come to play the predominant part in the creation of wealth. It is not simply about pushing back the frontiers of knowledge; it is also about the more effective use and exploitation of all types of knowledge in all manner of activity

The report suggests that 'knowledge' is more than just information and it goes on to distinguish between two types of knowledge: 'codified' and 'tacit'. Codifiable knowledge can be written down and transferred easily to others whereas tacit knowledge is 'often slow to acquire and much more difficult to transfer'. The knowledge economy allegedly differs from the traditional economy with an emphasis on what have called the 'economics of abundance', the 'annihilation of distance', the 'de-territorialisation of the state', the 'importance of local knowledge', and 'investment in human capital'.

In the attempt to re-position and structurally adjust their national economies to take advantage of the main global trends, British, Australian, Canadian and New Zealand governments have begun to nrecognise the importance of education, and especially higher education, as an 'industry' of the future. There is an emerging understanding of the way in which higher education is now central to economic (post) modernisation and the key to competing successfully within the global economy. This understanding has emerged from the shifts that are purportedly taking place in the production and consumption of knowledge which are impacting on traditional knowledge institutions like universities.

The role of the university is undergoing a transition in late modernity as a result of structural shifts in the production and legitimation of knowledge. The older goal of the democratisation of the university has now been superseded by new challenges arising from the dual processes of the globalization and fragmentation of knowledge cultures. These arise from a range of related developments: the separation of knowledge (research) from the post-sovereign state that no longer exclusively supports Big Science; the rise of new regulatory regimes that impose an 'audit society' on the previously autonomous society; a separation of research from teaching (education); the decoupling of knowledge from society and the replacement of the public by target constituencies; the functional contradiction between science and economy in the increasing specialisation of knowledge and the decline in occupational opportunities; the de-territorialisation of knowledge as a result of new communication technologies and knowledge flows; the crisis of scientific rationality under conditions of the 'risk society', reflexivity and the new demands for the legitimation of knowledge.

Universities And Knowledge Cultures

Readings asks how might re-imagine the university once have had to relinquish the notion of culture as the unifying idea. He argues that should not embrace the techno-bureaucratic ideal of the corporate university. He argues further that should attempt to live in the ruins of the university without romance or nostalgia. Since Kant the university has operated as a privileged model of free and rational discussion, one, based upon a notion of communication that ties the individual to the nation-state. Readings wants to critique this notion. He offers a new community of *dissensus* as a model for the post-historical university: not one based upon consensus and transparency but rather upon openness, opaqueness, incompleteness and difference.

Universities, traditionally, have been concerned principally with two main functions: research or the production of knowledge, and teaching or its dissemination and acquisition. Universities are, and have been historically, the central knowledge institutions of the modern state, although, significantly, they pre-date the development of the nation-state. Knowledge has been seen not only as an end in itself but also as an essential and defining element of the Western tradition, closely tied to scientific and material progress, cultural preservation, and the nature of both the market and democracy. The knowledge functions of the university, especially since the time of Kant, have also carried a critical function, together with certain privileges and responsibilities, built up over many generations. Accordingly, the university has served as the critic and conscience of society and the critical function has been protected from political interference and the vagaries of the market through the historical development of notions of institutional autonomy and academic freedom. This has been the essence of the idea of the liberal university. In an important sense, the liberal university epitomised the idea of a *public* institution designed to serve the needs of society through the development of knowledge as a public good where knowledge, especially during the Enlightenment, was tied not only to scientific progress but also general emancipation. It was the exemplar of a public discursive space where knowledge could be mpursued in a disinterested and scholarly fashion and ideas could be exchanged freely on the basis of academic interests. Today this ideal is undergoing radical change: in short, as the knowledge functions have become even more important economically, external pressures and forces have seriously impinged upon its structural protections and traditional freedoms. These shifts are most transparent in the discourse of the knowledge economy where traditional liberal values associated with knowledge—not only 'free inquiry', 'the freedom of thought' as an element of academic freedom, and 'liberation' and 'emancipation', but also the democratic virtues that are under girded by a notion of freedom—often come into conflict and suffer in decision trade-offs with values of utility, technical control, commercial secrecy and wealth creation.

The discourse on knowledge admits of different distinctions, which under conditions of knowledge capitalism may permit some variation at both the regional and institutional levels at least insofar as knowledge capitalism can be approached through different models: 'imperialistic' neo-liberal Anglo-American capitalism (the so-called 'Washington Consensus' issuing in structural adjustment policies), capitalism of Blair's Third Way that emphasises new 'public/private' synergies, French state capitalism, Scandinavian welfare capitalism, Rhine capitalism, Japanese corporatist capitalism, Chinese post-socialist capitalism. Each regional model will emphasise a different approach to conceiving higher education in the knowledge economy that may depend heavily on cultural factors such as learning traditions. The importance of regional models of the knowledge capitalism has not yet been studied or unpicked.

The discourses of the knowledge economy points to the new insights flowing from the economics of knowledge, the economics of information and the economics of education, whereas the concept of the 'knowledge society' helps to elucidate the concepts and rights of knowledge workers as citizens in the new economy, focusing on the subordination of economic means to social ends. In the former neoclassical economics and the revival of *homo economicus* brings together the ancient problematic of knowledge (that pre-dates capitalism and feudalism and dates from the first organised academies in classical Greece), with the problematic of capitalism that is less than a thousand years old and only recently (since WWII) a disciplinary formation or field. In the latter, the concept highlights the *juridical and legal infrastructure* that must accompany knowledge capitalism—knowledge and information rights of the citizen, not only rights of access to knowledge, education rights *per se*, and the rights of open and free information–a foundation of the free society—but also intellectual property rights (e.g., patents, copyright), the knowledge rights of the knowledge worker (human capital rights), and democratic rights concerning the governance of public science.

The term 'knowledge cultures' as it is crucial for understanding questions concerning the development of both knowledge economies and knowledge societies. The term points to the cultural preconditions that must be established before economies or societies based on knowledge can be properly understood or established. *Knowledge cultures* are based on shared epistemic practices, they embody culturally preferred ways of doing things, often developed over many generations. Simplified in the extreme, argument would be that knowledge production and dissemination requires the exchange of ideas and such exchanges, in turn, depend upon certain cultural conditions, including trust, reciprocal rights and responsibilities between different knowledge partners, institutional regimes and strategies.

If we were to admit this notion we could, perhaps, move from a single unifying idea to a constellation or field of overlapping and mutually self-reinforcing ideas of the liberal university. First, a preservation of the Kantian University and the Idea of Reason where Kant's critical philosophy or critical reason as a source of criticism, critique and reflection – pointed moderns towards the continuing relevance of the ideals of self-criticism, self-reflection and self-governance. As Michel Foucault put it so well:

> the thread which may connect to the Enlightenment is not faithfulness to doctrinal elements but, rather, the permanent reactivation of an attitude — that is, of a philosophical ethos that could be described as a permanent critique of our historical era.

Second, the Humboldtian University and the Idea of Culture, although modulated differently can be reconstructed in two senses: from *Bildung* as self-cultivation and moral self-formation to learning processes (pedagogy) based on an ethical relation of self and other; and from national culture to *cultural self-understandings* and cultural reproduction which implies a recognition of indigenous cultures and traditional knowledges, an awareness of 'nation' as a socio-historical construction, and an acceptance of the reality of multiculturalism. Third, the University of Literary Culture (Newman-

Arnold-Leavis) is understood where a national culture as a predominantly literary culture is revealed in the tradition of a national literature or canon. Crucial here is the shift from a literary to *post-literary culture*: the modern western university was a print culture shaped by print technologies for the creation, storage and transmission of knowledge. The shift to new techno-cultures is being shaped by digital technologies for the storage and exchange of information. We must begin to understand the new techno-cultures in relation to the university where the radical concordance of image, text and sound sets up new exigencies and promises for pedagogy but also new dangers. If we were to embody these new imaginings that reconnect to the threads of the modern university we may be able to encompass and redirect the energies of the Corporate 'Massified' Service University towards the democratic possibilities and impulses of the historic shift from cultural élite formation to genuine mass access and democratic participation.

References

Arrow, K. (1962). The Economic Implications of Learning by Doing, The *Review of Economic Studies*, Vol. 29, No. 3, pp. 155-173.

Bell, D. *The Coming of the Post-Industrial Society: A Venture in Social Forecasting*, Middlesex: Penguin.

Drucker P. *The Age of Discontinuity: Guidelines to our Changing Society*. London: Heinemann.

King, Banking on Knowledge: the new knowledge projects of the World Bank *Compare*, 32 (3), pp. 312-326.

Lundvall, B-A. *National Innovation Systems: Toward a Theory of Interactive Learning*, London: Pinter Publishers.

Reichert, S. *The Rise of Knowledge Regions: Emerging Opportunites and Challenges for Universities*, Brussels: EUA.

World Bank *Lifelong Learning for a Global Knowledge Economy*, Washington, DC:

4

Education, Research and Innovation

Over the past decade, new dynamics have emerged in each of the key domains of higher education, research and innovation (HERI), which are the integrated base for the Forum's activities. In higher education, these include:

(i) demand;

(ii) diversification of provision;

(iii) changing lifelong learning needs; and

(iv) growing Communication and Information Technology (CIT) usage and enhanced networking and social engagement, both with the economic sector and with the community at large.

In scientific research, the tension between basic and applied research is the core issue, thus linking to the "think global, act local" challenge. This necessitates more flexibly organized research systems, and pragmatic approaches which promote "Big Science" while also nurturing science which serves society in the widest sense. In the innovation field, the dynamic comprises both "research for innovation" and "research on innovation". Partnerships amongst governments, the economic sector and research universities are growing exponentially, so that new knowledge becomes linked to development goals. But innovation often occurs outside academic environments, as a result of inventive thinking and creative experimentation. Indeed, research system experts must understand the critical factors involved in order to advance this process.

Consequently a new meta-dynamic has also emerged, resulting from the interaction of these systems. In recent years, an analysis of research management has morphed into the observation and study of knowledge systems. In practice, this term denotes the synergy generated by the convergence of higher education, scientific research and innovation systems, which have now become strategically interlinked in terms of their objectives and modalities.

Throughout the current decade, the world has witnessed the advance of the Knowledge Society and its principal engine, the Knowledge Economy. This era has offered great hope, and certainly ground-breaking developments have occurred, often due to the pervasive forces of new communication and information technologies. As a result, all countries, whatever their level of development, have been obliged to review and reorganize their capacities for accessing and benefiting from the high-level knowledge which shapes social change. For those with weak or nonexistent capacity in this area, the risk of marginalization has accelerated sharply.

Since 2007, the current global economic and financial crisis has wreaked havoc on many well-established institutions, thus altering the landscape of wealth and stability within a very short time-span. Yet despite this harsh reality, the global and irrevocably interconnected nature of society in the twenty-first century remains fundamentally unchanged. Protectionism may well re-emerge, but technology has rendered interdependence irreversible. As a result, the search for more effective local, national and regional solutions must operate in tandem with ongoing global transformations, including those with unknown and possibly negative outcomes.

Against this background, the Forum's mandate for "research on research" has continued to gain importance. It is now widely held that understanding the Knowledge Society results from the meta-analysis of the crucial knowledge systems, namely higher education, research and innovation (HERI), which fuel its progress. This involves analysis of the current methodologies used to assess these systems, and the eventual design of alternatives better suited to different social contexts.

UNESCO is the United Nations Agency mandated to promote higher education and science. In keeping with this role the present Report takes a global view of the subject, which naturally covers the wide diversity of social contexts, from OECD Member countries to emerging economies, to middle-income countries (MICs) and low-income countries (LICs). This perspective was made possible through the wide experience of the Report's contributing authors.

Promoting Knowledge Systems for Social Development

Today, systems of knowledge production cover a vast range of entities *inter alia* universities, public laboratories, research centres and think-tanks run by policy and civil society groups, industry and the private sector, and the military complex. This process has brought with it major changes in the landscape of higher education, notably in the university sector.

Consequently, countries across all regions worldwide are facing increased demand to strengthen their capacities for research and knowledge production. This demand is rising across vastly different political, socio-economic and cultural contexts, each with their own capacity to respond; it has also given new importance to national knowledge-oriented institutions, and often necessitates urgent efforts to renew systems and structures of higher education in order that countries take their place in knowledge-based societies which are both competitive and volatile. In turn, reinforcing research and higher education multiplies pressures on the funding, content and structures of knowledge systems. These challenges have become particularly overwhelming for middle- and low-income countries, thus increasing the risk of their further marginalization.

Knowledge generated by research is the basis of sustainable social development. In this regard, three dimensions merit attention:

— Placing knowledge, including high-level scientific knowledge, at the service of development.

— Converting knowledge, in all its forms, into value via applications and impact assessment.

— Sharing good practice, to ensure widespread benefits.

Despite global uniformity in many areas of society, there exists no single answer as to what constitute the most appropriate systems, structures or policies for higher education, research and innovation. Because these crucial processes take place in varying historical, social, economic, political and cultural contexts, their outcomes cannot be uniform. It is conceivable that research and higher education could be structured in much more effective ways, which means that experimentation in this direction should be encouraged and its findings widely debated and shared at regional and global levels.

The Knowledge society varies widely in form and *modus operandi*, and this cultural diversity must be celebrated as an indicator of dynamism. For this reason, understanding local and indigenous knowledge through research is of the greatest importance. Excellence has many manifestations, and the search to define and conserve them can never be neglected because they witness the fundamental parity of cultures and their knowledge systems.

Nevertheless and from the perspective of social development, the ongoing serious inequalities in this area remain unresolved and have even assumed new urgency. The "Knowledge Divide" [concept used to describe the gap in living conditions between those who can find, manage and process information or knowledge, and those who are impaired in this respect and will become increasingly isolated and marginalized] and thus the "Research Gap", constitutes an issue to be remedied without delay.

Recognizing and promoting excellence, so as to discover and access new frontiers of knowledge, is an imperative which should be possible for all countries whatever their level of economic development. Yet these frontiers are often in the fields of science, technology and engineering, health care, agriculture and economics where highly-educated and skilled human capital (HC), along with large-scale investment, is essential to appropriate context of enquiry.

Social development embraces an array of complex aspects, including political governance, economic growth, employment trends and income distribution, education levels, access to health care, rural and urban population patterns, energy and use of natural resources; it also includes factors affecting quality of life, such as private consumption, life expectancy and access to communication technology. These and other indicators are traditionally used by leading global organizations (*inter alia* the World Bank, the OECD, WHO and FAO) to measure progress of social and human development in specific contexts. However, poverty remains a reality in many parts of the world and even exists inside high-income countries (HICs). While the fight against poverty has led to significant improvements in certain contexts (East Asian economies being one example), the problem remains dire in too many countries: sustained growth and productivity are currently proving very elusive. Until this battle is won, progress will remain the privilege of a minority; and winning will largely depend on equitable and affordable access to, and use of, relevant knowledge.

Research Function of Academia

The research function of academia remains a prime source of knowledge and innovation at national, regional and international levels. Yet, over the past decade, most industrialized states have been obliged to address the double challenge of providing wider access to postsecondary education and training and ensuring adequate investment in high-level research. This is proving to be a delicate balancing act, which hinges on visionary policies and a more diversified funding base. Governments pursue reforms to build world-class systems of higher education, which assure quality in both research and teaching. In contrast, the term "World-Class University" tends to denote research-oriented institutions, although this should also recognize those who achieve excellence through innovative approaches to learning.

For universities wishing to enhance their research reputations, the challenges continue to grow. Today, some twenty-two of the world's elite twenty-five research universities (known as "Super RUs") are located in one country, the United States of America (USA). While American higher education deserves full credit for the breadth and resourcing of this sector, this monopoly cannot be expected to meet global needs in terms of research. For this reason support for research universities, notably those with science, technology and innovation strengths, has become an important priority in OECD Member countries.

The rise in status and influence of various ranking systems (aiming to evaluate excellence in academic research) has influenced this situation. In this regard the Shanghai Jiao Tong Rankings (Institute of Higher Education, University of Shanghai Jiao Tong) are very controversial, since they originate from a strong S&T bias where output can be fairly easily measured (e.g. numbers of top scientists, published articles, citations etc.). The Higher Education Evaluation and Accreditation Council of Taiwan (HEEACT) use a similar approach. In contrast, the *Times Higher Education - QS World University Rankings* adopt a wider range of criteria including peer appraisal, graduate employability, teaching quality, and the presence of international faculty and students, some of which are much harder to assess. These systems are also frequently challenged for their weakness in measuring research in the arts, humanities and social sciences, and regarding the whole issue of interdisciplinary research, which underpins the Mode 2 Knowledge concept designed to resolve complex global development problems.

These issues are now at the forefront for a growing number of middle- and low-income countries, which face similar dilemmas in their policy-making procedures. Social justice would require that middle- and low-income countries not be allowed to fall behind in the knowledge stakes. Investment in research is increasing in emerging economies, such as Brazil, China, Singapore and South Africa. Postgraduate education and training has assumed new importance as an underpinning to this policy approach, and a dual agenda must be adopted: resources should be made available at this level, even where countries currently struggle with the provision of basic and secondary education.

Overall, the situation of research universities in low-income countries remains bleak and they are in need of rapid, effective solutions. For example, in the LAC region 80 per cent of Ph.D. graduates are concentrated in just four countries; average government expenditure on research in the Arab States is around 1.5 per cent, compared with 2.5 per cent in OECD Member countries - or, more starkly, 0.9 per cent in Egypt compared to 18 per cent in Japan. Even the poorest nations require research capacity, or access to research findings, to progress; and so it could be argued that support for the principle of a research university in these contexts is more urgent than ever before. Reaching this goal, and maintaining the quality and relevance of these essential institutions, requires national commitment and must remain a major objective for international cooperation in the years ahead.

Major Challenges for Research

Current issues facing the research function and its environment include equity; quality; relevance; ownership; and international networking. An ever-growing number of nations of varying size have now given priority to developing their knowledge base through higher education, research and innovation, and to commit the necessary resources to this goal. Success stories are becoming more common in all regions, and they are characterized by specific indicators:

- Innovative policies in higher education and research and in Science, Technology and Innovation (STI).
- A will to improve and profile the necessary infrastructure, including universities.

- Efforts to train and retain and attract highly-skilled human capital (HC).
- Increased levels of investment in research and higher education.

One clear example of this movement is the significant rise in the number of Singapore's Research Scientists and Engineers (RSEs), from 4,329 in 1990 to 11,596 in 2004. Another is the establishment of formal bodies, such as the Royal Moroccan Academy of Science and Kuwait's Private Universities Council (PUC), to assure an infrastructure for monitoring research and knowledge systems and to help organize national expertise in this field.

The mandate of the UNESCO Forum is to chart these important processes and help promote their replication and adaptation worldwide, in order to render the global knowledge society a more level playing field.

Knowledge Society: A Global Overview

The 1990s witnessed a process of swift and irrevocable change leading to what is now understood to be the Third Industrial Revolution, based on the advent of new technologies which have facilitated the ongoing march of globalization. Today, the Knowledge Society and the Knowledge Economy place cognitive resources at the centre of human activity and social dynamics. This has critical implications for a country's knowledge base.

What is a Knowledge Society? UNESCO's World Report, *Towards Knowledge Societies*, defines this entity as "… a society that is nurtured by its diversity and its capacities". Access to education and training for all is clearly a right for all citizens, and an obligation for governments. Furthermore each society already has its own knowledge assets, which should be recognized and protected so as to link and mesh with the new variants promoted by the Knowledge Economy. Several guiding precepts are important:

— Knowledge-based societies must foster the sharing of knowledge.

— Information and Communication Technologies (ICTs) create new opportunities for reaching this objective.

— Knowledge-based societies are much wider and richer than the narrower "information societies".

— Knowledge-based societies can offer a fresh and relevant approach for the development of countries of the South.

Managing knowledge-based societies is a complex process, involving a range of strategies and mechanisms which should operate effectively for optimal results. Elements range from traditional upstream aspects such as governance, policies and investment, to downstream management of knowledge institutions and workers with due respect for interaction and adaptation and for specific cultural and ethical values.

Role of HERI in Knowledge-Based Societies

Use of the plural "knowledge-based societies" suggests that countries should strive to foster their own individual version of the global Knowledge Society, whose cornerstone is higher education and advanced research. This principle of ownership is crucial in order to ensure that knowledge production *via* research and higher education are directly relevant to national development agendas. Governance, "brain drain", resource levels, and the widening "Digital Divide" (between those benefiting from digital technology and those not) are common challenges for both areas, but strategies should be tailored to specific contexts.

In higher education, the advent of massification has radically changed the traditional patterns of knowledge production, diffusion and application over the past two decades. In the wake of burgeoning enrolments from the 1970s to 1990s, demand has continued to rise and the world's student population could reach an estimated 150 million by 2025. While this demand has been obvious in OECD Member countries, it is certainly not confined to them. Strong population growth in Africa, Asia and Latin America, coupled with increased enrolment in primary and secondary education, has boosted demand at the tertiary level.

This demand is varied in objective and scope, covering traditional academic and research-based teaching and learning as well as specialized and more practically-oriented training. As a result, institutional diversification has become essential in order to achieve a range of provision: all forms find their legitimate place in the development of a nation's cohort of skilled human resources. Also, this diverse landscape has led to the emergence of a new tertiary educational paradigm with specific characteristics, namely the promotion of "learning by doing" and of individual creativity; the widening of access, through both face-to-face and open learning; and engagement with regional and local priorities. This new paradigm has also generated its own research agenda.

Regarding the particular role and contribution of research universities, these are characterized by top graduates, cutting-edge research, and vigorous technology transfer. Their critical dimensions are a concentration of talent, abundance of resources and favourable governance, which combine to assure excellence in graduate education and research output (Bienenstock, 2006).

In contrast, when countries lose their base for academic excellence – through outdated policies, neglected institutions, the exodus of their best graduates or woefully inadequate investment in research – their competitiveness in the global knowledge society will dwindle and eventually disappear. As the Forum's Special Initiative project has documented, 50 per cent of Colombia's science Ph.Ds. are abroad and an estimated 47 per cent of Ghanaian doctors' work in other countries. The dangers of this trend are evident and must be countered for at all costs.

Research and Innovation Systems

Systems of innovation may have varied scope (international, regional, national or local) and may have different organizational and institutional components:

— *Organizations* are formal structures that are consciously created with an explicit purpose, and are thus the principal players involved.

— *Institutions* can be defined as frameworks of norms, rules, legislation and routines which constitute the rules of the game

A total of ten critical activities occurring in these systems have been identified through debates Forum debates:

(1) *Provision* of R&D investment to create new knowledge, primarily in engineering, medicine and the natural sciences.

(2) *Capacity-building* to create a highly skilled group in the labour force to be used in R&D.

(3) *Establishment* of new product markets.

(4) *Quality assurance* mechanisms.

(5) *Encouraging* creative organizations which promote entrepreneurship and enhance the infrastructure to boost innovation.

(6) *Networking* through markets and mechanisms with interactive learning amongst the institutions involved.

(7) *Creating* enabling institutions which facilitate innovation.

(8) *Incubation* activities to foster innovative projects.

(9) *Financing* of innovative processes to facilitate the commercialization of knowledge.

(10) *Consultancy services* for technology transfer.

In such a climate, innovation can be generated from the synergies amongst opportunities, capacities, resources and incentives. Countries with robust innovation systems privilege research in a variety of contexts including universities and the private sector. In recent years, the changing external environment has seen OECD Member countries' governments place unprecedented emphasis on research as a key motor for national development. This has led to new challenges for research management, and to universities expanding their research links with industry, commerce and government, and the community at large.

However, innovation in developing countries poses very different challenges, in terms of understanding the process and of building systems. These issues were analyzed in two expert workshops organized by the Forum in 2009: "*Research in Diverse Social Contexts: Tensions, Dynamics and Challenges*" and "*Innovation for Development Converting Knowledge to Value*". Special factors identified include democracy and governance, investment in education and training at all levels and the state of the economy.

In Africa, gross domestic expenditure on R&D (GERD) as a percentage of the gross national product (GNP) continued to remain under 0.5 per cent between 1992 and 2000. Inadequate investment is also evidenced by a weakened university system and an often fledgling private sector with little government support. The decline of universities in Africa due to lack of investment has led to widespread calls for emergency assistance, including pledges from the Group of Eight (G8) at their annual summits in Gleneagles, UK in 2006 and Heiligen, Germany in 2007. The latter was preceded by a special pre-event on education, research and innovation as the base for sustainable development, hosted by Italy in Trieste, where Forum Experts provided a major contribution to the debate.

As for the private sector, it has considerable potential as witnessed by the success of microcredit schemes in Asia launched by Grameen Bank and similar bodies, and by the presence of small- and medium-sized enterprises

(SMEs) which survive frequently harrowing economic conditions to constitute a major part of business activity in developing countries. For instance, Benin's thriving textile industry is controlled by small entrepreneurs who are mainly women. Nevertheless, much stronger business infrastructure is needed to realize the innovative potential of these contexts.

Overall, it is not surprising that research on innovation has gained importance: it has become essential to understand why and how certain enabling environments encourage innovation and help optimize its various benefits. Among other things, research can identify how knowledge translates into innovative action and how diversity can drive positive change.

Globalization in Practice

Even before the onslaught of the global economic crisis, whose worst effects remain to be felt, there was heated debate on the long-term effects of the globalized economy in terms of equitable social benefits. Indeed, astonishing growth has taken place over the last few years as export-led economic policies brought sudden wealth to certain countries, thus reducing poverty levels. Significant opportunities were afforded to some of the poorest countries in Africa, Asia and Latin America; examples include the rapid rise of China since 2000, the ongoing creditable performance of the East Asian Tigers (Hong Kong, Singapore, South Korea and Taiwan), and the sharp upturn in commodity prices in agriculture and raw materials which rose 75 per cent in 2008 according to the International Monetary Fund (IMF). These gains have often been cancelled, in contrast, by the rapid downward spiral of the global economy, which has provoked chaos in the labour, banking and industrial sectors. This has shown the unpredictability of social transformation processes, including the need to anticipate rescue strategies when severe reversals occur. It is inevitable that HERI systems will experience some negative impact from this situation, and they must weather the storm.

Access to knowledge is another domain where serious discrepancies persist, with damaging consequences for production and dissemination. Two areas affected are CIT access and research productivity. Regarding the former, the extent of the "Digital Divide" is captured by comparing the distribution of Internet hosts with that of the world population; they are almost diametrically opposed, with 5.9 per cent of the web hosting done in developing countries although these have 80.4 per cent of the world's populations.

Indicators for research productivity (patents, scientific papers, numbers of active scientists, etc.) are also notoriously weak in middle- and low-income countries. The issue of health-related research, for example, helps to highlight attendant problems such as the questionable use of scarce resources, low patent production and limited publications in top scientific journals by researchers in the developing world. At the Forum's 2006 Global Colloquium, one citation from the WHO Commission on Health Research for Development contrasted the GERD/GNP expenditure of 2 to 3 per cent in OECD economies with levels below 0.5 per cent in developing Asian countries such as Indonesia and Thailand. Until this situation improves, access to knowledge will remain inequitable and sustainable development a distant goal.

African Higher Education, Research and Innovation

There is the strongly held view that higher education should respond in and through all three core function areas of teaching, research and community engagement, through the development of new curricula and qualifications to address new education and training needs, through developing appropriate research themes to address new knowledge needs, and through forging new partnerships and joint ventures with industry, small- and medium-sized enterprises (SMEs), government departments, community organizations and other stakeholders".

Social Development Challenges for Sub-Saharan Africa

The Millennium Development Goals (MDGs) for 2015 include the following:

— Goal No. 1: Eradicate extreme poverty and hunger.

— Goal No. 2: Achieve universal primary education.

— Goal No. 3: Promote gender equality and empower women.

— Goal No. 4: Reduce child mortality.

— Goal No. 5: Improve maternal health.

— Goal No. 6: Combat HIV/AIDS, malaria and other diseases.

— Goal No. 7: Ensure environmental sustainability.

— Goal No. 8: Develop a global partnership for development.

The international debate on African development must be reshaped. Aid will remain essential, but should be for the poorest populations and for emergency assistance. However, the greatest potential for sustainability lies in economic innovation, which can revitalize national economies and their private sector. African business is marked by high costs for capital, labour, taxes, transportation and communications, and by excessive government regulation. All these factors deter entrepreneurship, and impede productivity. The human capital base needed for this productivity, educated leaders and decision-makers, sound scientific research communities and skilled workers, is the long-term key to sustained progress.

Present problems date from the policies adopted in the last decades of the twentieth century, when this sector suffered severe reductions in donor investment in favour of the more rapid returns perceived from basic and primary education. This crisis in higher education and research was charted in a UNESCO Forum paper, entitled *"From Manpower Planning to the Knowledge Era: World Bank Policies on Higher Education in Africa"*. Two decades of reduced allocations to higher education resulted in the dramatic decline of African universities, and though demand for higher education grew in the region, the chances of a young person born in sub-Saharan Africa acceding to higher education were roughly eighteen to twenty times lower than those of their peers born in industrialized countries.

African HERI Systems

In the late 1990s the Knowledge Society and the CIT revolution induced changes in World Bank policy analysis, and the orientation of its advice altered sharply: tertiary education provided the necessary, diversified provision; CITs were seen as a fresh opportunity to access knowledge more easily, so that even the world's poorest nations could access "borderless" education. Africa was thus advised to prepare itself for the increasing role of market forces in tertiary education *via* a larger role for private higher education institutions, and also for the associated risk of increased "brain drain" that would result from favourable global employment opportunities.

The World Bank advocated enhanced governance and management skills; more adaptable regulatory frameworks and flexible curricula; and a strong emphasis on tertiary educational training, exploring the potential of distance learning and networked university systems. For low-income countries, the proposed approach was for targeted investment in advanced training and research in areas of comparative advantage.

In 2009 the challenges of governance, "brain drain", scant resources and the "Digital Divide" all remain. And African CIT faces problems of cost and reliability: the average university bandwidth is some 100 times more expensive than the same service in an American university. Yet opportunities exist, and according to IBM South Africa the Region is the world's fastest growing mobile telephone market. This and similar technologies can broaden educational access for excluded publics if the right policies are put in place.

The Future: A Three-Fold Challenge

(i) *Address* the multiple demands of tertiary education with diversified provision.

(ii) *Ensure* that research deals with the Education for All (EFA) agenda, where issues such as poverty reduction, literacy, teacher training, technical and vocational education and training (TVET), non-formal learning and preventive health care *via* education need in-depth analysis.

(iii) *Regain* an adequate level of high-level research, notably in STI fields, through re-energised academic investigation. African science which can help resolve development issues will depend on sound national research systems, the retention of top researchers, enhanced data collection and scientific publishing, and research-based policy-making

Recent projects to address these needs include:

— World Bank's Science, Technology and Innovation Global Forum.

— New Partnership for African Development (NEPAD).

— UNESCO Academics Across Borders (AAB) Initiative.

— UNESCO's Teacher Initiative for sub-Saharan Africa (TISSA).

— Despite the "height of the bar", support for African knowledge capacity in its entirety should be accelerated.

Research Imperative

Progressive nations achieve and sustain their levels of development through the benefits that accrue from their investment in knowledge. Specifically, figures for OECD Member countries show that investment to be a tripartite process comprising R&D, higher education, and communication and information technology (CIT); the actual balance amongst these three elements varies. The USA supports all three components on a fairly equal basis, while Greece and Portugal post a low investment in the CIT area.

Is this sort of investment justified in middle- and low-income countries, given the often overwhelming extent of their development problems? Although their capacities in the area of indigenous knowledge are well-recognized, their scientific and related knowledge systems are often extremely weak. Various factors can explain reluctance to support research in low-income countries, including that other areas require more urgent attention; that policy attention is directed towards the provision of basic education and health care; and that the results and long-term impact of research are poorly understood or ignored. In addition, there are the frequent suggestions for problem-solving *via* simple transfer and adaptation of strategies which have worked in other contexts, and which can be applied through "catch-up" or "leap-frog" approaches. This can be summarized as the "We can solve it for them" mantra, but though there are undeniably some success stories, the real underlying issues are not tackled.

- So, should poor countries limit their ambitions for accessing and using knowledge?
- Is it possible to identify, select and adapt new knowledge to local needs without a sound basis for its management via research capacity?

Of course, the answers are negative. The right of each and every nation to build its own solid research community should be reaffirmed and their important benefits reiterated such as:

- Contacts with international research.
- Provision of local analysis and advice.
- Identification of relevant research agendas.
- Critical thinking in higher education.
- Evidence-based criticism and debate for policy-making.
- Capacity to train future generations of researchers.
- Stimulation of national innovation systems.

Systemic strength can be defined as knowledge that is generated and disseminated from a solid, central productive hub. In industrialized countries this would be national research capacity, with its diverse components. In developing countries such capacity is often located in the principal universities (or even in a single institution), which must then assume a wide range of heavy and complex tasks. These include, *inter alia,* fostering a national commitment to research; promoting a culture of enquiry; assuring the acquisition of research skills; developing the capacity to utilize external research and knowledge; participating in the national budget allocated for research; and forging linkages with the international research community. These constitute the meta-level of activity necessary to "build" and "sustain" the knowledge system.

From Research to Socially Relevant Application

In middle- and low-income countries, certain forces tend to weaken the chances of building a basis for research:

— Dilution and redirection of possible resourcing for research.

— Challenges posed by the rapid expansion of higher education to meet increasing demand.

— Fragmentation of research-oriented action.

This has various manifestations, including privileging the seemingly immediate returns on investment; a focus on application-driven project funding or on problem-oriented research cooperation to the exclusion of basic, "blue skies" research; and support for vertical programmes, thereby ignoring the integrally linked nature of the overall sustainable development process, whatever the social context in which it takes place.

The familiar catch words of relevance and utility need to be treated with caution. Relevance is vital, but truly useful knowledge can be discovered in various ways. Often long-term and in-depth investigations are essential for ground-breaking knowledge to be generated - and often, great inventions are a sudden spin-off of a much more thorough and ongoing research exercise. Examples of the latter are the Internet, which derives from the advanced physics research of its inventor, Tim Berners-Lee, while he worked at CERN in Geneva, and similar CIT-based phenomena such as the Google Search instrument which has revolutionized access to knowledge (its inventors are academics, Sergey Brin and Larry Page, who met at Stanford University, USA). Thus, useful knowledge can be the outcome of lengthy and even seemingly esoteric research. Applications then follow as a crucial complementary process.

Moreover, research has an intrinsic monitoring and regulatory function, which can help prevent catastrophic situations involving loss of human life and destruction of communities through its anticipatory dimension. Examples here include research on climate change in the Pacific, which has helped build an early warning system to prepare for natural disasters, and research in economics and business such as that by Nouriel Roubini of New York University, who reported to the International Monetary Fund (IMF) in 2006 on the approaching crisis in the housing and financial markets. The foresight function of research renders essential service to social development, as Forum debates have often emphasized.

Benefits of Research Cooperation

This critical area should be given priority attention at all levels. Global research cooperation facilitates interaction and the sharing of benefits, and this includes work undertaken at regional and national levels. These perspectives gained from specific situations permit wide and varied analysis, thus supporting conclusions that are based on a broad base of evidence.

But participation in global research requires sound foundations. This is a *sine qua non*, and cannot be substituted for research support for isolated or vertical programmes which, though seemingly vital, cannot be resolved without a much wider repository of knowledge. Regional, national and even local research strategies form the cornerstone for this repository because they can guide the organization of research and available resources as well as assuring the interface with external research partners – including the donor community. Benefits from this interaction include support for a clearly-defined research base, a logical choice of projects and coherent reporting. In this way research capacity gradually but surely builds into a solid national or regional asset, with an institutional base and with credibility for international partners.

The benefits of research cooperation have led to the emergence of universities whose missions focus on promoting regional, and even local, excellence. Examples include the Universi-dade Federal do Rio Grande do Sul in Brazil, which has received government funding for sector-specific research often related to energy and advanced technologies; John Moores University, in Liverpool, UK, which is aiming to be a knowledge hub for the North-East of the country; and Waikato University in Hamilton, New Zealand, whose Law School specializes in Maori culture and institutions.

Given these trends, the plight of the poorest countries becomes even more critical as they risk losing all connection to the research process around them. These states must plan for, and receive support for, at least one research-based university which has the capacity for research training; other institutions of higher learning may deal with the needs for professional training. Three countries currently in dialogue with UNESCO for this purpose are Guinea Bissau, Haiti and Madagascar.

Equitable and Dynamic Knowledge Systems

Since 2001, the UNESCO Forum has pursued its mandate to help understand, build and maintain knowledge systems in both global and local settings. Central to these systems is research, a key function of academic higher education and a cornerstone of scientific innovation at national, regional and international levels.

Systemic analysis is a threefold process:

(1) *Understanding* the specific socio-political, economic and cultural dimensions of the research context: this is the essential framework for formulating advice. The examples cited have shown that contexts vary greatly and that the forces shaping research have changed radically over the past decade.

(2) *Documenting* research systems, whether national or greater in scope, *via* the collection of reliable data: this is a necessary base for action of improvement. Statistics and trends related to policies, infrastructure, human capacity (HC) and investment must be the basis of evidence-based policy-making, certainly that intended to advance a country's global competitiveness and connectedness and to address local challenges effectively. For developing countries the research dimension of the MDGs should be more clearly articulated, since only this can underpin long-term sustained solutions.

(3) *Nurturing* research universities is perhaps the single strongest component of knowledge-based systems, due to their crucial social, economic and cultural impact. Though well-recognized in most countries, inadequate policies and investment over a lengthy period has diminished this potential in the poorest states. Consequently, forward-looking strategies and a range of partnerships are now urgent in order to bridge the gap.

The UNESCO Forum has dedicated its efforts to ensuring that all Member States may have equitable access to these systems. Any future phase of the

Forum must build on the valuable lessons learnt to date, however the danger of the current climate cannot be underestimated; it must be addressed in the important debates of 2009, including the World Conferences on "Higher Education and Science" and the "World Social Sciences Forum". The first decade of the twenty-first century is drawing to a close in the midst of a major social and economic crisis.

The outcomes of this crisis are, as yet, unknown in their scale and severity, but they are already seriously affecting countries worldwide, whatever their level of development. In fact, this state of affairs creates the latest dynamic for higher education, research and innovation systems: Will gains in this area be further consolidated, or will the crisis cause a certain stagnation, or even regression, regarding the progress achieved to date? The latter scenario, which we cannot exclude, would be significantly detrimental to the advance of the Knowledge Society and would endanger "mega-dynamic" of interactive knowledge systems. Every effort must be made in order that these systems continue to address their dual challenge: safeguarding the benefits which accrue from the knowledge dividend, and identifying viable and equitable solutions to the complex problems at hand.

References

Bienenstock, A. (2006). "The Global Forum on International Quality Assurance and Accreditation". Papers presented at the UNESCO Forum's Global Colloquium on Research and Higher Education Policy. UNESCO Forum on Higher Education, Research and Knowledge, 29 November to 1 December 2006.

Edqvist, C. (2006). "Universities as Centres of Research and Knowledge Creation: An Endangered Species?" UNESCO Forum Global Colloquium, Centre for Innovation Research and Competence in the Learning Economy (CIRCLE), 20 November to 1 December. Lund, Sweden: Lund University.

El Kaffass, I. (2007). "Funding of Higher Education and Scientific Research in the Arab World". Presentation at the UNESCO Forum Regional Research Seminar for Arab States ("The Impact of Globalization on Higher Education and Research in the Arab States"), Rabat, Morocco, 24 and 25 May 2007.

Hazelkorn, E. (2009). "The Impact of Global Rankings on Higher Education Research and the Production of Knowledge". Occasional Paper. UNESCO Forum on Higher Education, Research and Knowledge. Paris: UNESCO.

Mouton, J. (2007). "UNESCO Forum Special Initiative: Study on National Research Systems. Regional Report on Asian Countries". Paris: UNESCO (mimeo).

UNESCO. (2005). *Towards Knowledge Societies*. First UNESCO World Report, with preface by Koïchiro Matsuura, Director-General of UNESCO. Paris: UNESCO Publishing.

5

Education and Development: Shifting Paradigms

No one today would argue the need for access to knowledge, and capacity for analysis, in all societies; and the funding of HERI is widely accepted as a productive investment in developed countries. Many middle-income countries see such investments as pivotal, and search ardently for mechanisms to enhance the impact and competitiveness of their systems. It is also being recognized that low-income countries will need strategic investments in HERI in order to escape a vicious cycle of ignorance and underdevelopment, however this is a relative latecomer to the development cooperation agenda, and remains comparatively neglected in support terms. Increasingly, governments of low-income countries are addressing the need to strengthen HERI in their development strategies, but so far the response from external funding agencies has been limited.

The need for investment in national research, including in low-income countries, is hardly a new insight. A high-level Task Force on Health Research, which set out to identify the knowledge gaps responsible for persistent ill-health in many parts of the world, concluded in 1994 that the major caveat in most areas was not a lack of global knowledge, but rather a lack of capacity for so-called Essential National Health Research (ENHR). In the absence of a basis for research in low-income countries, global research findings and advances could not be identified, evaluated and translated into locally suitable applications.

In spite of this understanding, axiomatic as it is in the global research community, in development circles there has been a long-standing habit of downplaying the role of intellectuals. One may recall the situation in the 1970s, when "degree disease" was an object of ridicule. African countries for instance had agreed, upon establishing the OAU in Addis Ababa in 1963, on a strategy to boost education as a foundation for postcolonial societies: they would hire foreign academics to help run some centrally located African universities, while also sending away young Africans for academic training. The idea was that, upon their return, these newly minted academics would replace the foreign staff and build universities that could produce qualified graduates and teachers for the other levels of the education system. The disappointing results of such early strategies, coupled with successive economic crises, spurred the development of alternate approaches based on a belief in "barefoot doctors" and other professions requiring only short-term practical training. Many of the students involved stayed abroad, looking for more lucrative employment.

The second wave of university bashing was more of an externally influenced phenomenon. By the mid-1980s most countries had established national universities, and were struggling to secure the capacities and resources for the latter's mission. With economies in decline, the social investments of developing country governments came under scrutiny, most importantly from the Bretton Woods institutions which comprise the World Bank Group and the International Monetary Fund.

A study commissioned by the World Bank suggested that the return on investments in higher education was far below that of investments in primary education, and governments were asked to cut back investments in higher education as a condition for education sector loans. Many aid agencies took a similar stance. The strong focus on primary education left higher education institutions on their own, to find ways of surviving and adjusting with little or no strategic guidance. Support for higher education more or less vanished from development cooperation, with only a few exceptions, including Swedish assistance.

UNESCO Forum on Knowledge Systems

Against this background, the UNESCO World Conference on Higher Education marked a crucial turning point: it attracted some 4,000 participants, was seen as an enormous success, and served as a "wake-up call" of sorts. The Conference reassessed the strategic importance of higher education and research to development, and it reconfirmed UNESCO's leading role as a source of normative guidance and advocacy in the field. Few had acknowledged the various protests against the above policies, but the UNESCO statement simply could not be ignored; a similar message came from the UNESCO World Conference on Science the following year. UNESCO clearly saw the value of higher education as a public good in contrast to the World Bank's advocacy of (privately funded) higher education as a private gain.

UNESCO decided that there was a need for informed debate on advanced knowledge systems, on the basis of evidence and not merely ideology. Therefore, it took the initiative to create a special Forum to promote the study of knowledge systems. The Swedish International Development Cooperation Agency (SIDA) stood ready to support this initiative given its resonance with the needs identified by its own Department for Research Cooperation, SAREC.

SAREC has worked for many years to support research for development. In addition to supporting research on and for development, it has striven to support research in and by low-income countries. Recognizing that knowledge of the conditions in, and the phenomena affecting, low-income countries has been comparatively neglected in international research efforts, SAREC funds a number of international, regional and national research efforts to address this deficiency.

Funding of research *on* and *for* development has been relatively easy; various initiatives have emerged to address neglected research areas, including research programmes linked to the UN Special Agencies and to some regional research organizations. Global challenges such as the development of effective vaccines against malaria and HIV, the breeding of drought-resistant crops, and mechanisms to make use of renewable energy resources and influence climate change also attract other international funding. The ambition of supporting research *in* and *by* low-income countries, however, has been more challenging. Regrettably, very little international development research funding has addressed this need in a systematic way; most research allocations focus on projects designed to address specific problems, and few grants are directed at the systematic build-up of research structures and institutions in low-income countries.

The Swedish experience has been a long and winding path of learning, partly through mistakes but also through elements of success. Such successes include the practice of "sandwich-based" research training, where doctoral candidates remained active in their (university) institutions while being connected to supervisors abroad. Instead of four or five years of study abroad, the home-based research training brought research activities to the faculty, as well as some equipment, library and ICT facilities which supported continued research after the candidate's graduation. Focusing on research activities in the home country of the doctoral students, rather than on scholarships, also gave SAREC valuable insights into local research conditions.

In the early 1990s the impact of economic crises, and ebbing external support, on higher education institutions became apparent. SAREC revised its policy, shifting its support from individual research and research training programmes to comprehensive support for research development in national universities. This approach has been successful to date, particularly in those cases where university strategies exist and can be used as a framework for the external input. Recent evaluations have in fact identified the SAREC experience as an approach to be considered by other funding agencies. Two limiting factors, however, currently weaken such efforts and need to be addressed. One is the relative absence of other external support efforts prepared to offer funding in line with institutional strategies. The other is the relative absence of overall strategies for the organization and funding of HERI at country level. Education strategies tend to cover higher education superficially, leaving the concrete steps to the market or to *ad hoc* decision-making. And strategies for research, to the extent they exist, tend to deal with research topics rather than its organization or funding; as in the case of innovation strategies, these are often blue-printed from literature that describes the systems of high-income countries.

Conditions for HERI, naturally, must be seen in the overall context of situational and socio-economic conditions, and need to be shaped locally. The gathering and compilation of experiences from other countries may guide decision-makers, but the available information on models has been limited to OECD Member countries – whose models may be unattainable for resource-poor societies. The debates of high-income countries often concern the refinement of an established system, whereas the immediate challenge in low-income countries may be to build the very basis for HERI. As it is often from the more affluent countries that external funding is planned and possible experts are recruited, it may therefore be difficult to identify and select appropriate pathways, and to formulate realistic HERI development strategies. Thus there is a need to assemble and supply information on HERI systems from different parts of the World, a task clearly linked to UNESCO's mandate.

Investing in Research

The need for investments dedicated to building a proper basis for HERI, until recently, has not been widely recognized by governments in low-income countries or by external funding agencies. Some argue that relevant research may be better done internationally, and that low-income countries should rely on research findings produced elsewhere rather than invest in local research.

Naturally, all countries need to draw upon international research findings, and Sweden for instance produces only a fraction of the scientific findings it actually uses. But Sweden can do this because of its vital domestic research community, which links into the world of science and makes it possible for the country to harness global discoveries for social and economic development. Low-income countries on the other hand, with a weak national research community, have fewer opportunities to identify, adapt and make use of new knowledge. Sadly, and in many countries, children still die from diseases that could easily be prevented through the use of internationally available knowledge.

Obviously, the understanding of various problems and their underlying factors is an important task for research. Increasing agricultural production for example is more likely to result from new knowledge than from finding better land; negotiating terms for the exploitation of natural resources, including mineral resources attractive to foreign investors, requires scientific data collection and analysis; and local problem formulation is needed in order to choose strategies for growth, for education and for international relations, not to mention for signing international treaties and conventions and for weighing their implications. If this is not sufficiently convincing, most will yet agree that qualified analytical capacity must at least be in place for countries to design their own development strategies (sometimes referred to as Poverty Reductions Strategies or PRS), to be used as "ownership"-based frameworks for development cooperation.

Usefulness of a National Research Community

The usefulness of a local research community goes far beyond direct research work, and a research community can facilitate access to informed advice. Decision-makers rarely turn to original research publications to find out about new resistance to life-saving antibiotics: they turn for advice to local scientists, who know the literature and can consult international colleagues if need be. What Prime Minister would accept the testing of an AIDS vaccine on his or her national police force, as is the case today in Tanzania, without local, qualified scientists to turn to and trust? Another important role for a domestic research community is the formulation of relevant questions for research, combining local observations with available literature in order to address relevant issues. This process also feeds articulated, situated perspectives back to the global scene.

Researchers contribute to informed debates and to critical reflection, not least in higher education. Indeed, national research universities constitute centres of excellence and act as hubs for national research development. The research-based university has the capacity for research training, and can "reproduce its own capacity" while also supplying qualified analytical competence to other institutions. Women participate in research training to a higher degree when doctoral studies can be pursued at home. Furthermore, the local research community stimulates and takes part in innovations which contribute to societal change and economic growth. In short, there are many uses for national research capacity in addition to research output *per se*.

Efficient Use of Scarce Resources

Unfortunately, investments in building a proper foundation for research, including skills in research management and in the basic natural and social sciences, remain problematic in many low-income countries. This is not merely due to lacking resources, but also to the use of available ones: patterns of funding for higher education and/or research may be inefficient.

The last decades have featured an enormous expansion of higher education, and many low-income countries have been pressed to establish new higher education institutions without corresponding increases in funding or in academic and management capacity. In addition to the new public institutions, a number of so-called "new providers" has also entered on the scene: these may be private colleges, branches of foreign universities, or distance learning facilities. These new providers often rely on the staff and resources of existing, overloaded public universities, whose academics might teach on the side in order to augment their income; potential research time shrinks accordingly. Library resources and other facilities are used by all and become severely strained. Quality does not ensue, and national universities no longer constitute a genuine alternative for those who can afford to study abroad or are offered scholarships to do so. Thus resources are exported, contributing to the income of institutions abroad instead of being invested at home. In some parts of the World, where accreditation mechanisms can ensure quality, the apparition of new institutions and providers of higher education may have been a positive development. In many low-income countries, this mushrooming has entailed a severe dilution of already weak capacity for academic teaching and research.

Here the need for policies and strategies, and for the design of regulatory mechanisms, is obvious. Governments need to find ways of concentrating sufficient resources into sustaining at least one research-based university capable of graduating Ph.Ds. Without such a strategy, the system remains completely dependent on (costly) external institutions for research and research training, and this for many years to come.

As for research funding, many universities do not have defined budget lines for research, nor do they have access to grant-funding research councils or similar public funding bodies. Unlike many high-income countries, which for efficiency purposes pool their research resources into one ministry, many low- and middle-income countries continue to view research as tied to various line ministries. Thus research may be funded as commissioned studies, or studies undertaken by specialized institutes also responsible for services (such as reference laboratories). The push for immediate return on investment leads to fragmented and *ad hoc* research funding, and both national governments and external donors appear to act on a short-term basis. In many cases research is funded merely from sector interest, by line ministries, or as part of aid to different sectors – rarely as a "research sector" or "cross-sector" to be built up as a common resource. In this regard, the increasing recognition of the need for actual research communities is a welcome change.

Strategies for Developing HERI

Such recognition of the need to invest in HERI is a good start, but it is not the same as knowing how to make it work. Today, an increasing number of low-income countries are recognizing HERI's important role, and some have taken initiatives towards strategies for research development. Few however have a tradition of planning for research, and many countries tend to neglect the need for a research basis to support a range of sectors. Policies and strategies for research in low-income countries, where Sida supports long-term collaboration, are either lacking or in an early stage of development.

Such strategies must be based on prevailing conditions and existing institutions, and preferably be developed by in-country researchers and policy-makers. Once produced, HERI strategies and plans will facilitate the involvement of partner countries and donors regarding the optimal expenditure of efforts and resources. A strategy may thus identify key institutions for focus-sed investments, in order to avoid spreading resources for research too thinly. The role of universities, as opposed to research institutes, needs to be clarified. In higher education, resources for research may be concentrated so that at least one university will develop capacity for in-country research training in critical fields.

Funding strategies will be decisive in order to balance core funds made available to institutions for research and those to be allocated on a competitive basis. Funding strategies will also determine the balance of grants open to proposals from researchers versus those targeted to defined priority areas. As mentioned earlier, strategies must consider the issue of funding research within sectors as opposed to funding a cross-cutting, "research sector". A further concern is the establishment of peer review systems, within countries or in regional collaboration to diminish interest bias.

Strategies for using research are also important, and the balance between building research capacity and using research capacity may be delicate in countries with many needs and few resources. Strategies may help to optimize scarcity, so that the basis for "reproducing capacity" in national universities is not unintentionally eroded.

Strategies for Innovation

Increasing attention has been given to the notion of strategies for innovation, which are intimately linked to research strategies but also involve actors in government and the private sector. So far, few agencies have supported research on a comprehensive basis as part of bilateral development cooperation; however the increasing concern for enhanced capacity impact in research funding is likely to lead to an enhanced interest in the development of HERI strategies as a basis for defining and aligning support modalities.

Supporting agencies may assist with direct advice, financial support, or initiatives to collect and disseminate experiences and ideas on research systems. Sida currently supports studies on higher education systems, including in the African Association of Universities (AAU) and the Council for the Development of Social Science Research in Africa (CODESRIA) and Latin American Council of Social Sciences (CLACSO) councils, and the elaboration of research strategies in collaborating countries. Based on initiatives to promote the notion of innovation, pilot innovative clusters have been funded in selected East African countries, and this has led to discussions on the creation of regional funds for innovation. Sida also supports African Un-ion/NEPAD initiatives to foster HERI strategies.

An important role of UNESCO is to provide the arena for sharing such experiments and experiences. To this end we have the UNESCO Forum on Knowledge, Higher Education and Research, which convenes researchers and aims to establish a reference base on such HERI systems.

Agency Perspectives

Aid agencies in, which implies that agencies have agreed to place their funding in the hands of partner governments, for the latter to use in line with their own strategies, has fuelled interest in and a need for careful analyzes. Ironically, in spite of the strong 'ownership' rhetoric, there has been much less understanding of the need to support the same partner countries' investment in a vital research community, able to underpin policy formulation and follow up on support activities.

The Paris Agenda

Against the background of fragmented aid, a number of countries and supporting agencies have agreed on new principles of development cooperation. The Paris Declaration on Aid Effectiveness underlines the responsibility of both parties, namely governments of low-income countries as well as supporting agencies: governments are responsible for presenting coherent strategies, as a common framework for domestic as well as external investments. External support should be aligned with these frameworks, and supporting agencies for their part should accept common reporting and audits (harmonisation). Such practices would reduce administration and transaction costs on both sides, and the Paris Agenda also recommends that funds be used to reach agreed, targeted results.

In support of sectors such as health and education, the Paris principles have been put into practice through a programme-based approach (PBA), sometimes referred to as "basket funding". The PBA has been defined as "... a way of engaging in development cooperation based on the principle of coordinated support for a locally owned programme of development, such as a national poverty reduction strategy, a sector programme, a thematic programme, or a programme of a specific organisation". This approach, so far, has not been adopted in support for research.

Research Funding

Few areas have been funded in a more fragmented way than research. Project support is still the most common, and in many cases grants go to researchers in the funding country with researchers from low-income countries as invited collaborators. Yet, there has been little talk of applying the Paris principles. Some have questioned whether such principles are suited to research funding at all.

In research funding aimed at enhancing research capacity in low-income countries, there may be limitations to PBA. In severe cases, countries may have neither policies, nor strategies, nor budget lines, nor transparent decision-making and follow-up processes. Is it then relevant to apply PBA principles?

We would argue that it is. In situations where both research systems and capacity are weak, and where research activities are poorly coordinated, the promotion of ownership, alignment, and harmonisation is just as important – if not more so – than when dealing with well-defined structures and plans. When conditions for complete harmonisation and alignment are not met, the opportunities for partial alignment and harmonisation should nevertheless be explored. Countries and organizations should be supported in their efforts to take control of their own development and planning processes.

Sida's experiences in supporting research capacity in low-income countries have recently been positively evaluated. The ambition has been to support research capacity and training, focussing on one national university as the hub for research development in each low-income partner country. In the early 1990s, Sida switched from mere project funding towards comprehensive support for the build-up of an institutional basis for research; this approach has many features in common with the Paris principles. Two major dilemmas however have hampered application: the weak and unstructured commitment to research in partner governments, and the weak commitment to research capacity in the donor community.

Role of Donors

Many research funding aid agencies subscribe to the idea of capacity-building; the problem is that, in most cases, this is a secondary ambition and not a primary objective. Sida recently commissioned studies which clearly demonstrate that most research funding addresses issues of importance on and for development. Few programmes have been designed primarily to enhance research capacity in and by low-income countries.

In funding research for development, we may distinguish between two central objectives: contributing to research capacity in low-income partner countries, and contributing to new knowledge of high importance to development. Most research funding is designed primarily to address important research issues; research capacity is often stated as a desirable secondary ambition. Many agencies hope to reach both objectives, however few programmes are designed primarily to strengthen research capacity in a partner country.

Aid agencies may support research as part of their contributions to a specific sector, which often means that studies may be commissioned. They may also offer participation in research programmes or projects, usually funded to include an external project leader. There are also cases without explicit capacity objectives but where co-operation is required for getting local perspectives or data into the analysis. Such initiatives offer opportunities for participating researchers, but they hardly contribute to the stable funding of a national basis for research.

Many research fundraisers hope that their project and programme funding, in addition to addressing priority topics, will contribute to enhancing local research capacity for research, and the "capacity nexus" may be an important alternative avenue for constructive support. Where this is a primary objective, the research conditions in the specific country must be addressed. Supporting agencies must see this as a long-term commitment, where the various components will support effective structures and systems.

Agencies often voice an ambition to support centres of excellence on a regional basis, but a regional institute housing high-level researchers could be a poor solution if it drains the national-level research communities. On the other hand the forging of nationally-based researchers into "networks of excellence" may be more constructive, as demonstrated by CODESRIA and CLACSO, the African and Latin American social science networks.

Cooperation offers from international research organizations tend to be well-defined as to orientation, content and design. This may suit in situations of established capacity to take on board new perspectives and contacts, but it will not automatically lead to capacity-building where the institutional basis is weak. Those offering cooperation from abroad seldom recognize the fragile basis for research in low-income countries, and the lack of basic research skills and methods across disciplines such as statistics, mathematics, epidemiology, the social sciences, biology, chemistry and physics. Those advising on research policy issues often assume the existence of such basic conditions, and argue for multi-disciplinarity in situations where the disciplinary basis remains to be built. The basis for research in low-income countries will not be built or sustained merely through vertical programmes that focus on particular issues or problems. In fact taken together, such "vertical" efforts risk fragmenting already scarce capacity and resources.

The UNESCO Forum will promote an improved understanding of the conditions for HERI across different situations, and point to constructive approaches for research cooperation, which unequivocally contribute to enhanced capacity for HERI.

UNESCO Forum: Rationale and Activities

Convening Research on HERI Systems

The UNESCO Forum on Knowledge, Research and Higher Education has established itself as a useful venue. It gathers researchers who study systems for research and higher education, and facilitates the sharing and compilation of available research findings; and it provides indispensable links to new knowledge, needed by UNESCO in its normative and advisory role and by Member States in their policy-making. The Forum facilitates access to front-line knowledge on systems, with particular emphasis on low- and middle-income countries.

UNESCO, in its advisory role, has long been able to tap into the information on national knowledge systems provided by the OECD; however this information has been limited to the systematic analysis of OECD Member countries. No similar overviews have been gathered concerning the situation in low- and middle-income countries, and the latter expect UNESCO to serve as a "knowledge bank" and clearing house in this regard. However, during the last decades, UNESCO has shifted its focus away from the analysis and support of knowledge systems, redirecting effort and resources to primary education. The two science sectors, for their part, have focussed their attention on specific research issues rather than on policies and systems for research. More recently however, following the external review of the two science sectors, steps have been taken to revamp the advisory functions in relation to advanced knowledge systems. These advisory functions, which correspond to UNESCO's core competencies, will greatly benefit from the deliberations of the Forum and its links to ongoing system-oriented research.

Initial Focus on Higher Education

In recalling the Forum's inception, we may touch upon some of the themes it has brought forward. The initiative started as more of an exploratory exercise, inviting reports on the state of higher education and research from various UNESCO regions. The first gathering identified problems and trends in higher education and research management: the commodification of higher education, and trade and GATTS issues were high on the agenda, as was the debate over research management at various levels (from system-wide policies, to the institutional level, to the management of individual research programmes and projects). The role of the Forum was never an advisory and supportive one, which is that of the UNESCO sectors; it is rather to convene and gather research on HERI systems and issues.

It was decided to establish a cycle of meetings, starting with workshops for researchers to share findings and studies on select issues, and proceeding to colloquia where they could share these findings with practitioners and decision-makers. An elaborate structure was established, with an inter-sectoral steering group within UNESCO to include representatives from the Social and Human Sciences (SHS) and Natural Sciences (SC) Sectors, and with a secretariat based in the Division of Higher Education. A network of relevant NGOs and institutes were invited as ob-servers. Scientific Advisory

Groups were formed in each of the UNESCO regions, whose chairpersons also sat on the Global Scientific Committee.

The first workshop in 2004 elaborated on epistemological issues around the nature of knowledge and knowledge systems. As regional scientific groups were formed, these groups set out to define priorities for further attention in Forum meetings. An important debate concerned higher education, and the need to resist a simplistic focus on primary education. The 2006 colloquium focussed on the role of universities in research, and was entitled 'Universities as Centres of Research and Knowledge Creation: An Endangered Species?' as an indication of overall concern. Clearly, the focus had shifted from particular issues to an overall framework, particularly for institutions dealing with the "handling of knowledge". Participants felt that universities needed to be rescued from the fate of dismantlement due to scarce resources, and massification into large-scale, lower-quality tertiary education. A solution should be sought in the formulation and implementation of clear national policies, and instead of allowing various old and new providers to establish themselves uncritically, regulatory mechanisms were sought to minimise academic drift and make it possible to concentrate resources into at least one genuine research university in each country.

Participants emphasized that the university sector must be dealt with in education as well as research policy terms. Research is needed to inspire critical thinking in higher education, which reflects back on society at large. Yet, higher education is not always dealt with through educational policies, as university research, and research training, is also part of the national research system. Few low-income countries however have produced research policy frameworks, partly because the need has not become obvious to decision-makers and partly because little is known about how to formulate and orient such policies. To the extent that research policies exist, they often address issues for research and research priorities. The framework for *how research functions* is less often addressed.

Understanding Research and Innovation Systems

This is why the Forum decided to look more closely into systems for research. A special workshop in 2006 identified the need for a template, able to capture elements of research systems in low- and middle-income countries alike. Simply applying the OECD Frascati Manual was not possible, as data are scarce and the issues covered may be less relevant in less-developed research systems. The template needed to be simple enough to present the overall situation, but sensitive enough to capture changes in incipient and fragmented systems.

The Forum thus decided to commission a special review of the literature on national research systems, with the objective of learning more about research systems in middle- and low-income countries, and, based on these findings, producing a framework for further country studies. Johann Mouton and Roland Waast accepted this challenge and brought in a large team of researchers.

Their ambition was not only to develop a template, or "heuristic mapping tool", that could be used by researchers in the future to undertake such studies first-hand; it was also to deliver (in many instances for the first time) integrated reviews of the research systems in fifty-two developing countries. The main findings (including four regional reports and a synthesis report) were presented at a workshop in Paris in January 2008. The study confirmed the challenges involved in undertaking such a review under conditions of poor data quality and limited endogenous research capacity; it also demonstrated the potential utility of a new research mapping tool which integrates traditional research and higher education indicators (mostly quantitative) with more qualitative, even narrative, descriptors. Despite some shortcomings (as far as certain country reports were concerned), the study also yielded helpful information in identifying regional differences and trends.

Further work is now under way to correct certain statistical data, improve on a small number of country reports and refine the proposed template. One challenge, identified at the recent advisory committee meeting, is to identify parameters which are sensitive to changes in very early, incipient and fragmented research systems so that also advances in such situations can be detected and monitored. Once guidelines have been produced regarding the use of the template, those who undertake studies will contribute feedback and further refinement can ensue. This will enable UNESCO to gather information from further studies undertaken amongst these countries. Regional observatories or reference centres may undertake the collection, storage and utilization of data (using the template) on research systems. UNESCO may thus be able to gather information with reference to countries and regions that have hitherto been nearly invisible on the international map of research systems. Such repositories will facilitate comparative analysis both for researchers and policy-makers.

The overall purpose of the special initiative is to help countries, and UNESCO in its advisory role, find and draw upon reference data and experiences as they articulate strategies for higher education and research; it is for countries to have ownership of HERI systems which are key assets for their development.

Some Common Issues

The initial impulse for the Forum was the need to understand HERI systems, and potential for system development, in low-income countries; this is not to say though that middle- and high-income countries cannot benefit from the type of research that the Forum generates. While levels of income and affluence may differ, many of the challenges facing HERI are similar in nature.

As mentioned earlier, the need of low-income countries for higher education and research should no longer be questioned. The question is how to realise ambitions in these fields. Several issues need to be addressed, such as:

- How to balance investments across various levels of the education system.
- How to balance investments in increased access versus those in improved quality.
- How to differentiate higher education institutions: professional development centres, academic research universities, colleges, etc.
- The role of research in universities as opposed to research institutes.
- The optimisation of scarce resources.
- How to invest in basic conditions for research, as opposed to high-profile projects.
- How to balance commissioned research with more open, academic research.
- How to ensure the utilization of research findings and to stimulate innovation.

The balancing of "access" and quality in higher education is a near-universal challenge. In Sweden, one of the countries able to provide solid funding for

HERI, the debate on diversification and how to balance quality and coverage has been fierce for decades. Some wish for a further concentration of research resources to only five universities, while others maintain that research funds should be extended, from the current sixteen, to all thirty-eight institutions for higher learning in the country. The rationales are not only driven by concern for high quality, research-based education, and research recruitment, but also by concern for quality in professional learning, where close relations with social services and industry are highly valued.

While Swedish higher education remains a public service, and is seen as a public good for society-at-large, other countries debate higher education funding as a means of adjusting to market needs and interests. Competition and market-driven supply of education then become engines, seen by many as drivers of quality; others see marketing as a waste of resources, and prefer that all resources be invested in quality enhancement. Private funding is sometimes argued as a necessary complement to limited public funds; Nordic countries, including Sweden, maintain that private funding would undermine the public revenue system and that costs for common goods such as education, research and health care, are to be shared via taxes. The actual outcome and impact of such different strategies is less well understood, and an important area for research.

Other oft-debated issues, also calling for policies and regulation, include quality-based accreditation; student funding systems, including loans and repayment structures; academic freedom; and salaries and promotion systems. One intensely debated issue in which experiential analysis is needed is the relation of higher education to nation-building and citizenship. The multitude of cross-border educational offerings ignores such ambitions and emphasizes the creation of individual, marketable skills. The notion of the "World-Class University", originally intended to describe a level of quality, tends to disassociate education from its cultural and political context. The Bologna Process, which aims to create a European Higher Education Area by 2010, and similar efforts at comparability seek to facilitate academic mobility and cross-border education; in other settings this mobility is decried as "brain drain", with its attendant negative connotations.

Taken together, these debates and views illustrate the need for research to underpin evidence-based information-sharing and analyses – for which the Forum is well-suited.

Looking Forward

The current Forum on Higher Education, Research and Knowledge has further potential as an arena for researchers to presenting original studies and research on HERI systems. UNESCO with its legitimacy and convening power is an important hub for such discussions and debates, both within the UN family of special agencies, and in relation to Member States. The development of a descriptive template will make it possible for its users to share and compare data. In the aggregate, such information can constitute a basis for assessing trends over time, as well as for making comparative assessments based on individual country studies. Another possible activity for the Forum would be to build a virtual reference library of available studies, to include comparative studies and assessments. Such information may be useful not only for UNESCO staff members in their advisory and normative role, but also for researchers in UNESCO Member States.

UNESCO, within the UN family, has the mandate for generic issues related to knowledge systems. In the current thrust towards "Delivering as One" also known as the "One UN" strategy, there is an obvious need to align the efforts of enhancing national research systems, linked to various specialized agencies, into a coordinated and comprehensive strategy. Several existing initiatives touch upon the need to understand HERI systems in greater depth. Within the World Health Organization (WHO), a policy on "research for health" is being developed for presentation at the World Health Assembly in May 2009. Linked to the Food and Agriculture Organization (FAO), the Consultative Group on International Agricultural Research (CGIAR) consortia address the need for stronger National Agricultural Research Systems (NARS). The UN's Research Institute for Social Development (UNRISD) calls for stronger systems for research on social development in low-income countries. More specialized research groups harbour similar ambitions, all to do with the inclusion of low-income countries in global research efforts.

In view and for the sake of optimal impact in its work, UNESCO should shift the balance, from research along specific issues and programmes to strengthening its core capacity for informed, evidence-based advice on HERI systems. In its advice to Member States and external funding agencies ("donors"), UNESCO should stress the need for investing in a basis for research, including research universities, as a prerequisite for targeted funds for "excellence" or specific research areas. The recent decision to create an inter-sectoral platform is a step in this direction, provided that it is adequately funded from the Regular Programme. However, further down the road, a formal merger of the current Division of Higher Education, the Social and Human Sciences (SHS) and the Natural Sciences (SC) Sectors would create a more powerful thrust towards UNESCO's role for advocacy and advice on advanced knowledge systems. If UNESCO is to shoulder the challenge of its mandate, of providing advice on the organization and funding of research, from a "One UN" perspective the Organization will have to rethink the current fragmentation.

From the outset, the Forum has succeeded in generating active interest, participation and support on an inter-sectoral basis, and this has greatly contributed to its success. Nevertheless, inter-sectoral activities themselves tend to suffer from sector-driven borders, funding practicalities and competition. If UNESCO is to be credible in its ambitions of driving HERI policy throughout the UN system and of becoming a Clearing House for other initiatives (such as the new International Council for Science engagement to strengthen research in Africa, the Global University Network for Innovation, and indeed the OECD's own broad engagement in these fields), it will have to put substantive commitment behind the cohesion of its internal efforts.

Above all, effective engagement by UNESCO in advising Member States on HERI systems will require the continuation of the Forum, as a repository of information and analysis and as a link to the system-oriented global research community. Given the Forum's proven potential, UNESCO's clear commitment to this important initiative in its planning and budgetary strategies is a critical factor. In this regard UNESCO's EFA Global Monitoring Report, with its autonomous status, presents a useful model for recording data and analyzing emerging trends. Moreover, the Forum has the potential to attract broader and continued external funding. Development cooperation agencies are likely to pay increased attention to knowledge systems, and for future reference they will certainly need the type of insights generated by the Forum.

The Forum has proven potential to attract researchers active in analyzing systems for HERI. It thus offers a vital link between UNESCO, its Member States, and the research community, which is crucial for understanding, shaping and assessing the advanced knowledge systems essential for sustainable development in all countries.

References

Åkerblom, M. (2007). "Study on Policies and Models for Research Funding". Report for Sida/SAREC, Stockholm: Sida.

Eduards, K. (2006). *Review of Sida's Research Cooperation: A Synthesis Report.* Swedish International Development Cooperation Agency (Sida). Stockholm.

International Association of Universities (IAU). (1987). 6th Round Table Harare Statement, Harare, Zimbabwe, 1987, in response to the World Bank's *Financing Education in Developing Countries: An Exploration of Policy Options.*

OECD. (2008). *Reporting Directives for the Creditor Reporting System: Corrigendum on Programme-Based Approaches.* DCD/DAC(2007)39 FINAL/Corr2. Paris: OECD.

Psacharopoulos, G. and Patrinos, H. A. (2002). *Returns to Investment in Education: A Further Update.* Policy Research Working Paper Series, World Bank.

6

Policy Dynamics in Education and Research

How governance and management in higher education are defined depends on the level of analysis: national, local, institutional, sub-unit or discipline level. Clark directs attention to three primary authority levels: the understructure (basic academic or disciplinary units), the middle or enterprise structure (individual organizations in their entirety), and the superstructure (the vast array of government and other system regulatory mechanisms that relate organizations to one another). The dynamics within each level, and the interaction between levels, differ according to context. The context, according to Clark, depends on where higher education institutions are located within a triangular field of governance/coordination constituted by academic oligarchy, state authority and the market. We find these three "ideal types" of coordination in developing and developed countries alike.

Explanations with respect to the ability of higher education institutions to exercise initiative in the context of system-wide authority structures have often been organized on a continuum. At one end of the continuum is the "bottom-up" type of system, where government policy follows, rather than leads, a change process initiated at the departmental, faculty or institutional level; at the other end of the continuum is the "top-down" type of system where institutions merely respond to government-inspired policy initiatives which are enforced by the power of the state. "Bottom-up" systems are characterized by high institutional autonomy; "top-down" systems are characterized by the opposite.

National systems differ substantially in the ways in which they have organized the governance of higher education. Moreover, the literature on higher education also throws up a number of different conceptual models of governance: collegial; bureaucratic; political; organized anarchy; and professional. The more recent literature adds to this list the entrepreneurial university; the service university; the enterprise university; and the corporate/ managerial university, to name but a few.

A central question in research on higher education governance is whether the university is an exceptional institution that has retained its core authority structure over the centuries, or is it to be understood in the same way as any other modern corporation? Some empirical research on the governance of higher education points to the resilience of higher education institutions and asks whether the changes we are now witnessing are a categorical break with the past or are merely the codification of existing practices. Clark, in his analysis of the entrepreneurial university, while recognizing the importance of strengthening the central steering core, nonetheless returns to what he terms the "stimulated academic heartland" as the fundamental ingredient of success. Others, such as Askling and Henkel, see the move of the university to the corporate enterprise as undermining the claim of exceptionality, where the challenges facing them are "... broadly similar to those of a range of public service agencies in the late twentieth century".

New Public Management (NPM)

Since the early 1960s, governance and management of higher education have come under attack from many directions. The governance reform movements of the 1960s and 1970s mainly involved issues of democratization and the inclusion of staff and students in decision-making. From the 1980s onward, the governance debate has shifted more toward issues of efficiency and accountability. This has been accentuated in particular by the introduction of NPM into higher education. Leisyte argues that:

> "New Public Management ... deliberately alters the structure and policy-development process of public-sector organizations with the intention of making them more efficient and effective. In higher education systems the management models of the 1980s and 1990s entailed a much more direct ideological and political attack on the institutional and professional autonomy of universities which continues to have ramifications. But the process of structural change was not just a simple centralization of power in higher

> education institutions; Henkel argues that there were parallel moves to decentralize, at least in the context of the UK higher education landscape. In other words, 'centralized decentralization', which is a management strategy based on the assumption that creative peripheries need strong central values and strategies, has become more important".

NPM approaches to higher education governance and management more resemble those of the corporate sector than the traditional norms of academic collegiality. Governments have introduced NPM in the hope of maximizing output while reducing unit cost, and in the process shifting the accountability for achieving these ends to the institutions themselves. Johnstone and Marcucci note that, in NPM, budget authority in a number of key areas is shifted from government ministries to the higher education institutions, for example, to:

— Establish wage and salary policies (formerly reserved to the ministry or parliament and to the government's financial, personnel, and civil service bureaucracies). — Reallocate expenditures from one category to another in response to institutionally determined priorities (formerly generally forbidden). — Carry forward unspent funds from one fiscal period to the next, thus encouraging savings and institutional investment and discouraging spending for no reason other than avoidance of loss or the appearance of an excessive budget. — Enter into contracts with outside agencies and businesses expeditiously and competitively (formerly too frequently politicized and prolonged). — Receive and own assets and sometimes even borrow and incur debt (not allowed in ordinary government agencies). The NPM approach tends to stress the centrality of the role of executive in the decision-making process to the exclusion of the professional scientists, which in turn may threaten the innovative nature of the so-called professional bureaucracy of which the university is a prime example.

Globalization, Marketization and New Directions

Changes to higher education governance have involved in many jurisdictions the stepping back of the state from direct control of higher education – the movement from a state control model of higher education governance to a state supervisory model. This has entailed greater freedom for higher education institutions, but a freedom nonetheless moderated by strict calls to accountability and, in many instances, harsh market competition. Many governments have moved towards the market steering of higher education institutions in the hope that this will enhance efficiency and accountability, while simultaneously reducing the financial burden of higher education on the public weal. Also, behind much of this change in overall governance structures is the need for individual nation-states to be competitive in the global knowledge economy. According to Ordorika:

> "Globalization has substantially modified the nature of contemporary Nation-States as the principal organizers of capital accumulation and as bearers and creators of national identities. The Nation-States' progressive withdrawal from higher education, expressed notably in the reduction of public resources, has implied an increasing competition for individual and/or institutional resources from the State and vis-à-vis the market. Consequently, traditional autonomy of academic institutions (universities and other postsecondary organizations) and its professionals from both Nation-States and markets, has been notably reduced".
>
> And, with respect to accountability, Ordorika continues to argue that:
>
> "Due to globalization and internationalization processes as well as changes in the nature of Nation-States, initiatives for accountability have been promoted in almost every area of societal life. The public sphere has been put into question and the weight of market relations in every type of social interaction has increased. Globalization has been a product and has in turn promoted a growing economization of society and an erosion of all that is considered 'public'; changes in the nature and capacity of Nation-States; and continuous expansion of markets, particularly within the realm of education and the production of knowledge; all of these contribute to explain the 'reduction of trust' from societies towards universities, institutions that rely heavily on public resources".

Finally, Ordorika concludes that:

> "The emergence of a higher education market poses a significant challenge for national research universities: the need to participate in the global realm of colleges and universities on the basis of their own nature and distinctive character, without diluting these in the face of hegemonic models and dominant international guidelines. For this purpose it is increasingly important to understand the loaded nature of concepts and notions of research performance and productivity that are so deeply linked to market oriented institutions of higher education. We need to be aware of the homogenizing effects of productivity driven policies, their impact on the narrowing of university goals and the detrimental consequences on the social responsibilities of the university. In the face of this hegemonic understanding of what constitutes a successful university in contemporary society, the challenge for peripheral universities is the preservation of diversity of traditions and responsibilities through a broad commitment to society".

Suwanwela is somewhat more optimistic about the benefits which the knowledge economy and society may afford developing countries, arguing that:

> "In the present era of the knowledge-driven economy and the knowledge-based society, knowledge policy – including policy regarding science and technology as well as knowledge management and tacit knowledge – is crucial. Developing countries must find appropriate positions and strategies to cope with change and to take advantage of this. Research on the research system itself, which must include knowledge production, innovation and knowledge utilization, offers this type of opportunity".

Meek describes the situation in Australia as a primary example of where NPM and market competition have replaced many traditional forms of academic governance. Within this changed policy context, many responsibilities have been devolved to individual universities. But, at the same time, institutions are held more directly accountable for the effective and efficient use of the funding and other freedoms they enjoy. Moreover, institutions are now placed in a much more highly competitive environment, and considerable pressure has been placed on universities to strengthen management, to become more entrepreneurial and corporate-like, moving to a situation where government funds less than 50 per cent of the operating budgets of public universities. The large universities, with more than 40,000 students and annual budgets that run to billions of dollars, rival in size and complexity many private corporations. Institutions must respond quickly and decisively in order to take advantage of market opportunities. There can be little doubt that the sheer size and complexity of Australian higher education demand strong and expert administration at the institutional level. Nonetheless, changes in the governance and management of Australian higher education directly concern the re-norming of the academic profession and possibly fundamental transformation of the idea of knowledge and of the university itself.

Kogan and Bleiklie also see dramatic changes in academic norms and values as the governance of higher education has shifted from one based on a republic of scholars to one based on the stakeholder organization:

> "How organizational and decision making structures within universities are organized may vary according to two broad sets of ideas about university governance that we may call the university as a *republic of scholars* and as a *stakeholder organization*. In the former case institutional autonomy and

academic freedom are seen as two sides of the same coin – which means that leadership and decision-making are based on collegial decisions made by independent scholars. In the latter case institutional autonomy is considered as a basis for strategic decision-making by leaders who see it as their primary task to satisfy the interests of major stakeholders and where the voice of academics within the institutions is but one among several stakeholders. Academic freedom is therefore circumscribed by the interests of other stakeholders, and decision-making is taking place within more hierarchical structures designed to provide leaders authority to make and enforce strategic decisions within the organization".

Governance and Management of Knowledge Systems

Governance of higher education is, in the end, primarily about the governance and management of knowledge and the formation of coherent knowledge systems. The knowledge system is, according to Choucri:

> "... basically the 'architecture' for the framework within which to 'locate' the knowledge-items. In well-developed areas of knowledge, usually the ontology serves that function. In domains where the foundations of knowledge are evolving and where part of the challenge is to develop the very fundamentals as well as the derivatives, then the first task is to address head on the need for a knowledge system. In practice, the framework provides the basic guidelines for organizing and managing knowledge.
>
> More specifically, we define a knowledge system as: *An organized structure and formal process for generating and representing content, components, classes, or types of knowledge.* Defined by its architecture, the knowledge system is (a) generic in form, but (b) specific in its domain content, (c) reinforced by a set of logical relationships that connect knowledge-items, (d) enhanced by a set of iterative processes that enable evolution, revision, adaptation, and change, (e) subject to predefined criteria of relevance, reliability, and quality".

The value of a knowledge system is based on four factors. First, "... a knowledge system provides a consistent venue for organizing knowledge and a coherent framework for addressing the challenges posed by the proverbial 'devil' of complexity and the associated 'details'". Whether organized around virtual or physical parameters, the basic principle is that knowledge must be accessible.

Second, there are "gains-from-organization", Google being a primary example. The third, added value of knowledge systems, is utilization – allowing "... people in different parts of the world to converge around common understandings of the issues at hand and collaborate for purposes of sharing knowledge, developing new knowledge, or even applying knowledge to their own needs". Finally, added value provided by well-organized knowledge systems is the re-use and reconfiguration of existing knowledge.

Increasingly, the governance and management of higher education are about the governance and management of knowledge systems and knowledge workers. In developing and developed countries alike, the utility of higher education governance and management models will be judged in terms of how well they allow the higher education institutions to contribute to further the knowledge society and knowledge economy.

Funding and Resource Conditions

Doing More for Less

Change in the governance and management of higher education institutions has been coupled with just as dramatic change in the way in which they are funded. A general worldwide phenomenon has been the movement away from near total public funding of higher education to a more heavy reliance on private funding and the principle of user pays. This in turn has questioned the public good nature of higher education.

Nearly everywhere, over the last two to three decades, higher education institutions and systems have experience growing austerity. This has been due to, in part, dramatic rising costs on the one hand fuelled by the massification of higher education, and the inability or unwillingness of governments to meet those costs, on the other. Johnstone and Marcucci note that:

> "These diverging trajectories of costs and available revenues, in turn, are a function of three principal forces: (1) rapidly increasing unit, or per-student, costs; (2) increasing tertiary level participation, or *massification*, greatly exacerbated in many countries by the combined forces of university-age population growth and the increasing higher educational participation rates of these increasing cohorts; and (3) a dependence on what in most countries is increasingly inadequate governmental revenue. These forces vary by country, but the result in most countries – and especially low- and middle-income countries – has been increasing austerity in both universities and other institutions of higher education as well as in national systems of higher education".

Tadjudin notes that market competition and competitive funding of higher education are aspects of higher education systems worldwide. Competitive funding can take the form of funding for projects, units, programmes or institutions. Drawing on the Indonesian case, Tadjudin outlines the following principles of competitive funding arrangements:

- *Competition*: the number of grants offered should be smaller than the number of units taking part in the competition ideally not exceeding 20 per cent of the participants.
- *Specific purpose*: the purpose of the grants scheme should be described in the guidelines for submission and in the performance indicators.
- *Autonomy and decentralization*: the grantee should be responsible and accountable for carrying out the project.
- *Consistency in applying policies*: competitive funding should be consistently applied if it is used.
- *Tiered competition*: there should be a reasonable chance of being awarded a grant which can be achieved by having healthy competition between institutions of a similar level.
- *Objective selection process*: the selection should be carried out by peer review and information about reviewers should be kept secret until the period of site visits.
- *Evaluation and monitoring*: after the announcement of the winners a periodic evaluation and monitoring process should be established.
- *Incentive and disincentive*: incentive is provided by a grantee being able to take part in more prestigious granting schemes and placement in a higher tier whilst punishment in the form of terminating a grant should be considered if the project does not perform well.

Tadjudin (2008: 87-88) believes that the success of competitive funding is based on a number of factors:

- There should be supportive policies at the level of the Directorate General of Higher Education (DGHE) and at the national level.
- The lack of understanding at a national level of the concept of competitive funding should be combated, particularly in the case of parliamentary leaders.
- Higher education institutions should look beyond competitive funding as just an opportunity to get funding from the DGHE and look at how it can improve their systems.

— In evaluating the results of this scheme some external review mechanisms like accreditation and university ranking should also be taken into consideration.

The cost of research is rising constantly, with many countries attempting to devote between 1 and 3 per cent of GDP. But for small economies, even this level of investment is not enough for some forms of research, particularly in the physical sciences and some of the health-related fields. Sörlin notes that:

> "The net results of these ever-increasing knowledge interests have contributed to an ever- increasing research budget in virtually all states around the world, albeit with certain plateaus and stagnant periods. Currently, it is newly industrialized countries in Asia, along with old industrial giants such as India, which are demonstrating the most rapid growth. Still, in most OECD countries as well, research funding is gradually increasing its share of GDP, although GDP itself continues to grow. The same is true, although to a lesser extent, of publicly funded R&D, which in many ENA countries is now approaching 1 per cent of GDP and in a few cases is exceeding that figure, which one generation ago seemed unattainable. In absolute terms this means that research funding has multiplied in the last two decades and since WWII the net growth is so huge that it would be hard to calculate with any reasonable precision".

Research is not only expensive, generally, but often carries many hidden financial burdens for individual higher education institutions. One of the big debates in many countries is the extent to which research should be fully funded, covering not only direct costs, but also contributing to overheads and infrastructure. Often, higher education institutions are asked to provide matching funding when biding for research grants. According to Sörlin:

> "Looked at from the institutional level, this enormous growth may seem less encouraging. It is often felt that, although budgets are constantly growing, they tend to be much harder to get and they come with more demands on performance. Also, a closer look at the gross R&D figures reveals that it is privately funded, and privately performed, R&D that grows at the fastest rate. The funds that go to universities and research institutes, and that these receive directly as block grants, have for a long time stagnated in most countries ... So the fact of the matter is that those institutions that carry out the higher education work and do the research have to do more and more work for less funding 'per unit', regardless of whether the unit is a student trained for three years or a scientific paper researched, written and published. In other words, productivity is going up in the research and higher education sectors".

While maintaining adequate public funding of higher education is a worldwide problem, it is most pronounced in developing countries. And here, the problem is not merely one of creating and maintaining an adequate higher education system, but allowing countries to participate fully in the global knowledge economy. Clearly, the amount of money devoted to General Expenditure on Research and Development (GERD) is much higher in developed than in developing countries. The immediate tangible effects of such funding differentiations are felt immediately in areas like health.The current situation has only marginally improved.

Table 1. Comparative Support for R&D (2002)

Country	*GERD $billion*	*GERD % of GDP*	*GERD per inhabitant $*	*Researchers per million inhabitants*
World	829.9	1.7	134.4	894.0
Developed Countries	645.8	2.3	540.4	3272.7
Developing Countries	183.6	1.0	42.8	374.3
Less-developed Countries	0.5	0.1	0.7	4.5
Arab States Africa	1.2	0.2	6.5	159.4
Arab States Asia	0.6	0.1	6.2	93.5
All Arab States	1.9	0.2	6.4	136.0
Brazil	13.1	1.0	75.0	314.9
China	72.0	1.2	56.2	633.0
India	20.8	0.7	19.8	112.1
Israel	6.1	4.9	922.4	1395.2

Source: UNESCO, 2005: 4, cited in Zahlan, 2007: 5.

Neo-liberal Ideology

Much of the recent debate over funding of higher education and research has been driven by a neo-liberal ideology. The policies of the World Bank, the International Monetary Fund (IMF), and the World Trade Organization (WTO) have been based on open market principles and free market competition. This has been particularly apparent and contested with respect to the introduction of the General Agreement on Trade in Services (GATS) and its impact on the provision of cross-border higher education. Bubtana argues that "... one of the main instruments of globalization and the emergence of the neo-liberal global economy is the creation of the World Trade Organization (WTO) and the launching of the General Agreement on Tariffs and Trade (GATT)". According to Knight:

> "While demand is growing, the capacity of the public sector to satisfy this need is being challenged. As a result, new types of providers such as international companies, for-profit institutions, corporate universities, IT and media companies are emerging. This scenario is changed further with providers – public and private, new and traditional – delivering education across national borders to meet the demand in other countries. Alternative types of cross-border programme delivery such as branch campuses, franchise and twinning arrangements are being developed. As a result, a rather complex picture of higher education provision is emerging".

Knight notes that "... the fact that the General Agreement on Trade in Services ... clearly identifies education as a service sector to be liberalized and regulated by trade rules is new territory for the education sector". However, Knight quite correctly recognizes that GATS is only one small element of the large mosaic of change in higher education:

> "There is much discussion and debate over four rather controversial trends or 'izations' of higher education. They include: commercialization (buying and selling including commodifica-tion), privatization (private ownership and/or funding), marketization (allowing the market to determine supply and demand) and liberalization (removal of trade barriers and promotion of education as a tradable service). Some would even add a fifth – globalization – and point to it as an underpinning cause for the other 'izations'. Some scholars and policy-makers would disagree and label education as an actor not a reactor to globalization and thus fully involved and responsible for these major shifts. Nevertheless, these trends or 'izations' are closely related to each other and are linked to the relationships between cross-border education, GATS and higher education policy and practice".

Competition and Globalization

Clearly, higher education operates in a globally competitive market and governments everywhere are concerned to maximize their higher education institutions' contribution to the knowledge economy. This has given rise to the notion of the so-called "World-Class" research university which has gained prominence in recent years. Global university rankings and the emphasis on creating world-class universities are part and parcel of globalization, as Ordorika notes:

> "Globalization has added a new element to competition and stratification in higher education. Research universities have always competed with each other for social and academic prestige, and also have long engaged in cross-border activity at their margin. Now for the first time we can identify a single system of world-wide higher education: a network of web-sites joined by

> instant messaging and data transfer, in which global connections run through the centre of institutions and governments and are integral to day-to-day practices. At the same time global people mobility in higher education has substantially increased. In turn global communications and mobility have created conditions for the emergence of a global market in higher education, i.e. competition among elite universities is now worldwide and is moving closer to capitalist economic forms.

The global higher education market is structured in two tiers: a super-league of global research universities, which are driven more by prestige and power than by economic revenues as such; and a larger group of institutions of lesser status involved in the commercial export of higher education, where the mode of development is that of an expansionary capitalism. This global market is mediated by comparative 'league tables' of research performance or university status

The Role of the Private Sector

It is important to note how funding and overall resource issues impact on diversity, or at least on the generation of new types of institutions. This is particularly apparent with the relatively new phenomenon of the rise of the private, for-profit higher education sector in many countries. These initiatives include the creation of physical campuses, the creation of cross-border initiatives by established public universities, and virtual universities. According to Guri-Rosenblit, Sebkova and Teichler, the positive aspects of such initiatives include:

— The widening of learning opportunities at various higher education levels by providing more choice for citizens in any given national jurisdictions.
— Challenging traditional education systems by introducing more competition and innovative programmes and delivery methods.
— Helping make higher education more competitive.
— Assisting in diversifying the budgeting of higher education.
— Benefiting through links with prestigious institutions, mainly in developing countries.

There are also negative aspects to the development of for-profit higher education: some providers may be unregulated, not subject to external quality control and offer degrees of dubious standard. "Programmes offered by private institutions tend to concentrate in the areas of liberal arts, business administration, and computer sciences and technology … to avoid investing in high-cost programmes in order to insure a higher profit margin". Prestigious institutions that establish cross-border programmes or campuses may not enforce the same quality assurance rigour overseas as they do at home. But, overall, the development of private higher education is playing an important role in helping to meet rising participation expectations in many countries.

Commodification and Marketization

Bertelsen observes that "... the commodification of higher education to serve the market is revolutionising entire practice from institutional image through to management, jobs and curriculum". She goes on to state that:

> "Once they have conceded that knowledge is a commodity to be traded, universities become subject … to the full and ruthless protocols of the market. Time-honoured principles of truth and intellectual rigour are rapidly superseded by cost-effectiveness and utility, and market rules are systematically applied. First, research is only done if it creates new products, and courses which don't feed job skills are a waste of time. So managers dutifully prioritise 'core business' and eliminate 'peripheral' activities, and funding becomes an investment decision based on short-term production goals".

It appears that the modern university has shifted its orientation from social knowledge to market knowledge and that the "... development of a market oriented university supersedes academic decision-making. According to Newson, "These new forms of decision-making fundamentally undermine a conception of the university as an autonomous, self-directing, peer-review and professional-authority based institution, and thus changes the politics of how academic work is accomplished".

Clearly, the commodification of knowledge has led to new types of relationships within the academy based on what Slaughter and Leslie refer to as academic capitalism, and the academic capitalist professor has become a powerful position within many universities. According to Henkel, "academic scientists and the institutions in which they work have become more or less willing actors in a range of markets and so in the commodification of scientific knowledge". She goes on to state that "... capacity for profit-making sits alongside intellectual reputation as high value currency in an increasingly competitive academic labour market". But this does not mean that the university is being transformed out of all recognition. Marmolejo and Puukka's summary of the current situation is worth quoting:

> "Higher education institutions are seen historically as key actors in the production, preservation, and dissemination of knowledge. Since the foundation of the Bologna University, almost a millennium ago, the idea of a university as a place in which learned individuals transmit information and knowledge to learners has been evolving. In today's world it is understood that higher education institutions in societies all over the world are the main factor for the social and economic mobility of individuals and, in the long run, for societies. Moreover, in a context characterized by complexity and accelerated change, higher education faces important opportunities and challenges, many of which are new and unexpected".

Role of Civil Society Stakeholders

The term "stakeholder" originates from the business/management literature, and is defined by Freeman as "... any group or individual who can affect or is affected by the achievement of the firm's objectives". The appeal of the concept is that it emphasizes that an organization's long-term success is not solely dependent on the financial interests of its immediate shareholders, but that it must take account of a broad range of social, political and cultural agents in order to achieve long-term success. For the university to be an effective institution in an increasingly complex environment, this means that it is not just a matter of generating sufficient income to "remain in business", but that it is just as essential that it proves "... its relevance to society and the various entities in society that the university regards as important".

There are at least three different stakeholder theory types: normative, instrumental and descriptive. The *normative* approach concerns how managers should deal with the organization's stakeholders. The *instrumental* approach sees stakeholders as a means towards an end. The *descriptive* aspect of stakeholder theory deals with specific organizational characteristics and managerial behaviours regarding stakeholders.

There are many kinds of stakeholders, and the interests of some may be in competition with those of others, and, depending on where one is located within an institution's environment, some may be considered more of a stakeholder than others. However conceptualized, the interaction between stakeholders and institutions has a direct impact on knowledge production.

Knowledge Economy and the Third Mission

While the globalization of higher education has been emphasized over the last couple of decades, a more recent and just as important phenomenon has been the notion of regional, social and economic commitment. In a number of important ways, global competition has led higher education institutions to discover or re-discover the importance for their survival of local support and engagement. Marmolejo and Puukka comment that:

> "Higher education institutions can and do make a significant contribution to regional, economic, social and cultural development. In a globalized economy, the relevance of the various activities conducted in those institutions is growing in importance and is subject to increasing scrutiny. Too often, however, failures of communication between regional stakeholders and higher education institutions reduce the effectiveness of their teaching, research and public service efforts and limit the understanding at the local level of their impact. These communication failures are often … due to weak or unclear policy signals, and conflicting agendas".

And they conclude that:

> "Preliminary findings suggest that, if countries want to be globally competitive, regional innovation systems need to be strengthened. In order to achieve this, cooperation between higher education institutions, public authorities and the business sector becomes vital. Currently, many regions are characterized by an abundance of activity involving higher education in regional development in some way, but there is limited evidence of coherent action. It is also evident that there are often no proper incentives, indicators nor monitoring of the outcomes of this type of activity. Finally, a cultural change within HEIs is necessary since regional engagement, academic excellence, and research are often not seen as complementary activities".

In Table 2 Laredo provides a very useful summary of the various dimensions of higher education institutions' third mission.

Research and the Knowledge Economy

The increasing recognition of the importance of research and the training of a highly skilled workforce in positioning nations in a global knowledge-based economy at once elevate the importance of higher education institutions and threaten many of their traditional values. The process is part and parcel of the advent of the post-industrial society and the commodification of knowledge – commodification taken here to mean "... the phenomenon in which non-material activities are being traded for money".

Table 2. The "Radar" of Third Mission Elements Proposed by the PRIME–OEU Project

Issues	*Focus, main indicators and descriptors*
1. Human resources	*Focus*: Transfer of embodied knowledge in Ph.D. students and graduates. *Comment*: This axis screens the transfer of "competences trained through research" to industry and "mission oriented" public services. *Indicators*: The number and share of Ph.D. diploma going to industry and public services (distinguishing between R&D and non R&D positions).
2. Intellectual property	*Focus*: Codified knowledge produced by the university and its management (patents, copyright). *Indicators* concern not only patents owned by the university, but university "inventors" (whatever the grantee is). Patent numbers should be complemented by licences granted and fees received.
3. Spin offs	*Focus*: Knowledge transfer through entrepreneurship. *Indicators*: Simple counts are not enough, a typology of relationship between spin-off firms and labs has to be considered (staff that left, staff still involved, research contracts, licences granted ...). *Descriptors* are needed to characterise university involvement and support: dedicated teams, incubator, funds provided (in whatever form, including shareholding).
4. Contracts with industry	*Focus*: Knowledge co-production and circulation to industry. This is taken as the main marker of the attractiveness of universities for existing economic actors.*Indicators*: Number of contracts amount as a share of total resources, type of partners (global, large firms, SME) are the key aspects. Level of concentration (sectoral and/or on a few partners), types of contract (research, consultancy, services) and duration are important complementary aspects. Delineating in large labs the degree of concentration (thematic or on given teams) is also often of strategic interest.*Comment*: This is often complemented by a "soft" dimension where account is taken of membership to professional associations (and role played in given professional networks), professional publications, activities in continuous training, consultancy activities (often not paid to the lab) and internships (master students accepted in "stages").

5. Contracts with public bodies	*Focus*: The "public service" dimension of research activities.*Indicators*: Similar aspects as for contract with industry apply, especially differentiating between co-research and services.*Comment*: It is important to complement contracts by non-market relations which are often critical when labs focus on social and cultural dimensions (this has often important implications for identity building but also for economic activities such as tourism). This is also very present in health research (with clinical trials for new therapeutic protocols ...).
6. Participation in policy-making	*Focus*: Involvement in the shaping and/or implementation of policies (at different levels). This is often captured under the wording of "expertise", including policy studies, participation in the formulation of long-term programmes or to "formalised" debates on S&T&I policy, involvement in standard setting committees, in committees and work on safety rules ... *Descriptors*: The usual mode is to consider a description in the annual report in order to build an indicator of presence and "relative importance" (number of different activities and entities, number of persons involved).
7. Involvement in social and cultural life	*Focus*: Involvement of the university in "societal" (mostly "city") life. *Comments*: — A number of universities have lasting "facilities" that participate in the social and cultural life of the city (museums, orchestra, sport facilities, facilities like libraries open to schools or citizens ...). Some involve themselves opening "social services" (like law shops) — Besides these "structural" investments, a number of labs involve themselves in given social and cultural events (expos, concerts, urban development projects ...).*Descriptors*: There is little accumulated knowledge on how to account for such activities. Two approaches are being experimented: accounting for relative importance in all university investments and/or activities, positioning these within their own environment (as can be done for museums).
8. Public understanding of science	*Focus*: Interaction with society. *Comment*: The choice has been to focus here only on "dissemination" and interaction with the "general public". All growing aspects upon involvement in

	public debates are considered to be part of dimension 6 (participation in policy-making). *Descriptors*: Follow sets of activities deployed (open days, involvement in scientific fairs and the like, involvement in general press and science journals for the public, involvement in the different media, construction of "dissemination" and "interactive" websites, involvement in activities directed towards children and secondary schools ...). Differentiate between individual initiatives and proactive policies of labs and of the university (as a whole or through its departments).

Neave writes that:

> "Knowledge has always been power as well as a public good. Access to it and its role in innovation determine both the place of Nations in the world order and of individuals in society. But, commodification displaces the creation and passing on of knowledge from the social sphere to the sphere of production.
>
> Displacing and reinterpreting knowledge under these conditions raise fundamental questions for the university above all, in the area of academic freedom and in the 'ownership' of knowledge. They also pose questions about the ethical obligation to make knowledge freely available to those who seek it".

In the mid-1980s, Lyotard hypothesized that "...the status of knowledge is altered as societies enter what is known as the post-industrial age and cultures enter what is known as the post-modern age". According to Roberts, knowledge "... is becoming 'exteriorised' from knowers. The old notion that knowledge and pedagogy are inextricably linked has been replaced by a new view of knowledge as a *commodity*". Or as Oliveira puts it, "... there is an essential difference between 'science as a search for truth' and 'science as a search for a response to economic and political interests'". Lyotard maintains that:

> "Knowledge is and will be produced in order to be sold, it is and will be consumed in order to be valorised in a new production: in both cases, the goal is exchange. If knowledge ceases to be an end in itself, it loses its 'use-value' ...
>
> Knowledge in the form of an informational commodity indispensable to productive power is already, and will continue to be, a major – perhaps *the* major – stake in the worldwide competition for power".

According to the OECD, "... knowledge is now recognized as the driver of productivity and economic growth, leading to a new focus on the role of information, technology and learning in economic performance. The term *knowledge-based economy* stems from this fuller recognition of the place of knowledge and technology in modern ... economies". Several writers have extended the concept, arguing that science and research are transforming the whole of the social structure, creating a knowledge-based society of global proportions. Concepts depicting this transformation are formulated by Gibbons and his colleagues in terms of Mode-1 and Mode-2 science, and later Mode-2 society. Etzkowitz and his colleagues provide the less ambitious conceptualization of the "Triple Helix", representing the complex interplay between universities, government and industry in the innovation framework.

Of course, neither knowledge nor its utilization is equally distributed within or between nations. However, the divide is starting to be bridged, at least partially, as the developing nations begin to create their own competitive research systems.

There is clearly a reciprocal relationship between the massive and unprecedented expansion of higher education during the second half of the twentieth century and global economic restructuring based on the advent of the post-industrial or "knowledge" society. In the post-industrial society, knowledge supersedes agriculture and manufacturing as the main means for wealth production, and becomes the primary resource of society. It is not that agriculture and manufacturing disappear, but rather that technology has made both agriculture and manufacturing so efficient that they demand the attention of only a minority of the workforce.

As the knowledge society continues to develop, market relations based on knowledge production increasingly permeate all aspects and institutions of society, and the university is faced with a growing number of competitors in both research and training. Also, the commodification of knowledge is impacting heavily on the internal social structure of the scientific community.

What is remarkable is the continuing importance and centrality of the university as knowledge is increasingly brought within market and political exchanges.

Institutions: Structural Differentiation and Patterns

There are many different types of diversity in higher education (programmatic, systemic, procedural, etc.). This theme will concentrate mainly on systemic diversity which can be defined as the "existence of distinct forms of post-secondary education, of institutions and groups of institutions within a state or nation that have different and distinctive missions, educate and train for different lives and careers, have different styles of instruction, are organized and funded differently and operate under different laws and relationships to government". One also needs to distinguish between vertical (or hierarchical) diversity based on the status of institutional types and horizontal diversity based on institutions' teaching and, to a lesser extent, research functions.

Diversity, it is claimed, affects nearly every aspect of higher education: access and equity, teaching methods and student learning, research priorities, quality, management, social relevance, finance, etc. Stadtman, for example, states that diversity:

— Increases the range of choices available to learners.
— Makes higher education available to virtually everyone.
— Matches education to the needs and abilities of individual students.
— Enables institutions to select their own mission and confine their activities.
— Responds to the pressures of a society (complex and diversified in itself).
— Becomes a precondition of college and university freedom and autonomy.

However, views about both the character and extent of diversity vary substantially. Guri-Rosenblit, Sebkova and Teichler ask the following questions:

— What range of heterogeneity or homogeneity is preferable?
— To what extent should diversity be arranged inter-institutionally or intra-institutionally?
— How clearly should differences be demarcated or softened and blurred?
— To what extent is diversity best served by formal elements of diversification (i.e. different types and levels), or by informal elements (i.e. differences in the reputation or profile between individual institutions or their sub-units)?
— Does diversity prevail predominantly according to the vertical dimensions, i.e. ranking according to quality, reputation etc., or does

horizontal differentiation, e.g. according to curricular thrusts and institutional profiles, play a role as well?

With the continual expansion of higher education following the Second World War, the issue of diversity has been a recurrent theme in debates on the steering and management of higher education institutions and systems. But the debate has resolved neither how diversity is to be achieved, whether or not it is an inevitable result of expansion, nor even if it is a worthwhile goal. Responses to the issue by different national systems vary widely. Much of the writing on higher education in the USA assumes that diversity is an inherent good, best achieved through market competition rather than by centralized planning. Many European countries until quite recently have not only developed centralized systems of higher education but have also in the name of equity and quality enforced a high degree of homogeneity amongst institutions, particularly universities. Other countries have attempted to manage diversity through structural means, such as the binary systems in Australia, Germany and the United Kingdom which differentiate between "theoretically based" universities and "vocationally oriented" polytechnics. While the binary arrangement has been discarded by Australia and the UK, it appears to remain entrenched in Germany and is being introduced and/or reinforced in such countries as Finland, the Netherlands and Norway. In addition, according to Guri-Rosenblit, Sebkova and Teichler, "... trends of globalization, supra-national policies, bottom-up initiatives of founding private for-profit higher education institutions, continuous cuts of higher education budgets by governments, the emergence of the digital technologies and the growth of transnational higher education in the last decade have added additional layers to the debates on diversity and massification in higher education".

Structural Differentiation or Integration

One thing that is known about diversity is that it cannot be understood in isolation from the way in which governments manage and structure higher education systems. The great debate over the last thirty years is whether higher education systems around the world are evolving towards integrated, unitary systems or formally differentiated systems. So far the empirical evidence does not support the ascendancy of one trend over the other. Nonetheless, it is important to understand the basis of the two arguments for they impact directly on how we think about both the character and the efficacy of higher education.

Bleiklie argues that "... higher education systems in much of the Western world have become steadily more integrated". But he also comments that this is a very complex and far from inevitable, or one-directional process. He notes that, from the literature, there are two opposing views on the development of diversity of higher education systems: convergence and divergence. The convergence school argues that, for example, with the increased emphasis on similar compliance schemes in the areas of quality assurance and accountability, increased student mobility, the blurring of basic and applied research, and cross-border initiatives such as the Bologna Process, all higher education institutions are assuming similar characteristics, norms and values. The counterargument has it that institutions in competition with one another will "naturally" seek a niche market and differentiate themselves from their competitors. Governments also take a direct interest in diversity because, with growth in function, complexity and size, they find it extremely difficult to fund all institutions on the same basis.

Research and different knowledge regimes are also potentially powerful differentiators of higher education systems. No country can afford to fund all of its universities as world-class research universities. But in integrated, unitary systems, there is a tendency for non-research universities to emulate research-intensive institutions. However, due to the lack of resources, this emulation results in second-rate imitations. Moreover, those institutions that emulate research universities without sufficient resources to adequately do so, cannot provide their students, particularly their research students, with appropriate tuition. Emulation of research universities also diverts institutions away from engaging in extensive programmatic diversity which appears imperative for mass higher education. The important question is how to foster diversity by preventing institutions from converging on some preconceived gold standard of what is proper higher education. But how this is to be accomplished is not at all clear.

According to Bleiklie, there are basic political-economic concerns driving the development of higher education everywhere: "The first concern is that the level of education in the population affects the competitiveness of a nation". Nations will attempt to structure their higher education systems in order to produce the highest educated population at the lowest possible cost. The level of education in the population is directly related to a nation's ability to compete in the global knowledge economy. "The second concern is that higher education systems need to be flexible". Specialization both within and between institutions is necessary to match graduates with the needs of the labour market. Nations' response to these concerns is influenced by a number of factors:

— Firstly, institutions within today's integrated higher education systems constitute a complex set, in which different categories of institutions have had vastly different relationships with public authorities and demonstrate considerable variation with respect to their degree of autonomy.

— Secondly, institutions may try to adapt to the integration process by means of different strategies.

— Thirdly, national systems vary considerably with regard to the degree that they are placed into a hierarchy, both across categories of institutions, and within categories.

— Fourthly, knowledge has gained importance in society amongst other reasons, because of the emergence of mass education and the steadily more extensive use of research in private business and public administration.

In a similar vein, Guri-Rosenblit, Sebkova and Teichler argue that:

> "The extent of diversity and homogeneity of higher education systems in each national context depends on various variables. Each national higher education system has external and internal boundaries that portray its horizontal and vertical structure at various levels. The external boundaries define basically which kind of institutions are included in or excluded from the higher education system ... The internal boundaries reflect the horizontal and vertical structures of any given higher education system in relation to a variety of variables: overall structure (unified, binary or segmented into several sectors), the interrelations between the public and private sectors, access policies, study programmes, budgeting patterns, research and teaching policies, academic traditions and cultures, evaluation and accreditation, etc.".

Rankings and the Pursuit of Prestige

One form if not aberration of vertical differentiation in higher education on a global scale is the current university ranking craze. The obsession with university rankings and league tables is driven by several complex factors and is coupled with the notion of world-class universities. Basically, as the global competition of the knowledge economy heats up, nations are concerned that they create the best research universities possible in order to maximize their competitive advantage. World rankings are one means for nations to judge how well they are doing in the competitive global knowledge stakes. "Preoccupations about university rankings reflect the general recognition that economic growth and global competitiveness are increasingly driven by knowledge, and that universities can play a key role in that context".

Putting the more bizarre aspects of university rankings to one side, it is important to note that the creation of world-class, research-intensive universities is the preoccupation of nearly all OECD Member countries, and many if not most developing nations are realizing that they require at least one, though not necessarily world-class in all aspects, research-intensive university. Thus, it is worthwhile to explore what is actually meant by a world-class university.

In general, world-class universities are distinguished by a few basic features, the most important appearing to be: excellence in research, highly qualified faculty, high levels of government and private sources of funding, and highly talented students. According to Salmi, achieving the level of excellence required to be categorized as world-class can be attributed to three complementary sets of factors:

— A high concentration of talent (faculty and students).

— Abundant resources to offer a rich learning environment and conduct advanced research;

— Favourable governance features that encourage strategic vision, innovation and flexibility, and enable institutions to make decisions and manage resources without being encumbered by bureaucracy.

While recognizing the importance of both research and research-intensive universities to the development of knowledge economies in developing and developed countries alike, it needs to be recognized that no nation can afford to fund all of its universities at a level commensurate with world-class research universities. Moreover, many nations may be better positioned in a competitive global market by creating "world-class systems" of higher education, rather than devoting the majority of their resources to creating a few so-called "World-Class" universities. Even in the USA, "... of about 5,000 tertiary education institutions no more than thirty universities are among the best in the world".

There is evidence to suggest that world-class systems of higher education are differentiated systems. These are systems that address the increasing needs of society and the diversity of student backgrounds that result from massification. Higher education institutions require a variety of missions and need to cater to a range of stakeholders. The core business of higher education will remain teaching and scholarship, and, in an increasingly complex and volatile global environment, the relevance of their activities to local communities will become all the more important.

Role of Universities

"The proper role of the university in a national innovation system", according to Xue, "or, more broadly, in a knowledge economy has become increasingly controversial …" While there may be agreement on the role of the university in disseminating knowledge through teaching and related activities, there are "… disagreements regarding its role in generating knowledge, and even less agreement on its linkage to the industry and the commercial market". Nonetheless, the advanced industrialized countries are all concerned to maintain and enhance strong research and innovation systems. But, as Johnstone and Marcucci note:

> "Research capacity is important as well for low- and middle-income countries: for the sake of their economies, for the requirements of effective management and sound policy-making in their governments as well as in the entities of their civil societies, and for the preservation of their national histories, cultures, and identities".

According to Johnstone and Marcucci, R&D does not depend on universities: "Most R&D in OECD countries, which constitutes some 80 per cent of the world's research and development and which has been growing significantly in the last two decades, is carried out by business and industry". Nonetheless, the authors note that the proportion of R&D that is conducted in universities and university-affiliated research centres has grown substantially in recent years. The growth of higher education-based R&D has been funded by both governments and the private sector, although in those countries lacking a strong private sector, much of the funding of higher education-based R&D falls to government.

In most systems of innovation, according to Edquist, the following activities appear to be important:

1. Provision of research and development (R&D) creating new knowledge, primarily in engineering, medicine and the natural sciences.
2. Competence building (provision of education and training, creation of human capital, production and reproduction of skills, individual learning) in the labour force to be used in innovation and R&D activities.
3. Formation of new product markets.
4. Articulation of quality requirements emanating from the demand side with regard to new products.
5. Creating and changing organizations needed for the development of new fields of innovation, for example, enhancing entrepreneurship to create new firms and intrapreneurship to diversify existing firms, creating new research organizations, policy agencies, etc.
6. Networking through markets and other mechanisms, including interactive learning between different organizations (potentially) involved in the innovation processes. This implies integrating new knowledge elements developed in different spheres of the SI and coming from outside with elements already available in the innovating firms.
7. Provision (creation, change, abolition) of institutions – for example, IPR laws, tax laws, environment and safety regulations, R&D investment routines, etc. – that influence innovating organizations and innovation processes by providing incentives or obstacles to innovation.
8. Incubating activities, for example, providing access to facilities, administrative support, etc. for new innovating efforts.

   Financing of innovation processes and other activities that can facilitate commercialization of knowledge and its adoption.
9. Provision of consultancy services of relevance for innovation processes, for example, technology transfer, commercial information and legal advice.

According to Ho, the knowledge cycle "... consists of knowledge acquisition, assimilation and development".Ho explains that "... knowledge development may lead to creating or discovering new knowledge/technology or creating new value by applying knowledge/technology to societal or business challenges. The knowledge development stage is where value is created, in other words, innovation".

Commercialization and Knowledge Transfer

As mentioned in a global knowledge economy, knowledge becomes a commodity to be bought and sold. The importance of knowledge and having a highly skilled labour force to utilize that knowledge are the backbone of the economy of many if not most nations.

Suwanwela has recognized that massification in a knowledge-based society leads to or forces innovation both within and without higher education. Distance education, recognition of prior learning, new courses, new types of institutions, new disciplines and technologies are but a few examples. As part of this process, Suwanwela (2008) argues that knowledge is becoming generally more accessible to the public and that knowledge transfer and the growing ties between universities and industry and commerce are increasingly becoming more important.

One needs to be cautious about the degree of the impact of commercialization and knowledge transfer on higher education institutions, particularly with respect to return on investment. A recent Australian study suggests that "... even at its best, research commercialization is likely to generate no more than 3 to 5 per cent of university revenue ... Salary costs are high and considerable funds are needed to meet expenses in taking out patents and in consulting fees". Very few if any universities anywhere are in a position to entirely support themselves through the commercialization of their research products. In the USA, "... annual licensing revenue has grown from $160 million in 1991 to $862 million in 1999, but still only accounts for about 2.7 percent of university research and development expenditure". Also, "... it is easy to overstate the value of industry funding for university research". In the USA, industry funding for research has remained stable at around 6 per cent for the last twenty years, and is today about the same proportion that it was in 1960. Interestingly, "60 per cent of USA industry funding for university research is for basic research". The argument that university/industry commercial partnerships are turning the attention of research universities away from the more fundamental, knowledge for knowledge sake questions can be challenged.

Suwanwela argues that the commercialization of research tends to favour not only a few elite institutions, but also disciplines that are more directly capable of turning their knowledge products into commodities (e.g. biomedicine, certain areas of engineering, etc.). This has left many academics in the social sciences feeling marginalized. However, the importance of "social knowledge" and interdisciplinary teams that involve social scientists as well as scientists and technologists in the innovation process is being recognized. It is becoming accepted that "... there is a growing need for firms to have knowledge about the social and regulatory pressures that will partly determine whether innovations succeed or fail".

However, several commentators have argued that a major drawback to greater commercialization of university research is the threat it poses to "open science" and academic freedom. The fear is that commercial-in-confidence joint ventures limit the free exchange and dissemination of ideas between both academics and students. Academics may be hindered in the open publication of research results, and research students may find themselves caught between dual loyalties to the university and the firm. "Universities thrive on the idea of publishing the research results, while firms may want to keep much of the information as a trade secret". It appears that strategic alliances between universities and industry in the area of biotechnology are particularly prone to such problems.

There is some empirical evidence to suggest that academics involved in commercial ventures are more secretive, but other studies have shown that they are also more productive and publish more. While some studies have noted concern for the academic freedom of graduate students working on projects involving university-industry partnerships, other studies found no evidence that academic freedom was under threat. There has been a growing trend for joint publications between university researchers and those based in industry and government, which appears to have actually increased the significance of the university researchers' contribution. In Canada, for example, "... over a period of eighteen years, the industry and federal government sectors have doubled their collaborations with universities, while provincial governments have increased such collaborations by more than 50 per cent, thereby increasing their links with institutions of higher education".

"The emergence of public-private research partnerships reflects a fundamental change in the way in which knowledge is generated and applied as well as changes in approaches to the management of industrial research and development". "Simply put", according to Poyago-Theotoky, Beath and Siegel, "... university-industry partnerships appear to accelerate technological diffusion". Thus, "it is not surprising to observe the formulation of policies that stimulate the formation of university-industry partnerships" in many if not most countries. But it must be admitted that "... we still know very little about the global impact of the rise of university-industry partnerships". Governments everywhere "... have sought to bring about institutional 'framework conditions' that are favourable to industry-university relationships and that encourage the development of channels through which these relations can develop". But how best this can be done remains unknown.

Nonetheless, a few generalizations about university-industry partnerships are possible. First, it seems that the quality of the relationships and the free flow of information, particularly tacit knowledge, are as important if not more so as the actual commercialization of a research product. Second, interactive partnerships are becoming more the norm rather than simple contractual arrangements designed to develop a specific product – Suwanwela provides several examples of this. Third, university and other forms of publicly funded research provide the core support for knowledge transfer and innovation. Fourth, while in many jurisdictions, universities and industry are coming closer together, the distinctive qualities of each must nonetheless be preserved as well. Fifth, university-industry partnerships are beginning to be regarded as an important policy instrument for regional development and are seen in an overall context of community engagement that extends from the local to the global, rather than a simple university department/industrial firm arrangement. Finally, and related to the last point, a more multidisciplinary approach to university-industry relationships is starting to emerge where it is being recognized that social and cultural factors and the involvement of social scientists are as important in bringing about successful innovation as the more scientific and technological oriented aspect of such ventures.

There is no one best model for enhancing university-industry relationships or for the commercialization and application of publicly-funded research. The types of successful linkages, transfer channels and partnerships appear to depend greatly on the context in which they occur. The national context is important, but so are the regional and the global. Suwanwela makes the very important point that:

> "The escalation of the cost of technology-intensive commodities such as drugs, energy, tools and services has created a widening divide between knowledge-producing/exporting and knowledge-importing countries. Intellectual property right leads to monopoly and power of pricing. Profit maximization leads to price setting based upon the level of need for the

> product and the ability to pay by those in need to use it. If the technology is needed, the knowledge-importing countries have to buy at a high price with their limited resources".

Academics often form networks and alliances nationally and internationally to promote their disciplines and research agendas with little or no regard for immediate financial return. Universities form consortiums not only to further their financial interests, but to assist one another to further key areas of development, such as in the area of medicine. Through competition, higher education institutions enhance resources and prestige. Through collaboration they can build on strengths and compensate for weaknesses in building successful research and teaching partnerships.

Relationship between Research and Teaching

The Teaching/Research Nexus

Analysis of the teaching/research nexus is not only a complex technical task, but also one fraught with many political overtones and vested interest. There is little doubt that higher education plays an essential role in the knowledge economy, and there is evidence to suggest that every nation needs at least one university with a degree of research intensity. However, whether every university or higher education institution needs to pursue a research as well as a teaching mandate is quite another question.

At the undergraduate level, it is easier to identify the negative aspects of a heavy emphasis on the teaching/research nexus than the positives ones. The main dysfunctions are: devaluing teaching and diverting staff time from teaching; forcing staff who have little interest and/or skill in research to become research active; and diluting scarce financial resources. Of course, at the postgraduate level, research training must be supported by a strong research culture. However, not every institution or every field in particular institutions necessarily needs to be engaged in postgraduate research training activities.

Mission Diversity and the Teaching/Research Nexus

The question of the relationship between the teaching/research nexus and institutional mission diversity is highly complex. Meek has explored this question in some detail in *Higher Education, Research, and Knowledge in the Asia-Pacific Region,* summarized below. Meek begins by referring to

Nowotny, Scott and Gibbons who maintain that the scientific and social roles of the university, rather than being mutually exclusive, are actually mutually sustaining:

> "The development of higher education and research policies in many countries has been based on the belief that it is necessary to insulate the scientific functions of the university from its social functions, often equating the former with 'elite' and the latter with 'mass' education. The intention often has been to create a clearer separation between research, in which the elite university still plays an important but no longer exclusive role, and the higher education … of mass student populations where such a separation either does not exist, or to reinforce it, where it does exist, by encouraging the emergence of more differentiated systems".

Nowotny, Scott and Gibbons argue that "... high-profile attempts to maintain, or promote, differentiation between research-led and access-oriented institutions have not always been successful because of the political difficulties such attempts create". It is difficult to segregate research-led universities from access-oriented higher education institutions in open, democratic societies, which may "... help explain the tendency to seize on quasi-market, or actual market, solutions". As a consequence, "... not only has the number of 'researchers' within higher education systems increased as a result of the expansion of these systems since 1960; research is now undertaken in a wider range of non-university settings which extend far beyond freestanding research institutes or dedicated R&D departments into government, business, community and the media".

> Clearly, "... the old division of labour between fundamental and applied or problem-oriented research has almost disappeared, and with it, the functional distinctions between universities, public labs and industrial and other private research". Also, according to Rip, "... the contrast between fundamental (and scientifically excellent) research … and relevant research … is not a principled contrast. It has more to do with the institutional division of labour, than with the nature of scientific research".

Moreover, there can be little dispute that many societies have become more knowledgeable and that with the advent of the World Wide Web and other forms of modern telecommunications, access to knowledge has become more widespread and nearly instantaneous. At the same time, society has successfully challenged the elite position, autonomy and exclusivity of many professions, including academic researchers. The knowledge society is simultaneously more dependent upon science and less trustful of it and its proponents – "... enhanced understanding [of science] tends to diminish rather than increase public confidence".

Nonetheless, differentiation both within and between institutions remains an important policy question and the empirical evidence strongly suggests that research remains the primary differentiator. The important research question is how to foster diversity by preventing institutions from converging on a single preconceived "gold standard" of what is proper higher education.

Much of the argument plays on the meanings of "research" and "knowledge". In adopting a fairly traditional definition of research (publications, grants, patents, etc.), questions of differentiation of function both within and between institutions remain important concerns. Arguments based on the fundamental importance of the nexus between teaching and research in higher education are often self-serving, particularly when we take into account the fact that in all higher education systems something like 80 per cent of the research output is produced by 20 per cent of the staff. Since research attracts prestige, everyone wants a share, despite the legitimacy of their claim.

From a research management point of view, it does not appear that research is a democratic, widely dispersed activity, and, as stated above, one might question the nexus between teaching and research – at least in terms of research that generates external funding. A case probably can be made that all university staff should be engaged in scholarship at a high level, which means staying informed about the latest research in their areas of expertise. However, with respect to research itself, concentration and selectivity appear to be the order of the day.

This issue is not so much the separation of teaching and research. The evidence suggests that this occurs regardless. What is important is the policy context that structures the way in which the boundaries between teaching and research are created and maintained. It is probably true that "... economic growth is affected not only by the quantum of funding but by the way funds are allocated (for example, in terms of the institutions, fields and industries to which they are directed, and the mechanisms used to finance research) and by knowledge dissemination and research commercialisation practices that are adopted …". On the other hand, a narrow priority-driven and overly utilitarian approach to public support for research may in the long-term be counterproductive. Henkel cites investigations that suggest that "... since outcomes of inquiry are often wholly unpredictable, imposing limits in terms of future relevance or applicability is likely to reduce, rather than enhance, the social or economic benefits it may generate".

The research university is unlikely to disappear, though it is being transformed as it interacts with an increasingly complex and turbulent environment. According to Rip,

> "... the key challenge is to diversify and recombine its components, both cognitively and institutionally, into what call a post-modern university. Such a university will include overlaps and alliances with Centres, public laboratories of various kinds and various private organizations managing and performing research. The boundaries between the university and the outside world are porous, and such 'porosity' is sought explicitly".

While the boundaries between the university and the outside world may be becoming more porous, this does not necessarily mean the comprehensive dissolution of the normative structures that maintain scientific communities specifically and academic organizations generally. According to Henkel, the extent of category collapse implied by some observers is questionable, although "... it is not necessary to subscribe wholesale to a post-modern perspective to perceive a variety of ways in which the boundaries between academic and other worlds are being blurred and to conclude that this is a growing trend". The university, even under mass conditions of higher education, "must remain relatively stable in order to continue to fulfil two primary functions: the production of the next generation of researchers and generator of cultural norms". The question of diversification versus homogenization of higher education institutions and systems is one of the most important areas for further research for all nations.

Building Research Culture

Higher education institutions must provide a supportive environment if research is to flourish. In some developing countries, higher education institutions were originally established mainly to engage in teaching and it will take a good deal of effort and an appropriate policy environment to nourish a research culture. For example, Salazar-Clemeña, writing about the Philippines, notes that that country has a number of general policies which emphasize the development of a research culture and environment. These include the recognition that research:

— Is the ultimate expression of an individual's innovative and creative powers. Higher education institutions shall ensure that the academic environment nurtures and supports Filipino research talents.

— Thrives in an environment characterized by the free flow of information, honest and analytical exchange of ideas, and supportive administrative structures. Higher education policies shall enhance the individual's capacity to conduct independent and productive research.

— Is one of the main functions of higher education institutions. Universities, in particular, are expected to lead in the conduct of technology-directed and innovative/creative researchers who are locally responsive and globally competitive.

Yutronic argues that successful development of research capacity in universities should involve:

— Research and development with relevant impact, that is, the creation of local pertinent knowledge integrated with global knowledge advancement and transfer to produce relevant impact.

— The renovation of professions in order to solve development problems and take advantage of new opportunities.

— The creation of new development frameworks for societies and countries based on their own particularities.

Yutronic also maintains that, in order to create successful research universities, the following areas need attention:

— Critical capabilities ("critical mass") must be achieved particularly in terms of the creation of research webs and communities.

— Assessment procedures need to be defined in order to guarantee high quality staffing.

— There should be clear criteria for the institutional organization of research universities.

— Research universities should also strive for involvement in R&D initiatives.

— A process of continuous R&D operation and production with relevant impact should be started.

Meek's recommendations for better management of the Australian research enterprise include:

— Universities should identify strengths and make hard decisions about allocating resources based on these.
— Care should be taken that the social sciences as well as basic research in the sciences are not neglected.
— In shifting the financial pressure to students, the government should recognize that student fees will not support increased research efforts.
— Increasing the number of private providers in the market is unlikely to increase research levels.
— Increases in funding coming from business and industry are needed but should not diminish the investment from other sectors, particularly government.

What Counts as Research and Indigenous Knowledge?

Much of the writing on the relationship between higher education and the global knowledge economy concentrates on Western systems of innovation. However, non-Western traditions of knowing and cognitive engagement with the environment have existed for centuries. A challenge in many countries is to effectively blend Western constructions of knowledge with indigenous ones. Chanana, for example, analyses "Situating the Indian Academic Profession in Guru Tradition". In comparing the Guru tradition in India with that of the modern university professor, she notes that the indigenous academic tradition in India both existed since ancient times and held advanced learning in higher esteem. The contemporary Indian professor is a British transplant and introduced a significant degree of distance between teacher and student. Of course, the Western academic tradition is itself going through a transition, the trajectory of which needs to be understood, at least in part, in terms of the indigenous circumstances into which it was initially introduced. "Because the faculty role is essential to the functioning of the higher education system, it is transformed along with the transformation in the functions of the system. However, if only the Western framework of values and practices is considered, then important points that impact the academic profession are likely to be missed".

Thaman argues for the inclusion of Pacific "indigenous knowledge systems" in the discourse on knowledge production and dissemination in higher education, particularly in higher education institutions in Oceania. Like indigenous peoples everywhere, the inhabitants of the islands of the Pacific Ocean have for centuries used local knowledge of themselves and their environment to live, work, trade and communicate with one another. Western influence commencing about 300 years ago constitutes a small fraction of the thousands of years of history of these peoples. Thaman uses the term "indigenous knowledge systems" to refer to "... specific systems of values, knowledge, understandings, and practices developed and accumulated over millennia, by a group of people in a particular region, which may be unique to that group or region".

"Indigenous knowledge systems" and "Western knowledge systems" are different but have equally valid ways of knowing and interpreting the world. Western knowledge claims universality, while "indigenous knowledge" is peculiar to the culture that owns it. In recent years there has been a concerted effort by some educators to incorporate indigenous knowledge into the formal education systems in Oceania, both to improve results and to preserve the cultural heritage of the Pacific people. Western scientific interest in indigenous knowledge is increasing. For some time, Western scholars have been interested in local agriculture and farming technologies. .

References

Askling, B. and Henkel, M. (2000). "Higher Education Institutions". In: Kogan, M., Bauer, M., Bleiklie, I. and Henkel, M. (eds.), *Transforming Higher Education: A Comparative Study*. London: Jessica Kingsley, pp. 109-130.

Lyotard, J.F. (1984). *The Post-modern Condition: A Report on Knowledge*. Minneapolis: University of Minnesota Press.

OECD. (1996). *The Knowledge-based Economy*. Paris: Organisation for Economic Cooperation and Development.

Perkin, H. (1991). "History of Universities". In: Altbach, P. (ed.), *International Higher Education: An Encyclopaedia*. Garland: New York, pp. 169-204.

Stadtman, V.A. (1980). *Academic Adaptations: Higher Education Prepares for the 1980s and 1990s*. San Francisco: Jossey Bass.

UNESCO. (2007). *Summary Reports of the 2007 Regional Research Seminars: Main Findings & Conclusions*. Paris: UNESCO.

7

Globalization and Cross-border Education

Globalization, technological changes, the rise of the knowledge economy, and changing skill requirements in the labour market seem to influence changes in the landscape of higher education, worldwide. Since the emergence of these phenomena, knowledge-based sectors have become the primary drivers of growth, and the demand for skills and higher education qualifications is on the rise. The move towards a knowledge economy has been characterized by a change in the pattern of deployment of the labour force and an increase in the knowledge content of products. Knowledge economies have experienced a migration of workers from manufacturing activities to service sector activities, making the latter a dominant sector both in terms of level of employment and income generated. The share of the labour force engaged in service sector occupations doubled or trebled in knowledge economies in the 1990s.

The quantity of knowledge embedded in the goods produced and exported has increased considerably. While the knowledge content has increased, the goods have become, as it were, lighter in weight – in fact, 'weightless' – facilitating their exportation. Knowledge economies engage in knowledge production (R&D) and in the production of knowledge-based goods. Investment in knowledge production is financially rewarding to firms, increases national income, and helps maintain the potential for growth and national competitiveness for the future. While returns to investments in knowledge-based production may be achieved in the short term, those from investments in research and development (R&D) activities may only be realized in the long term.

Knowledge economies require people with theoretical knowledge to promote research activities, with professional skills to develop production, and with technical skills to produce and support production. These skills correspond to a level of education imparted in universities and institutions of higher education. The International Labour Organization (ILO) estimated that, in some knowledge economies, nearly 70 per cent of all new jobs require a post-secondary level of education. While the more advanced countries have universalized school education and massified, if not universalized, higher education, most of the Commonwealth countries are far from reaching this target. Further, it has become essential that the developing countries expand their higher education sector if they are to catch up with the technological advances of other countries and accelerate their economic growth. In other words, for developing countries, higher education expansion is becoming a prerequisite for progress towards a knowledge economy.

The quantity of skills required has outstripped the capacity of the existing higher education institutions to produce them, even in countries that have the largest networks of higher education institutions. The choice for these countries was either to expand the capacity of their higher education systems to produce these skills domestically, or to import skills from the global market. While the former may be a desirable option in the long run, it would require heavy investment and take some time to build the necessary infrastructure. Thus these countries have preferred a more immediate, ready-made solution and encouraged skill migration, especially from developing countries, leading to a 'global hunt' for talent.

Many developed countries have thus made it easier for highly skilled workers to obtain a visa, with the aim of boosting skill migration. For example, the introduction of the H1B visa in the United States (USA) helped to attract skilled workers, especially from Asia. Nearly 1 million highly skilled workers entered the USA under the H1B visa between 2000 and 2003). The European Union is introducing the Blue Card visa to attract skilled workers from developing countries. Countries such as Australia, New Zealand, and the United Kingdom (UK) have introduced point-based migration policies that give preferential treatment to candidates with higher-level qualifications.

Even so, it seems that the level of migration has not been sufficient to meet global demands. Further, the quality of the skills possessed by migrants has not always been at the level demanded by the production sectors. This called for a greater output of skilled workers, either domestically or abroad, from institutions with established credibility to assure quality. Attention, therefore, turned to cross-border education, to alternatives such as institutions of higher education in developed countries (student mobility), certified institutions/branch campuses in developing countries (institutional mobility), or distance modes of education (programme mobility), which proved to be reliable in ensuring quality.

The cross-border mobility of students was encouraged, especially since it was found that a majority of those who entered OECD countries as students would stay there after their studies. For example, it was found that nearly 90 per cent of Chinese and Indian doctorate students in the USA did not return home after their studies. It is clear from this that, in many developed countries, cross-border education has become fertile ground for recruiting future highly skilled workers. In addition, there were institutions and corporations willing to invest in cross-border institutions or programmes as profit-making ventures. The private sector and transnational institutions play an important role in this mode of cross-border skill development, which relies more on individual than on state funding. In other words, cross-border education has helped transfer the cost of skill development from the public to the individual domain, and was also a necessary condition for the expansion of market operations in this area.

Mobility of Students, Graduates and Scholars

Physical Mobility

Physical mobility–of students, graduates, scholars and possibly administrators–is by no means a new phenomenon in the sphere of higher education and research. Rather, looking and cooperating across boundaries was more widespread in this sector than in most other sectors of society, and it has always been its most visible international activity. But most experts agree that mobility has accelerated in recent years, as a consequence of increased opportunities, declining national controls and global economic and societal interconnectedness. As regards student mobility, for example, it was argued in a contribution to the UNESCO Forum that "... the opportunities and the problems linked to student mobility have certainly changed substantially under conditions of expansion of higher education, the changing economic and social order as well as the doorsteps towards what is called a 'knowledge society' ".

Mobility in higher education and research tends to be discussed notably in four respects: (a) the role physical mobility plays for knowledge transfer, (b) the contributions of mobility to quality of teaching, learning and research as well as the risks as far as quality is concerned, (c) the impact of mobility on the knowledge, values and subsequent life course of the mobile persons, and (d) the ambivalent setting of costs and benefits of mobility for the mobile persons, the higher education and research institutions, and the nations experiencing an influx or out-flux of persons.

Quantities and Patterns of Student Mobility

Education statistics collected by UNESCO show that the worldwide number of students studying abroad, i.e. in a country different from that of their citizenship, has increased substantially in absolute terms from less than 200,000 in the early 1950s to more than 2 million in most recent statistics. However the overall student population has increased at a regular pace and the rate of foreign students has remained more or less constant at about 2 per cent.

A recent methodological account came to the conclusion that data on foreign students are losing their relevance as indicators of student mobility, because the more persons move internationally in the course of study, the less studying in a different country (from that of citizenship) indicates genuine student mobility, i.e. the crossing of a border for the purpose of study. Moreover, international data on foreign students are far from complete in including temporary mobility and doctoral study abroad. Yet the available data suggest that incoming students from other countries comprise more than 10 per cent of all students in various economically advanced countries, and that of the students from some low- and middle-income countries, more than half study abroad.

Recent overviews frequently point out that most foreign students are citizens of China and India. Such an emphasis on absolute data does not take into account the extent of study abroad, i.e. the proportion of students from certain countries studying abroad or the proportion of foreign students among all students in a given country.

Various trends and policies have contributed to increasing student mobility more or less in tune with overall enrolment trends. On the one hand the sheer necessity to study abroad for students from low- and middle-income countries (because hardly any study programmes exist in the desired areas and levels) is on the decline, as a consequence of expansion of higher education, and of graduate education, in most countries all over the world. On the other hand, a multitude of factors favour an increase of mobility. Among others:

— The more higher education expands, the more attention tends to be paid to distinctions in quality and reputation.

— In some low- and middle-income countries, a lack of study opportunities in certain fields of study might lead students to seek study opportunities abroad, or governments might support their students to study abroad. Two experts from Egypt stated: "Students study abroad for many reasons, but mainly to seek admission in fields either not available in Egypt or in which admission to them is streamlined by the authorities. One such example is to obtain a degree in molecular biology and genetic engineering, both of which are in the list of priorities for overseas scholarships".

— Many students hope that "vertical mobility", i.e. mobility from less reputed programmes and institutions or national systems towards more highly reputed and hopefully "better" ones, will turn out to be valuable. One should bear in mind, though, that the frequency of "vertical" mobility to certain countries and institutions is by no means determined solely by the academic quality of the host institution: "... now, it is more often influenced by colonial or post-colonial ties or more recent networks, language learning, opportunity for immigration".

— More students from low- and middle-income countries can afford and are willing to take the economic risk of investing into study abroad.

— An increasing number of institutions of higher education in economically advanced countries, in many cases supported and pushed by national policies, are active in trying to attract growing numbers from low- and middle-income countries.

The widespread claim that student mobility is highly valuable and is expanding "exponentially" might create the misleading impression that barriers to mobility tend to fade away. Various experts presenting surveys and first-hand experience in the UNESCO Forum named a broad range of barriers: "lack of administrative capacity at the institutional level as well as the lack of state incentives encouraging the institutions to increased mobility", inability to afford the living costs and student fees abroad, exorbitant tuition fees charged to foreign students, security concerns, discouragement of women in some countries to study abroad, mistrust in propagandistic information policies, etc.

The Varying Rationales

In the framework of the activities of the UNESCO Forum, it was pointed out that economically advanced countries differ dramatically in their policies and strategies of stimulating student mobility. Notably, three distinctions are worth mentioning here.

First, some countries have shaped the regulatory system for financing higher education in such a way that their higher education institutions are strongly interested in generating income through fees paid by foreign students. Some experts consider this the most successful strategy of increasing mobility: "Academic mobility (students, programmes, providers) is considered by many as a huge commercial business and is expected to increase exponentially"; others argue: "But there is a danger ... if the perception builds overseas that international students are subsiding Australian higher education and getting little in return, it will eventually reduce enrolments". In contrast, other countries stimulate student mobility by other means and pursue a broader mix of educational, cultural and economic objectives including assisting the developmental objectives of the sending countries.

Second, some countries put prime emphasis on non-reciprocal intake of students from other countries and primarily favour "South-North" flows. Other countries appreciate reciprocal and "horizontal" mobility. The European Region Action Scheme for the Mobility of University Students (ERASMUS) programme in Europe supports temporary mobility, and is the largest programme stimulating reciprocal exchange on the assumption that "horizontal" mobility is most valuable for learning from contrasting experience.

In many cases, the rationales differ in governmental policies, institutional strategies of higher education institutions and students opting for study abroad. As regards intra-European temporary mobility, Rivža observes a growing role of student options. "Taking into account the increase of possibilities due to the information and communication technologies, students, on the one hand, have more possibilities to organize periods themselves. On the other hand, increased independence of students in this aspect diminishes the role of teaching staff and higher education institutions in organizing mobilities".

Third, student mobility takes place in varying contexts of professional mobility. The United States of America (USA) is often named as an example where student mobility serves the recruitment of highly-qualified labour from other countries; Japan and Germany (the latter as regards students from outside the European Union), in contrast, are named as countries where policies to attract foreign students are clearly severed from policies regarding labour mobility.

Links between Student and Professional Mobility

In principle, international student mobility is linked to professional mobility and migration in various ways.

— Many students in low- and middle-income countries opt for study abroad in general, or choose the field of study or host country, in the hope that study abroad will provide access to a career after graduation in an economically advanced country.

— As already pointed out, some countries pursue immigration policies notably in the sector of highly-qualified labour and take foreign students as a talent pool for recruitment.

— There is an increase of jobs in the process of economic globalization and of growing international links across sectors which call for internationally experienced and competent graduates. Thus, the professional value of study abroad is often viewed as high for graduates, irrespective of whether they return to their home country or find employment abroad.

Actually, little is known about the extent to which student mobility has resulted in subsequent enhancement or, in reverse, to which the high-flying hopes of the mobile students were not fulfilled. As regards South-North mobility, "successes" are named often and "failures" occasionally, but sound data are hardly available. As regards temporary mobility within economically advanced countries, elaborate research has been undertaken: "Studies addressing the professional impact on short-term mobile students in Europe show that the study period abroad turned out to be helpful in the job search process. With respect of income and status, formerly mobile students do not perceive any clear advantage to formerly non-mobile students. Two professional effects of short-term mobility are most striking: formerly mobile students are more frequently professionally active abroad and those who are not employed abroad take over clearly more frequently visible international assignments such as communicating with foreigners, using foreign languages, travelling abroad for professional purposes, using knowledge on other countries, etc.". However, a recent study points out that the professional impact of study abroad in another country starts to decrease "... because study in another country gradually loses its exceptionality as compared to general experiences of internationalization and globalization affecting the daily life of others".

"Brain Drain" and "Brain Circulation"

Many low- and middle-income countries face a substantial outflow of graduates – either at the beginning of the course of study or after graduation – who eventually get employed in other, often economically more advanced countries. "Brain drain" is the most frequently employed term in this context to underscore the loss of investment and talent through outflow.

> "Brain circulation", in contrast, is often used to point out that countries facing an outflow of talent (also an outflow of scholars) often experience a "return" in terms of remittances (i.e. part of the outgoing persons' income sent back to the home country), collaboration of the foreign "diaspora" with their home country, or eventually "reverse mobility". Knight, for example, wrote: "More developing countries are seeing the diaspora as a source of expertise, knowledge and networks rather than only a source of income." Kearney summarized the arguments presented in one of the Forum workshops as follows: "While the Brain Drain continues to be a reality for many developing countries … returning experts or the circulation of expertise can offer positive aspects, but require innovative approaches to academic and professional credentials. Examples of this include Silicon Valley IT experts returning to India … mobilization of the diasporas from Africa and the Arab states, and burgeoning cooperative arrangements such as joint professorships, dual research appointments and laboratories (known as 'collaboratories'), and jointly awarded graduate degrees".

Altogether, however, as was frequently pointed out in the Forum, there seems to be an inflationary use of the term "brain circulation" in order to play down the net losses many low- and middle-income countries suffer from the international mobility of highly-qualified labour, and notably from the international mobility of researchers. Thus, it cannot come as a surprise that calls are often made for the receiving countries of mobility to compensate financially the enormous losses of the sending, "drained" countries.

It was also pointed out in the Forum that some countries are not just passively and involuntarily affected by "brain drain", higher education policies rather seem to be an integral part of international flows of the workforce. In some countries, graduates in high demand internationally are "produced" in such a magnitude that they are bound to find jobs related to their study in other countries. Often, one cannot clearly disentangle whether this is an inadvertent "loss" which might be true of the "exodus" of Nigerian medical doctors.

The UNESCO Forum on Higher Education, Research and Knowledge, as one might expect, paid attention primarily to the international mobility of scholars – academic staff at institutions of higher education and research institutes in general, or specifically graduate students, doctoral candidates, young researchers or senior scholars. No worldwide statistics exist on the international mobility of scholars; yet available data on individual countries and regions show on the one hand that the majority of scholars from some low- and middle-income countries in science and technology work abroad, and on the other that in some low- and middle-income countries the majority of scholars are expatriates. Most available data do not allow to disentangle clearly how frequent the South-North, North-South, North-North and South-South flows are.

Most highly-skilled persons migrate to the major Anglophone economically advanced countries. Actually a substantially higher proportion than that of students studying abroad are in these countries. Considering the population size of these countries, however, we note that Australia, Canada, and Switzerland have a relatively higher influx of highly-skilled persons from abroad than France, Germany, UK and the USA.

Collaborative and Strengthening Policies

Low- and middle-income countries respond quite differently to the potential and risks of the outflow of talent (those who become researchers in other countries). For example, South-South mobility and collaboration is promoted in some regions among neighbouring countries, in order to stem long-term outflow and to facilitate mutual enhancement. Collaborative and twinning arrangements are made with laboratories and institutions in economically advanced countries, as well as arrangements of joint supervision of doctoral candidates. Some countries are highly efficient in tapping the diaspora of experts from their country all over the world, and thus ensure that the most talented emigrants contribute to the enhancement of research in their country of origin. Some countries are very successful in the repatriation of those citizens who have become highly reputed researchers abroad. Improved information on "success stories" of that kind might stimulate similar actions in other countries as well.

Improving the Research and Societal Environment

Experts from low- and middle-income countries active in the UNESCO Forum for Higher Education, Research and Knowledge point out that the threat, or actual experience, of losing talent and potential (for research, economic wealth and social well-being) might turn out to be a creative starting point for reconsidering and redressing the situation in the home country. Awareness might grow of deterrent societal and financial conditions for research and academic life in the host country. For example, we note efforts:

— To secure appropriate remuneration which allows scholars to concentrate on research rather than on "moonlighting" in order to make their living.
— To establish rewards for research activities and participatory decision-making processes.
— To reduce "red-tape" bureaucracy.
— To strengthen academic freedom as well as freedom of movement and collaboration.
— To address gender parity and encourage respect of young scholars.

These activities could increase the attractiveness of countries that, historically, have been less welcoming for scholars than most economically advanced countries. Consensus emerged that many low- and middle-income countries could do much more to make conditions attractive for their own research talent.

Some problems of research environments and scholars' living conditions are similar across low-income countries and might not be taken into sufficient consideration. Professional isolation was named as such an example by an African expert:

> "Scientific knowledge advances through dialogue and exchange of views. This will not happen if the local scientific community is not large ... This means that the scientist will not be able to subject his or her ideas, hypotheses or research results to informal peer review through regular contacts with his or her colleagues. The result is that the capacity of the individual to do research withers away ... In fact, escape from isolation is one of the contributory factors to brain drain".

Experts addressing these issues in the UNESCO Forum called for detailed analyzes in individual countries in order to identify areas of improvement. In one country, the salaries of scientists might be quite low in comparison to salaries in other sectors; in another case, lack of incentives might be more crucial than the level of salaries as such. In some countries, talented women might be severely disadvantaged; in other countries, freedom of creative thought might be missing. In some countries, improvement could be realized within the universities and research centres without major environmental change. Finally, self-critical analysis might show that poor management practices and lacking respect for academic creativity discourage high-quality research.

Internationalization and Globalization

In some respects higher education institutions and research centres have always been international institutions, as efforts were traditionally made to seek the most advanced stage of knowledge all over the world. Getting acquainted with world-wide knowledge was a clear imperative for fields with a universalistic knowledge base, but in many other fields as well, learning from contrast, comparative study and study of worldwide interaction was imperative. In addition, cosmopolitan values were widespread among leading scholars. However it remains customary to talk about higher education and research systems while referring to nations: the regulatory system, the policies and funding practices, the institutional settings, the careers and employment conditions, the study programmes and degrees are all shaped nationally.

Rapid processes of internationalisation and globalization have been observed in this domain. Experts agree that both terms refer to changes in higher education and research itself, as well as to changes in the context of higher education and research. Internationalization often points to a growth of border-crossing activities amidst a persistence of borders and nations, while globalization often implies that borders and nations as such get blurred in this process or might even disappear. Moreover, specific issues tend to be linked to the individual terms. Internationalization is often discussed in relation to physical mobility, academic cooperation and knowledge transfer, and international education. Globalization, as the preferred reference since the 1990s, is often associated with competition and market-steering, transnational education, and commercial knowledge-transfer.

As we have pointed out, the physical mobility of students and scholars is often the most visible element of international activities. Internationalization and globalization, however, refer to the wider range of knowledge transfer activities, which might include cooperation across borders, dissemination of knowledge through various media, provision of study programmes across borders, etc.

Trends and Causes

In describing internationalization and globalization both in the context of higher education and research as movements *within* higher education and research, we note four changes:

— The increasing global interconnectedness of economy, technology, society and culture. More enterprises act as "global players"; governments consider actions in the national framework more frequently as determined by the international setting, and more often take actions on national level with one eye on the worldwide "map".

— Communication, cooperation and knowledge transfer are facilitated by information and communication technology, and by greater opportunities for travel.

— National governments (or regional governments within Federal systems) in many countries of the world have turned to a gradual de-regulation and de-nationalization of their higher education and research policies. This is partly driven by changes in governance concepts whereby detailed governmental supervision is less effective and efficient than a combination of general target-setting, decentralization, and incentive-steering (followed by an expansion of evaluation and reporting activities ex-post steering). Partly, these policies are a response to the insight that the growing global interconnectedness of knowledge is bound to relativize national policies anyway.

— Finally, we note a growing "commodification" of knowledge and education, where activities of research and teaching are undertaken by institutions regulated by commercial logic; we note a growing streamlining of the purposes of research and education for economic utility.

Consequences for Low- and Middle-Income Countries

The various analyses presented in the framework of the UNESCO Forum underscore that the recent trends provide opportunities for low- and middle-income countries to get easier access to, and participation in, high-quality knowledge production. And various examples were put forward to illustrate recent improvements in study programmes and research activities. But experts also pointed out the risks involved and the failures. Among the problems named, the following stood out:

— Investments in higher education and research are so impressive in many economically advanced countries that other countries hardly have any chance of catching up. Investments by industry in research and development largely concentrate on economically advanced countries, and only a few other countries (such as Singapore) succeeded in getting a substantial share of research funds from abroad.

— On the other hand, many low-income countries do not consider themselves to be in a position to make the necessary investments and benefit from the increasing opportunities for access to high-quality knowledge. Sanyal and Varghese point out that "In fact little research in Africa is funded by the national authorities and ... research in these countries is essentially a donor-driven activity".

— The increased global competition in higher education and research, and the related information systems on "World-Class Universities" and indicators of "cutting-edge" research are more likely to underscore gaps than to motivate the less privileged to "catch up".

— Transnational education provided or assisted by economically advanced countries might be low in quality, and might exploit those paying for it in many cases; the low- and middle-income countries have limited capacity for reviewing the quality of programmes and preventing the obvious low-quality programmes from spreading on their territory.

— The resource pools for research in many low- and middle-income countries, even if financially sufficient, might be too small to compete with the larger pools of other countries.

— The programme goals of transnational education programmes and the paradigms of research might be so driven by the perspectives of economically advanced countries that the needs of low- and middle-income countries are neglected or even suppressed.

Altogether, the findings of the Forum suggest that the current trends are more likely to widen, or at least maintain, the gap of higher education and research between the economically advanced countries and the majority of low- and middle-income countries. Targeted measures were called for in order to improve the actual developments in low- and middle-income countries, increase the likelihood of quality improvements, and serve their specific needs better than in the past.

Cross-border Education

Learning across borders, recently often called "cross-border education", is by no means predominantly realized through the physical mobility of students. In recent decades, "transnational education" spread in terms of cross-border study provisions such as distance education, "offshore programmes", "branch campuses", or higher education institutions or study programmes jointly carried out and supervised by institutions and actors from economically advanced countries and host low- and middle-income countries.

The initiative for transnational education often came from economically advanced countries in which the national funding regime encouraged the "import" of foreign students and the "export" of study programmes, and where the native English language facilitates such activities. Even though the financial considerations might have explained these initiatives at the beginning, countries such as Australia increasingly acknowledge an educational value of increased international activity for Australian students and scholars, in that it can "... increase their understanding of other cultures and broaden their scholarship", they "... benefit socially and culturally from the presence of overseas students", and "Collaboration with international colleagues enhances the capacity of Australian academics to produce high quality research".

As regards low- and middle-income countries, one overview mentioned the following possible benefits of virtual-type universities and other transnational educational arrangements: "The positive aspects of the initiation of these new institutions include: widening of learning opportunities at various higher education levels by providing more choice for citizens in any given national jurisdiction; challenging traditional education systems by introducing more competition and innovative programmes/delivery methods; helping make higher education more competitive; assisting in diversifying the budgeting of higher education and benefiting through links with prestigious institutions, mainly in developing countries.

In a document by Bubtana high hopes were set on the envisaged GATS agreement for treating higher education programmes as a service commodity, with "... the advantages that foreign providers would increase access to higher and adult education, develop higher education and research infrastructures, increase the mobility of students, academic staff and researchers, and increase competitiveness which leads to improved quality". But many observers see problems and risks inherent in the increase of transnational education:

> "Risk can include: an increase in low-quality or rogue providers; a decrease in public funding if foreign providers are providing increased access; non-sustainable foreign provision of higher education if profit margins are low; foreign qualifications not recognized by domestic employers or education institutions; elitisms in terms of those who can afford cross-border education; overuse of English as the language of instruction...".

As regards the perspectives from Australian higher education, Meek writes:

> "... international students who are in institution programmes through offshore schools have become a worry regarding the quality and reputation of Australian education. This is because these students are often enrolled in the courses using different assessment standards and criteria from their onshore counterparts. Further, there have been discrepancies in teaching standards, quality of education and support services in these offshore campuses relative to onshore campuses..."

Another risk was pointed out:

> "Real collaborative education programs require responsibilities from both sides. There are examples, however, of one-sided offerings with one partner

> involved only by name, which is used to bypass certain regulations. The worst case is the one hidden under profit incentives, exploiting the local university's name".

The views of the low- and middle-income countries are reflected in Bubtana:

> "All these types of providers are capable of crossing borders without adhering to the rules and regulations of any state. In the absence of national and international regulatory frameworks, the concepts of quality, accreditation and recognition of studies and degrees remain questionable areas." He also states: "The fear in developing countries is that … cross- and trans-border providers will lead to negative rather than positive consequences such as increased social costs for higher education, the return of the elitist systems, and gradual disappearance of national systems that cannot compete with foreign providers. Some critics consider the agreement as a pretext for the total takeover of higher education by the corporate community, and for monopolizing research for commercial purposes".

An expert from New Zealand points out the tensions between what is relevant in the providing countries and what is needed in the countries the learners come from:

> "With the increasing internationalization of higher education, developing countries are ill-prepared to absorb and appropriate yet more foreign influences and demands of international organizations … The needs of institutions to develop within a global academic and research community and thereby adopt the predominant Western models of higher education and the development needs of these countries are often clashing, posing a dilemma between satisfying market forces and the need to nurture education within socio-cultural specificities of the country. The challenge of how to be locally relevant and at the same time with international standing is a big challenge for these higher education institutions. The internationalization of higher education is making it more difficult for local knowledge to prevail".

Research and Research Training

The internationalization of research, and also of research training, is often hailed as important in raising the quality of research in low- and middle-income countries. Many examples of "good practice" were named in the analyses presented at the UNESCO Forum. For example, in Latin America and the Caribbean, as experts from these regions stated in a comparative study, "... in all the national cases … we found that there is generalized agreement that an international orientation in education and training at the doctoral level is worthwhile to help countries position themselves in a world and economy that have changed significantly, and that extensive stays abroad are an important way of achieving this. Motivations are varied: on the one hand, a desire to improve the quality of research graduate training; and on the other, at the level of international politics of countries, an internationality to increase the capabilities of participation and negotiation in an international scientific community and other domains of the economy that require a greater familiarity with increasingly globalized regimes of regulation and control".

An interesting case for international collaboration in research was reported in Egypt, in "... the Unit of Environmental Studies and Development (UESD) established at the Aswan Branch of Assiut University, South Valley. This unit has the status of a UNESCO-Cousteau Ecotechnie Chair and all research activities are executed by projects with foreign funding. The Chair is strengthening research capacity in the university, which benefits, in particular, postgraduate studies, by promoting interdisciplinary education and applied research. Highly motivated university researchers and postgraduate students from different departments are working voluntarily for the unit and, in return, the Chair provides facilities for research, training and communications. In addition, the Chair provides small grants from research projects funding for newly graduated B.Sc. students enabling them to work on subjects related to the Ecotechnie concept for their M.Sc. and Ph.D. degrees, supervised by senior staff of the UESD team... The Chair trains junior staff members in research and in proposal and publication-writing".

There are many cases where an insufficient balance is noted between the partners from the North and the South:

> "Research into donor-based programmes of 'cooperation' between institutions from the North and South has indicated an inequality in the relationship. 'Because the Northern donor provides the funding, ... knowledge, ... often decides on the model and activities to be chosen, despite the fact that the Southern institution is obviously being better placed to determine the needs and priorities'... The Northern institutions benefit from these programmes in terms of the internationalization of courses, attracting researchers, establishing collaborations with partner institutions in the South, and getting access to research grounds in developing report vividly states how the local relevance of research can be undermined in the search for enhancement of research quality:

> "Chagas' disease is essentially one of poverty ... At this time only one drug is available, Ben-znidazol, it is produced by one international laboratory (Roche), was developed over 40 years ago and is used only for the acute phase of infection... no drug exists for the chronic phase ... Chagas' disease is thus considered one of the 'most neglected illnesses', affecting the poorest populations of developing countries and enjoying no R&D attention from pharmaceutical companies".

Paradoxically, the researchers working on this disease have gained international visibility and are involved in international networks. However, these researchers "... must work on the priorities identified by the leaders of each network", which are "... largely determined by the industrialized countries, supra-national institutions and developed country private enterprises...". The authors define this situation as "subordinate integration", where

> "... the groups suffering from unfavourable local conditions, can in theory, and sometimes in practice surmount them and gain access to new, significant resources for their activities. This seems to feature 'democratization', in the universalized relations around the production of knowledge. However, this abstracting logic for local conditions, at work in the process of internationalization, can lead to increased subordination... The most important effects come from the latest iterations of research and funding policy, themselves a product of the competition between the USA and the EU... Thus traditional models for the promotion of S&T are increasingly being replaced with new policies and new instruments: the 'project' as a funding unit is being replaced with 'programmes' and 'networks'".

Pooling Resources between Neighbours

Collaboration between countries in research is increasingly viewed as a necessity in small, economically advanced countries. This was for instance true of the Nordic countries in Europe: "To take part in international relations is generally considered to be of great importance for a small advanced country like Norway, particularly to increase the breadth and quality of research". "In addition to Denmark, Finland, Iceland and Norway are small nation states. In recent years there has been a growing concern about the need for extended Nordic collaboration on education, research and innovation, in order to reach the critical mass necessary to fulfil national goals of educational and research excellence in relation to the EU policy and the increasing global trade in higher education.

In some poor regions of the world, including Africa, regional cooperation is viewed as a necessity to ensure minimum resources. Concerning human capacity-building, "... it is quite clear from the nature of the challenges that most countries will not be able to act alone to successfully build their capacity. The training resources are weak. The scientists are isolated and the threat of brain drain prevents the search for training outside the region. Under such circumstances, regional cooperation offers a good alternative. Such cooperation can have three benefits: information sharing, resource sharing and resource mobilization. Information sharing will prevent attempts to re-invent the same solutions or to repeat the same mistakes … The challenge associated with isolation of scientists will be overcome through regional cooperation. Through resource utilization, sharing the strengths of some institutions in certain subjects will even out the weaknesses of the others. Thus, through cooperation it will be possible to undertake high-level training within the region and thereby minimize the threat of brain drain".

The obvious benefits of regional cooperation might even lead to the establishment of a single university for several small countries, instead of separate small, national universities. The University of the West Indies, founded almost sixty years ago in the Anglophone Caribbean, is such a case. But there are cases where cooperation of that kind is missing: "… cooperation between Arab scientists is almost non-existent, despite the presence of a number of Arab regional organizations whose objective is to promote such cooperation. Neither national nor regional Arab organizations devote any real resources to cooperation", and this holds true even though common problems exist (which could be addressed jointly).

> "The Arab States share a wide range of common scientific and technical problems, thus there should be considerable incentives for co-operation. Most of the Arab World is in a dry zone where water is scarce; this dictates certain research issues in water use in agriculture and in water management. Likewise several Arab countries are oil and gas producers; this provides common technological challenges and opportunities for sharing experiences. Moreover they all share a number of problems in health, and in the application of codes and standards as well as in many other fields" (ibid.).

Many efforts have been undertaken to stimulate cooperation in higher education and research within various African regions.

Various other experts name additional problems: non-hosting countries of the region might feel marginalized; some countries do not contribute financially on a regular basis; if joint centres are decentralized, quality control can be an issue because different rules and practices apply for the various countries involved. Two Latin American experts conclude that strong mechanisms are needed to ensure success in regional cooperation:

"At least three entities will need to be created to ensure regional and functional cooperation in higher education and research. These are:

1. Coordinating and regulatory mechanisms to promote exchanges, advise governments and institutions, and grant approval for the establishment and operation of higher education institutions.
2. A quality assurance mechanism that ensures high standards in all areas of study in higher education institutions.
3. A clearing-house which facilitates nationals of one country undertaking study in another area agreed by the Governments concerned, such that Governments pay in part or whole the economic cost of their students".

All experts addressing the issues of regional partnerships in the UNESCO Forum agreed that, in spite of the difficulties experienced in various cases, many regions of the world have to form regional partnerships in order not to be left behind in terms of research quality and relevance.

The Changing Academic Environment

Experts addressing for the Forum the situation of the academic profession by and large agree on four, interrelated major changes in the environment shaping academic professional roles. The terms vary, but often refer to popular jargons: "massification", "knowledge economy", increasing power of management or "managerialism", and "competition". In all cases, the terms employed and analyses presented are ambivalent: potentials for improvement are acknowledged, but risks and dangers are underscored. Altogether, the notion of a "profession under pressure" is more often presented than one of improving quality and relevance and than one of an increasingly satisfying professional situation).

— *"Massification"*: The increase of student enrolment all over the world is generally seen as a valuable contribution of higher education towards enhancing the living conditions and career perspectives of graduates, as a step towards reduction of historically rooted inequities, and as forming the necessary basis for the "knowledge society". But enrolment increases are often also seen as creating resource squeezes and undue efficiency pressures. Last but not least, in many countries the growth of enrolment encourages policies of differentiation of higher education institutions, whereby some strive for a close link between research and teaching, while others are clearly shaped by their teaching function. Kogan and Teichler characterized the consequences of massification as follows: "Expansion of student enrolment was identified as the major driver of change, moving the intellectual discourse of the teachers and learners to organized curricula and instruction techniques, leading to a separation of the teaching and research function for many academics, undermining a social exclusiveness of the professoriate, increasing pressures for efficiency, and thus elevating the status of university management and possible government as forces of establishing a compromise between the traditional ideals and the new pressures of efficiency and coordination."

— *"Knowledge economy"*: Most academics believe that higher education and research has to contribute to technological progress, economic growth, societal well-being and cultural enhancement. The increasing expectation, in the context of a "knowledge society" or "knowledge economy", of relevant results of higher education is widely viewed as an opportunity for growth and for quality enhancement. However, fears are widespread that undue pressures for visible utility might undermine a creative environment in higher education and research, and might consider certain stakeholders, certain purposes and certain directions of innovation while neglecting others.

— *"Managerialism"*: In many countries of the world, the role of the institutional leaders and the departmental leaders has been strengthened in recent years in higher education and research institutions within the overall steering and governance of that sector. On the one hand, governments were willing to devolve part of their powers, notably those of detailed administrative supervision; on the other, the collegial power of academics to administer their affairs decreased. This is often seen as having led to more rational decisions and higher efficiency, but there are widespread critiques as well: that managers often became the servants of unbalanced external pressures, that managerial control undermined the motivation of academics, and that academic rationales have lost ground in shaping the goals and processes of teaching and research.

— *"Competition"* is a normal state of affairs in the highly selective and intellectually demanding academic profession, and those academics who strive continuously for the highest level of achievement are generally viewed as desirable. In recent years, however, academic work was increasingly put under the regime of incentive mechanisms, evaluation measures and indicator-based steering, and many critics note a growth of counterproductive effects. These include an over-burdening of academics, too much attention to externally well-funded research objectives, overemphasis on short-term, visible success, imitation of the goals and process of select "World-Class Universities", and neglect of the less well-paid and less incentive-supported functions of higher education. It is interesting to note that experts tend to describe the major changes in low- and middle-income countries in similar terms to those in economically advanced countries. This suggests that the trends are in fact similar, often as a result of the global influence of the economically advanced countries – and the spread of higher education governance concepts from the north to the south. However, there are some issues relating to the academic profession which are indicative for low- and middle-income countries.

Employment Conditions

In a substantial number of countries, the salary level of academic staff in higher education and research institutions is far too low to earn a living. "Within developing countries the conditions of work and remuneration of the majority of academics is inadequate … Academics have to hold more than one job to make ends meet". This might lead to irregular presence at the university. For one low-income country, an expert reported: "Many professors increase their earnings by selling books and photocopies, such as of lectures and notes, to students. The professors prefer large classes because they can make more money". Some look notably to consultancies for additional income. In some countries, the low pay causes a serious understaffing or staffing on a minimum quality level, because many staff members "... leave for better-paying jobs". Most frequently, the bad pay of academic staff arguably leads them to neglect research, because research duties are less formally controlled in most universities than teaching.

In most economically advanced countries, senior academic staff at universities and public research institutes traditionally had permanent employment contracts, while the situation varied for junior academic staff. In some countries, they had similar contracts as seniors from the very beginning, in others their employment security grew gradually over time, while in others permanent contracts were only awarded with the appointment to senior positions.

In recent years, employment security for senior staff was called into question. "Job security, once and assumption, is under attack … Permanent employment is no longer a given and tenure is becoming increasingly rare". In Japan, for example, the civil service status for academics at national universities was discontinued. As a consequence, most newly appointed academic staff gets short-term employment, and permanently employed persons could be dismissed if structural changes are made. In Latvia, "... permanent professorships are all but abolished, and faculty members who wish to stay on have to apply again for their own chairs every six years, perhaps competing with young aspiring talents who were recently their own graduate students".

In some countries, and notably in the private sector, teaching assignments are made predominantly on a part-time basis. This might lead to financially unsustainable living conditions of academics, although, as was pointed out for example for Mexico, "... it is not uncommon to have part-time academics that, by virtue of several part-time contracts, are in fact 'full-time faculty'". In other countries, as in Mongolia and some Central and Eastern European countries, officially full-time employed staff of public institutions work part-time at private institutions, in order to make up for the unbearably low salary.

In many countries, institutions of higher education forego pay for social security and medical benefits. Apart from the hardships for the individuals, excessive part-time work is criticized for leading to overworked teachers not caring well for quality of teaching and learning, neglect of teaching-related tasks outside the classroom, and reduction of the research role of these institutions. Therefore, minimum standards are set in some countries for the employment of full-time staff. In Mongolia, "... the legal requirement concerning staffing of higher education institutions is that a minimum of 60 per cent of teaching staff have to be full-time faculty members".

Salary levels are diversified in some countries. This might reinforce "... the rise of the academic 'star' ... and the compulsive 'winner-takes-all' phenomenon with high salaries for successful and entrepreneurial professors". The conditions for promotion are an issue of concern:

— In various low- and middle-income countries complaints are widespread that promotion is a routine which undermines efforts to enhance one's own achievement and might actually block talent. A report published by the Human Rights Watch (USA based, international NGO) "referring to Egyptian academicians, stated that promotion at all levels is close to automatic provided one does not stray too far into red line areas. The progression moves from assistant to lecturer, once the Ph.D. is complete. Usually lecturers become assistant professors after five years, and full professors after ten years. Promotion depends on tailoring research to state-imposed standards rather than increasing knowledge in the field. Once a scientist has become professor no other academic promotion opportunities exist and there are no mechanisms for monitoring both research and teaching".

— Views vary regarding the strengths and weaknesses of external academic recruitment. It encourages the collection of experiences at various locations, and assessment of external candidates might be less particularistic. On the other hand, internal recruitment might increase institutional loyalty and the long-term build-up of areas of expertise. Therefore, some "... institutions have their own career procedures and development, and offer possibilities for promotion for the best of academics who are not moving". However as one expert pointed out, institutional loyalty could be reinforced in such a way as to undermine "academic integrity".

— At many institutions promotion is tied to formal criteria, such as publishing a certain number of papers in journals (or in specific, highly select journals). These procedures seem to underscore achievement-oriented, fair selection at first glance, but are often criticized as encouraging formal achievement rather than substantive quality, and as neglecting the varied functions of the academic profession.

Various analyses presented in the framework of the Forum touched upon the issue of gender equity in careers. Some experts point out the small percentage of women among academic staff in select countries. Others underscore that the percentage of women varies dramatically among countries in similar stages of economic development or of higher education expansion. Some experts argue that too little is done to support women in coping with their double role as academics and mothers. Others refer to the research: academic productivity varies less according to gender, family status and child care than conventional wisdom might suggest.

Growing Complexity of Academic Work

In addressing the work situation for academics in higher education and research institutions, many experts in the Forum emphasized that lack of facilities and poor working conditions are major impediments to quantity and quality of research in low- and middle-income countries. Also, the working conditions for teaching are often characterized as deplorable; for example, "Working conditions in Asia commonly consist of large classes, lectures, few laboratories and rote learning. Often direct teaching is some twenty hours a week. Needless to say, little time is left for research".

The analyses undertaken in the UNESCO Forum for Higher Education, Research and Knowledge addressed two other issues which might be viewed as equally challenging for low-and middle-income countries as well as economically advanced ones: first, the growth of complexity of the academic work role and its implications, and second, the links between growing managerial power, increasing evaluation activities and the objectives set for teaching and research work.

Altogether, many experts expressed the view that the professional role of academics was already quite complex in the past, as leaders in their fields setting norms for teaching and research, as responsible persons for curriculum development, as mentors for junior academic staff, as being involved in many matters of administration, as persons in charge of many external and internal functions. As a consequence of rising expectations of their work, many senior academics are expected to take over a larger set of activities or handle their activities in a more "professional" way than in the past.

The bundle of expected tasks tends to vary across regions and institutions:

— Mexican experts presented the following description of extended functions: "... teaching, research, participation in the institution's collegial life, administrative work, participation in technological development, counselling and taking a central role in service activities, both to the productive and social sectors".

— A French expert, describing the scene in economically advanced countries, points out that the job roles of academics had traditionally been more closely centred on core functions of research and teaching, and that explicit reward had been centred on these core functions. "Today, this is no more the case. Writing proposals, developing contracts, elaborating e-learning programmes, being engaged in technology transfers, etc. are part of the tasks achieved by faculty members ... recognized as important aspects of academic work. In Germany and in the USA for instance, the ability to raise money and to manage research projects based on external funding is one of the criteria of judgement when hiring professors. This diversification of tasks also holds true for teaching. Activities around teaching have evolved and represent a larger scope of tasks nowadays. Giving a class and supervising doctoral students are only one part of the training work. Teaching, engineering, designing learning programmes, finding internships for students also belong to "teaching" today. Furthermore, new missions (or the so called "third mission") are emerging. They include links with regional, national and international bodies and decision-makers, interaction between scientists and the public at-large and involvement in public debates, public expertise, support to public policy at-large, etc.".

— Changes of teaching and learning functions are described by other experts: "Another challenge is the transformation of teaching and learning. The traditional lecturer delivered the lecture, usually of fifty or sixty minutes' duration, to packed lecture halls, which could hold anything up to 600 students. During the last ten years more and more emphasis has been placed on the importance of 'student-centred' learning, where the teacher acts as manager and facilitator, helping the students to learn at their own pace, and in their own time. The use of technology, with the delivery of technological and resource-based learning materials, changes the nature of the university teacher's interaction with the student. Many would point out that the time needed to act as an effective and efficient facilitator is considerably more than that needed to deliver a traditional lecture".

One way of coping with the growing complexity of the academic role is to differentiate the roles among academics. Some institutions are in charge of both teaching and research, others focus on teaching. Some institutions focus more strongly on basic research, while others strive for immediate utility. Some professors emphasize the core role of teaching and research, while others understand themselves as academic entrepreneurs. In many cases, they have to adjust to teamwork – a competence not always developed among academics.

As regards the link or division of labour between teaching and research, an expert reporting on India underscored that both facilities for research and the possibility to get along with the complex demands of teaching and research play a role in the options academics take. In India, a "... teacher survey reflects their attitude towards teaching and research. A total of 68 per cent of the teachers complain that it is difficult for them to manage research along with their heavy teaching schedule. About half of the teachers therefore abstain from any form of research along with their teaching. Teachers have very poor exposure to scientific meetings and international conferences. Sharing ideas and information with others who are working in the same or related areas are minimal in the campuses. Teachers expressed their willingness to pursue research if adequate facilities and support for infrastructure are provided in the institution. However, contrary to their complaints on infrastructure facilities only 16 per cent found that it is difficult to get adequate research support from public or private agencies. Teaching and research are not treated separately and no career advancements are provided to the faculty member who has a proven track record in research".

One expert points out that some functions are increasingly expected at specific stages of the academic career, thus reinforcing the division of labour between academics of different career stages: "Specialization occurs through the evolution in the distribution of tasks during the career achieved by permanent academics ... experimentations are generally achieved by doctoral students and post-docs under the supervision of the *maîtres de conférences* (tenured assistants/associated professors), while the professors raise funds, develop contacts and write project proposals. This increasing share in project management, administrative responsibilities and maintenance of partnerships which occurs with seniority is again not new, but it becomes more and more important, clear and explicit". In addition, "... the increasing part of contingent staff allows for a specialized distribution of activities among them", i.e. undergraduate classes given by part-time or adjunct staff (USA), doctoral students with teaching duties (France) or increasing numbers of post-docs taking place in research activities (USA).

The growing complexity of assignments in higher education and research institutions is taken care of by an increasingly specialized staff, which in part alleviates the functions of the academics and in part calls for greater cooperation:

> "The role of academics further changed as a consequence of the expansion and increasing status of 'new HE professionals', 'professional administrators', 'middle-level managers' or similarly termed university-trained persons in HE whose prime roles are managerial support or service provision and who have to be both highly qualified in their domain of shaping the institution and highly knowledgeable in the core functions of the academics. Academics have to adapt in this communication, and acknowledge the fact that while professionals in academic matters, they are amateurs in matters of shaping the university (and must cooperate with a new group of experts who are amateurs in academic matters, but professionals in shaping the university)... However, simple diarchic assumptions do not hold. There are mixtures of colle-gial, academic-based decision-making and bureaucratic/hierarchical working. Academics do take over the roles of HE professionals or those of administrative leadership".

The growing managerialism in higher education and research institutions was not viewed as a factor reducing the complexity of the academic job role. Powerful university leaders and faculty deans do not seem to reduce the administrative and decision-making activities of the academics, but they do affect the targeting and modes of involvement.

Decision-Making

As a consequence of growing managerial power in recent years, several experts contributing to the Forum cite a change in the internal institutional climate within higher education and research. Obviously, many academics consider the new climate as alien.

— The strong managerial power has changed, as some point out,

"... the nature of the relationship between each academic and his/her institution. The university is no longer a place welcoming and sheltering academic activities, it has taken over the role of an employer. The affiliation (or sentiment of affiliation) to one's institution is progressively transformed into work relationships. The responsibilities and duties of each academic are not only defined by his/her professional group but also by his/her institutional work arrangement".

— "A powerful force lending support to the growth of managerialism has been assertion of quite penetrative quality assurance procedures that replace the hitherto 'trustful' relationships between academics and their institutions as the belief in 'transparency' has replaced trust in expert and professional knowledge".

— "And alongside them may be colleagues whose expertise and experience lies mainly in the business or professional rather than the academic world. Thus, changing boundaries within the academic profession come to change boundaries between academic and other professional worlds. And as boundaries change, they become more permeable".

— "Moreover, the context in which the above tasks are to be performed has also changed. Among its main characteristics are the following: more students to attend to, internal and external performance-based economic incentives, professional development programmes stressing the attainment of formal degrees rather than competences for actual work, in many instances less than ideal working conditions, a highly rigid and segmented academic job market, and a career structure that is not well defined".

The increased pressure for efficiency and visible productivity generated by the management of universities and research institutes is viewed in many respects as successful. Often, it seems to lead to a clarification of job roles, to stronger efforts to take into account the needs of students, to use available facilities and other resources in a more targeted manner, etc. But various questionable consequences of the managerial regime are named: most of them are stated more frequently with respect to private than public institutions.

First, incentives become so important in guiding academic work that low achievement in the case of limited extrinsic rewards seems to be reinforced:

— "It had been, to some extent, the case that faculty members at universities in third world countries, in general, and Arab countries in particular, would embark on research work only when directly connected with efforts leading to their promotion. It is noted, in many cases, that once a faculty member in many of these countries attains his full professorship goals, he/she would tend to retire from doing research altogether, or do little, if any. In the absence of any targeted direction for research from the nation's strategic planning, this is worsened by the fact that research conducted by incumbent faculty members does not serve the needs of any viable industry that would serve the local community".

— According to a research project on faculty perspectives regarding the prevailing research culture in the Philippines,

  "... many faculty members consider teaching as their main task whereas research is only an add-on activity ... A weak belief in the importance of research certainly affects productivity and the trifocal function in general. The active researchers among the faculty interviewees disclosed that their involvement in research had sometimes reached a point when they began neglecting other functions". On the other hand, "... faculty from private universities emphasized that the policies in their universities pertaining to criteria for faculty promotion are very clear. The quality and quantity of research that they produce are given appropriate merit and have a bearing in their promotion".

Second, various authors discuss the impact of increased evaluation and managerial policies to increase research output. Among others, the ranking of "World-Class Universities" is seen as calling for increased research productivity, and various factors seem to reinforce it. For example, the of a comparative study in the Netherlands and the UK concludes: "... as noted by some respondents, the push for accountability and research quality assessment resulted also in more productivity since the system did not tolerate the 'idle' academic anymore. Further, the speed of building the credibility in basic research units increased from the pressures for 'relevance' and 'efficiency' coming from the environment". Some experts, though, name undesirable consequences, such as:

— The search for success in "safe" areas: "... the major concerns for academics in terms of research were the pressure for high performance in research from funding agencies and university management, while also tackling the ever-increasing teaching loads, stratification of research groups, and threats to individual academic freedom... Research units are afraid to lose out in the competitive environment and be 'punished' (e.g. closed down) in case of underperformance. This makes them to go for 'safe' research themes that will be more likely to secure funding, rather than to be innovative and take a risk".

— The loss of research talents who note that the utilitarian and applied research they are increasingly asked to do at universities is better resourced and paid in other secto..

— Some experts point out that concern for formal achievement is reinforced rather than that for academic quality. For example, Mexican experts note a race towards the attainment of advanced degrees:

"In the first place, Mexican faculty need to continue their specialized training beyond the formal higher degree that the vast majority holds at this moment. In this regard two main issues need to be confronted. One, faculty training and professional development need to be re-conceptualized. Some programmes such as the Programme for the Improvement of the Professoriate, and the internal merit-pay systems that public HEIs have in place, have promoted an atmosphere in which the goal, both institutionally and at the individual level, is to obtain a higher degree in the fastest possible way, and without necessarily much respect for traditional academic values".

Third, the dominant funding, assessment and management regimes are viewed as serving only specific interests and as undermining the search for non-conformist and creative means of knowledge generation. Some experts report such views as widespread among academics, while others point out that they share these concerns. Some examples:

— "The academy's desired state was one in which 'autonomy' or 'academic freedom' was thus the necessary safeguard for the discharge of the university's primary duty, which was to permit intellectual non-conformity as the means of advancing knowledge".

— "The Australian Institute made a survey of academics on this issue. 'The survey found widespread dissatisfaction with the erosion of academic freedom, with many respondents complaining of management pressure to produce commercially favourable research and student results … Among 165 teachers and researchers who responded, 92 per cent expressed concern about the general state of academic freedom. Of those, 81 per cent blamed the increasing commercialization of their university … About one in five reported that they had been prevented from publishing contentious research results, and 41 per cent said they had experienced discomfort with publishing such results … Almost half had experienced reluctance to criticize institutions that provided large research grants or other form of support. Approximately 5 per cent said they had experienced pressures to admit and pass full fee-paying students and more than a quarter expressed low levels of satisfaction with the freedom to determine student standards … The effect of competition, together with the administrative restructuring, on the academic profession has indeed been both positive and negative. The resulting efficiency and quality in education and research can be expected, but in reality it can be the opposite by reducing intellectual creativity. Complementarity of competition and collaboration allows for a better balance".

— "There is a lot of money for universities, but only if they accept to do what the funding agencies, including the state, want them to do. The more money they receive, with decreasing margins per researcher, the more ensnared they will become in their deprived condition. They will grow into grand deliverers with little freedom. They may keep up their high performance academically, and they may even contribute increasingly to research, which is the sought-after version of this logic. But they may as well end up being mediocre in both branches, plus dissatisfied from stress and a mounting identity crisis".

— "… knowing the specific culture of basic research units, research units were very slow to adapt to changes in the environment and they created strategies to preserve their core activities untouched. For example, despite the national research programmes and thematic funding, they still preserved their own research topics by diversifying their funding base. In that sense, sometimes other external donors, such as industry, were influential when it came to problem choice of research. Research units got involved in more applied type of research if they wanted to retain contracts with industry. This was mainly true in the biotechnology field, though even researchers in medieval studies found themselves going for 'popular' topics, as for example, the link between Robin Hood and the 'hoodies' of today in the UK to get external funding so that they can appeal to a broader audience".

— In developing countries,"... the dependency on donor agencies for funding research activities poses risks for the independence of academic research, forcing academics to tailor their research depending on donor needs. This dependency is not sustainable, as research is carried out not on a continuous basis but whenever the funds are available".

— The increase in controls over academic tasks is marked. Some controls are national, such as the Research Assessment Exercise (RAE), UK which results in a classification of research achievement within university departments and awards funding on that basis. Those who fail to achieve to expectation can find their promotion and salary prospects affected.

— "In small states, where most educational research is funded by the state or by independent international donor agencies, through the state, educators who find themselves confronting evidence that policy prescriptions are not producing the desired outcomes, make a very rational decision not to speak 'truth to power' in order to preserve their employment opportunities. What is of even greater concern is the fact that the more funding that has been invested in the policy prescription, the greater the risk to educators of highlighting its limitations or deficiencies".

— "Rather than an increase in academic power, there is an emergence of other forms and other actors of control on top of academic regulations. As a result, academics are no longer evaluated only by their peers, but also by their own institution or through national devices that public authorities develop in order to control, rank and benchmark their activity. As a whole, there is a global increase in the level and intensity of controls, which often relies on the peer review process".

— "The problem of unethical science has increased because of the quest for money, visibility and reputation due to competition for survival among not only institutions but also individual faculty members. Recently, a series of remarkable cases have occurred featuring corrupt behaviour in science".

Altogether, the discussion in the UNESCO Forum indicates that strong managerial power and a multitude of evaluation devices have become a matter of procedure. The debates of the 1990s about the opportunities and dangers of governmental deregulation and about the principal opportunities and dangers of evaluation mechanisms are not repeated or continued anymore in a similar way in the early years of the twenty-first century. But concern are expressed frequently that the dominant rationales of funding, management and evaluation are geared towards the interests of the financially most potent stakeholders, and towards over-utilitarian strategies in teaching and research. This critique implicitly does not call for the "ivory tower", but rather for increased opportunities for non-conformist, unexpected and creative knowledge creation as well as for greater consideration of various stakeholders and societal needs.

Recent Developments in Research Training

The move towards the "knowledge society" and "knowledge economy" has spread research over various sectors of society. As a consequence, the universities in some economically advanced countries are (according to statistics of research expenditures) no longer the "... major players in carrying out research", but "... continue to play a dominant role in research training".

In recent decades, an expansion and re-structuring of doctoral training and similar research and academic training can be observed in economically advanced countries. Obviously, more attention has been paid to doctoral training in higher education and research policy discourses since the 1980s than in preceding decades.

Most experts and policy-makers called for a growth of doctoral degrees, notably for the following reasons:

— Higher education continued to grow in those economically advanced countries, where senior positions are predominantly filled by doctoral degree-holders. Thus, more persons with a doctoral degree were in demand in order to take over the teaching and research tasks characteristic of teaching positions in higher education.

— A doctoral degree became the typical entry prerequisite for high-level academic positions in universities, including in those countries where this was not the case a few decades ago, e.g. Japan and the UK.

— The number of research positions outside higher education, for example in public research institutes and in private R&D, has increased in recent years even more strongly than the number of academic positions in higher education.

— The number of doctoral candidates at universities in economically advanced countries who originate from low- or middle-income countries is growing more rapidly than the number of doctoral candidates from economically advanced countries. Provisions for doctoral work are expanding rapidly in low- and middle-income countries.

Valid international statistics on the number of doctoral candidates do not exist. In the USA, for example, all students at "graduate schools" might be viewed as doctoral candidates, while in other countries only those who have already been awarded a master's or similar degree are included. Mostly, the available statistics only include those doctoral candidates who are registered as "doctoral students"; this might include all doctoral candidates in countries where a graduate school is a "must", but only a minority of doctoral candidates where the majority of them are employed or where no obligation exists to enrol as doctoral candidate for other reasons. As a consequence, only statistics on the number of doctoral *awards* can serve international comparison purposes.

Table 1 provides an overview of countries with high numbers of annual doctoral awards, as well as those with a relatively high rate of doctoral awards within their overall population.

Table 1. Trends in Net Graduation Rates at Advanced Research Qualifications, ISCED 6 Level (1995-2005)

Country	***Graduation rate 1995***	***Graduation rate 2000***	***Graduation rate 2005***
France	m	1.2	m
Switzerland	2.3	2.4	3.1
Portugal	m	1.0	2.6
Germany	m	2.0	2.4
Sweden	m	2.5	2.2
United Kingdom	m	1.4	2.0
Russian Federation	m	m	1.9
Australia	m	1.3	1.7
United States	m	m	1.3
Israel	m	0.9	1.3
Brazil	m	m	1.3
Poland	m	0.8	0.9
Japan	0.4	0.6	0.9
Turkey	m	0.2	0.2
Mexico	m	m	0.1
Chile	m	m	0.1

Doctoral training in the USA is very attractive for young researchers from all over the world, notably, in the science and engineering fields, and the mode of organizing doctoral training in the framework of graduate schools has had an enormous impact on other countries. This does not mean, however, that the current practices of doctoral training are necessarily viewed as more or less satisfactory. In a recent summary of the debates in the USA, doctoral students are believed to be

- Educated and trained too narrowly.
- Lacking key professional skills.
- Taking too long to complete their degree, or too often not completing it at all.
- Ill-informed about employment opportunities outside academia.
- Experiencing an overly long transition period from Ph.D. completion to stable employment.

Most of these problems are referred to in Europe as well. Most recent studies in Europe "... have identified altogether eleven problem areas in the traditional forms of doctoral education in European universities:

- Traditional master-apprentice models versus schools and programmes.
- Highly regulated and competitive versus rather informal and unregulated admission.
- Status of doctoral candidates: students versus salaried junior research staff, but also regulation of rights and duties of both sides.
- Frequent financial insecurity.
- Increase in numbers of doctoral candidates and degree holders but often not in the 'relevant' subjects; competition for the best talent and brain drain.
- Long average duration of the phase of doctoral qualification, with large differences among subjects.
- Lack of proper supervision and quality control of doctoral education and training.
- Mobility and international exchange of doctoral students is lower than expected, but there is increasing competition to attract and keep best talent.
- Large differences in the processes of assessment and validation of performance; problems with issues of independent assessment.

— New trend of 'professional doctorates' (and 'fast track' options), with relevance and quality concerns.
— Transition into (academic) careers featuring 'holding positions' in the post-doc phase".

In various countries, efforts are made to train doctoral candidates to do and to write-up a masterful work of research, but also to deliberately foster a broader range of related competences. Eggins, for example, names:

— "Acquisition of formal research methods.
— Development of transferable skills.
— Studies in professional applied activities.
— Innovative teaching methods.
— Training in reviewing methods.
— Publishing in research journals".

Many experts perceive a trend toward major restructuring of doctoral training, through the spread of doctoral training within doctoral programmes and graduate schools. In fact, there seems to be an increase of collective responsibilities for supervision of doctoral work, of taught courses as part of doctoral training, of enhancing skills beyond the ability to write a research master piece, and of central management of doctoral training within the universities.

It would be misleading, though, to assume that doctoral training in economically advanced countries is adapting to the North American graduate education and graduate school model. Rather, many changes are underway in various European countries leading to various kinds of compromises between the Humboldtian tradition of the individual supervision of the doctoral candidate by a single professor and the American model. Some variations might be mentioned, which are noteworthy for economically advanced countries:

— In Germany, the Netherlands, the Nordic countries in Europe and some other countries, the majority of doctoral candidates are employees at universities and research institutes, expected to be trained and to do productive work concurrently: either fully concentrated on the doctoral dissertation or having additional research assignments. They might be regular employees within the university budget and on regular pay scales, employees within special financial arrangements for doctoral candidates, or employees paid through financial means of research projects. In most European countries, the term doctoral "students" would not be viewed as desirable, even if the candidates re-ceive a fellowship or are officially registered as students for purposes of administration and benefits.

— In various European countries, doctoral programmes or "research schools" emerged as one possible option, keeping the opportunity for other universities without such programmes to award doctoral degrees and for professors not involved in such programmes to supervise doctoral students. Thus, doctoral candidates can opt either for programmes or individual doctoral work supervised by one or two professors.

— Opportunities to work for a doctoral degree without long residential requirements are widespread in many European countries. Often, residential requirements are at the pleasure of the supervisor of the individual dissertation.

— In most economically advanced countries, the doctoral training phase is not viewed as a movement from the "bachelor" to the "doctor", but rather from a master-level qualification towards a doctorate. Average "time to degree" in the USA is calculated as about eight years from the bachelor toward the doctoral degree, but for example as about five years on average in Germany from a master-level degree onwards. Various economically advanced countries do not make the American distinction between "undergraduate" education up to a bachelor and "graduate education" thereafter. Even though European countries move in the framework of the so-called Bologna Process towards the introduction of a bachelor-master system, this does not necessarily result into a move towards a similar conceptual divide between the character of bachelor programmes and that of master's programmes as is customary in North America.

— In the USA, a clear distinction is made between academic, "Ph.D.", and other professional doctoral awards, whereby the former are viewed as clearly preparatory for subsequent academic careers, while the latter are viewed as academically less demanding and as clearly leading to other highly qualified professions. In the UK, activities have increased recently to establish "professional" doctoral programmes.

Most low- and middle-income countries have relied, as far as doctoral training is concerned, on the provisions for doctoral training in economically advanced countries. For example, about 80 per cent of students from Arab States involved in graduate training in 2000 were actually enrolled in OECD Member Countries. Many young people went to economically advanced countries upon completion of secondary education, or after the award of a bachelor degree, in order to eventually be awarded a doctoral degree. Also, many universities in low- and middle-income countries send some of their academic staff to economically advanced countries for doctoral study. These activities have turned out to be successful in many cases, but high costs are incurred, the risks of failure are high, the work on the doctoral dissertation is not directly in interaction with other research and teaching activities at home, the work might follow other ra- tionales than those relevant to the home country, and those eventually awarded a doctoral degree might not return.

Over the years, however, a number of low- and middle-income countries began to set up their own graduate programmes and doctoral training. In most of these countries, the process of embarking into graduate education and notably doctoral training was cautious and initially on a small scale. The research base often was too small to embark into these training efforts. In many countries, even the percentage of professors with a doctoral degree has been small. Often, bachelor education was so much based on rote learning that a transition towards independent and creative learning on the graduate level turned out to be difficult.

Belal and Springuel, argue for example with respect to Egypt:

> "Gaps in education exist at all undergraduate and postgraduate levels for teaching how to perform research and to write up results. Students are not trained to do research, nor taught how to write scientific papers. This essential part of education is completely neglected in both undergraduate and even postgraduate studies. With very few exceptions, the research topics for post-graduate students are proposed by supervisors who have instructed the students and do not encourage the personal student's thinking. They use a student as the tool for doing the practical or field work but not for research. 'Egyptian university graduates are capable only of waiting for orders and executing them. No thinking, no arguing, no questioning; no objecting and not even dialoguing: a personality that does not (and cannot) create or think. This graduate is usually stuck with this type of passive personality for the rest of his or her life'."

One expert describes undergraduate education in India as follows:

> "In many campuses the teacher acts as information-delivering agent who tends to promote memorization rather than conceptual understanding. The authoritarian nature of teaching-learning practice existing in universities turns students as respectable receptors of a pre-constituted knowledge package. ... "The existing science courses must be improved by incorporating an active component of student engagement in the learning process ... Teachers should train students in the way to handle the information flood around them ... The assessing mode existing in the universities needs immediate attention. Properly tested and effective evaluation instruments must be used for assessment purposes".

Consequently some experts suggest enhancing research capacities in various developing countries, whereby research training is also viewed as one of many steps rather than as a key activity, as in a list of proposals put forward by Zakri:

— "... to create and strengthen centres of leadership and excellence, especially in least developed countries, by identifying leaders and research teams, providing them with autonomy, financial stability, modern equipment and access to IT and international peer groups;

— to support fellowships and training programmes that keep researchers up-to-date with the latest information and connected with other research and educational centres around the world;

— to promote cooperation in the South through South-South exchange fellowships for doctoral and postdoctoral researchers...;

— to create institutional networks to address common problems relating to the region ...;

— to publicise and share successful experiences...;

— to create and support merit-based academies in the South that will help promote and sustain scholarship, recognise and reward good work, interact with other academies and scholastic bodies, serve as role models for the young, and engage governments;

— to mobilize expatriates and institutions in the North enabling the 'brain drain' to be converted, in part, into a 'brain gain'...;

— to provide equitable access to knowledge...;

— to engage the private sector as agents for national development by supporting R&D through in-house research, training, recruitment and related modes of support; ‾ to persuade governments to commit to R&D by investing more…"

Often, masters and similar professional programmes were established first and doctoral programmes followed some years later. Many institutions and countries started involvement in doctoral training in cooperation with scholars and universities from economically advanced countries before taking over responsibilities themselves.

While a doctoral degree has become more or less an indispensable qualification for academic careers at universities with a teaching and research function in economically advanced countries, masters education in many other countries could lead to academic careers. Table 2 shows that about three quarters of doctoral graduates in Latin America subsequently work at higher education and research institutions, but also about half of the masters' graduate.

Table 2. Destiny of the Holders of Masters Ph.Ds in the 1990s (percentages)

Type of activities	*Masters*	*Doctors*
Business and public services	20.7	10.9
Public and private companies	21.1	5.9
Universities	34.5	68.8
Research Institutes	5.4	8.3
Offices/Consulting	12.5	4.5
Others	5.7	1.7

Some countries have succeeded over the years to build up an impressive scale and quality of doctoral training. The Republic of Korea and Mexico are often named as countries with a feeble system of graduate education three or four decades ago, but a highly successful one at this time. The consolidation of graduate studies took place in a period of economic growth, which eventually led to the membership of these two countries in the OECD.

Brazil is often named as a country pursuing a systematic strategy of enhancing research potentials, through sending large numbers of graduate students abroad as well as gradually expanding graduate education in the country. In the mean time, more than 10,000 doctoral degrees are awarded annually in Brazil.

China is among the countries in which, in recent years, strong efforts have been made to extend the training of young researchers. Since 1999, the number of graduate students increased annually by more than 20 per cent. In 2005, fifty-six graduate schools were established and 349 universities and research institutes were authorized to award doctoral degrees. The overall enrolment in doctoral education increased from less than 1,000 in the early 1980s to about 15,000 in 1990, to about 50,000 in 1998, and eventually to about 200,000 in 2004.

This expansion obviously has met a mixed response in China. Critiques are widespread, to the effect that access to doctoral education has become too easy and that a substantial proportion of doctoral students do not seem sufficiently prepared. Many candidates are awarded a doctoral degree, even if invited experts have voiced substantial criticisms of the assessment process. On the one hand, many experts and actors are concerned about the quality; they point out that many supervisors are not well-prepared, facilities are lacking, doctoral training takes place in large classrooms, and the number of doctoral candidates per supervisor is very high; moreover, they claim that high quality cannot be achieved in a large sector of part-time doctoral students. Other actors and experts argue, in contrast, that massification is bound to affect doctoral training as well, whereby high quality is likely to be preserved only in the leading universities and research institutes.

A report presented to the Forum shows that various measures are being taken to assure the quality of training. Among others, professors must be appointed to become "doctoral supervisors". In 2005, less than 60 per cent of full professors at thirty leading universities in China were entitled to supervise doctoral candidates, and this proportion was lower at other universities. In addition, many of the (roughly) two-third of persons awarded a doctor degree who are subsequently employed in higher education and research institutions must complete a "preparatory training programme" in order to become fully qualified for academic work.

Experts addressing general issues regarding training of doctoral candidates and other young researchers in the framework of the UNESCO Forum agreed in suggesting that low- and middle-income countries should embark onto those training activities even if perfect conditions cannot be assured, but they should develop strategies of mid-term quality improvement. They pointed out that conditions in the various countries are too divergent to suggest general strategies. Finally, some experts suggested that research and other advanced training in developing countries should differ from training abroad in ensuring, strategically, the relevance of that training for the development of the respective country and region.

The Changing Discourse on Quality

Efforts to formulate what constitutes excellent teaching and research have sounded similar over the last few decades and across the world. A representative of Stanford University stated in the framework of the UNESCO Forum for Higher Education, Research and Knowledge that research universities share the following "characteristics":

— High-quality faculty committed to research and teaching.

— High-quality graduate students, who want to learn to perform research or function with advanced expertise.

— An intellectual climate that encourages scholarship.

— Facilities in which teaching and research can be performed effectively.

— Funding for operations and instruction.

— Research funding.

— Research infrastructure.

— High-quality leadership.

Similarly, two Malaysian experts propose that

"... to attain research excellence, the university must have the following:

— Top-quality professors.

— Favourable working conditions (including job security and appropriate salaries and benefits).

— Academic freedom and intellectual excitement, including freedom to pursue knowledge and to publish freely.

— Conducive internal self-governance and an entrenched tradition which ensures that the academic community controls the central elements of academic life, such as student admission, degree criteria, and the selection of new academics.

— Adequate facilities; and

— Adequate funding for research".

Many characterizations of excellent universities and research institutes of these kinds are similar in:

— Defining excellence by "quality", i.e. by taking for granted that "quality" does not have to be defined but rather is based on common notions.

— Emphasizing quality without any explanation of whether "relevance" is implied in the criteria of quality or is distinct, and whether there are any conflicts for universities and research institutions as far as efforts to enhance quality and relevance are concerned.
— Assuming that a close link exists between excellent research and excellent teaching and learning.
— Pointing out a link between the quality of the environment, the competence of the persons involved, and achievement-oriented behaviour.

Across countries and over the last three or four decades, we note divergences as far as the management of universities is concerned. Of the characteristics quoted above, some put emphasis on university management while others call for strong academic self-governance.

Over the years, the discourse on the quality of teaching and learning in economically advanced countries, and to a large extent in low- and middle-income countries as well, was strongly shaped by the notion of "massification" of higher education. In the process, quality increasingly has been viewed as endangered:

— By the increasing proportion of students prepared for and motivated by quality education, against a declining willingness of governments to keep average expenditures per student on a high level.
— By increasing provision of private higher education, inclined in some cases to "sell" higher education on a low-quality level.

Private higher education often claims to offer study provisions closely linked to the needs of the employment system: concentration on fields in high demand, curricula geared to presumed job assignments, more teaching by practitioners, more practical experience during the course of study, more active help in the job search process etc. As above, various experts stated that often the study provisions at private institutions of higher education are very low in quality. In some cases, the quality might be so low that graduation from these institutions does not open up job opportunities in the areas targeted.

As regards "profit-seeking higher education institutions" in Brazil, Ribeiro argues that "... teachers are not properly qualified and lack job stability, and a great number of students come to higher education with an insufficient education and a desire for no more than a professional degree."

Moreover, "Most students who go to private, profit-seeking higher education institutions in order to get a degree in law or business (which in Brazil belong to the level of undergraduate studies) are unable to exercise their respective professions when they end their four to five year study … A very important reason for this failure is the bad quality of studies in Brazil, with the sole exception of those on the graduate level".

Discussions about ways of ensuring quality in higher education concentrated on two themes: (a) measures to enhance quality, and (b) diversification as a means to ensure high-quality education in some sectors of higher education, while accepting other standards and objectives in other sectors.

The discourse on the quality of research was somewhat different. Experts observed that there was a more or less steady growth of research expenditures over the years in economically advanced countries, and that there was a trend towards an increase of the quality of research as well. The expectation of relevance of research also grew along the way to what often is called the "Knowledge Society" or "Knowledge Economy", and the spread of neo-liberal ideas encouraged some actors to call for or actually implement a reduction of public research expenditure. According to Sörlin, the rise of neo-liberalism (which does not support state intervention in cases of marked failure), resulted in "... stagnation of research funding and the first serious dip in the rising curve of research spending that characterised OECD countries for four decades". It is interesting to note that the Lisbon Declaration (2000) of the heads of governments of the European Union calls for an increase in the proportion of the GNP spent on research; but it leaves open the extent to which this aim should be achieved through increased public research expenditures or through increased private investments in R&D.

Incentives, Competition, Evaluation

In the majority of economically advanced countries, teaching and research in higher education was shaped by a funding and supervisory system based widely on trust. Government played a role in general target-setting and bureaucratic supervision on the one hand, but on the other provided funds for education and research with a substantial degree of academic freedom, i.e. little restrictions as regards the substance of teaching and research; it trusted that the individual academics would do their best in striving for the quality of their work, and eventually produce relevant results. Over the recent two or three decades, this regime of trust was increasingly substituted by efforts to ensure the quality and relevance of teaching and learning as well as research. This was realized notably through:

— Increased incentive steering.
— Various means to increase competition.
— Establishment and extension of evaluation schemes.
— Strengthening managerial power within higher education and research institutions.
— Ensuring greater stakeholder influence.

Advocates of such a move, from an environment of trust towards a mix of operational steering instruments to increase effectiveness and efficiency, tend to claim that these mechanisms enhance the quality of higher education and research, while leaving open what the consequences might be for the relationship between quality and relevance.

Relationships between governments, university management and academics, as well as funding conditions, were much less based on trust in most low- and middle-income countries. This notwithstanding, the majority of these countries has taken reform steps in recent years similar to those of economically advanced countries. Many discourses as regards quality and relevance of education and research are similar in low- and middle-income countries to those in economically advanced countries.

Quality and Relevance under New Management

Strengthening incentive and competition mechanisms within higher education is often advocated as a guarantee of quality enhancement. "The current 'Zeitgeist' assumes that increasing competition as a rule leads to enhanced quality in higher education". However, experts note many instances where increased competition might actually lead to a quality decline: ¯ "... experts also point out counter-productive consequences of over-competition, such as increasing imitative behaviour among institutions and scholars ... [and] efforts to improve according to indicators rather than according to substance and increasing activities of deliberate disinformation".

— "Moreover, some higher education institutions, in order to increase their competitiveness within given financial frameworks, send home students abroad and admit larger numbers of foreign students which might require more administrative, consultative and academic support. This in return might imply greater risks of quality of learning and successful graduation".

— "Increasing competition between universities is generally expected to cause increasing vertical diversity of higher education institutions. The widespread advocacy of ranking and league tables ... leads to increasing quality awareness of consumers and more targeted choices and, in effect, steeper quality differences between higher education institutions." Analyses on ranking only underscore the quality of the leading institutions, but do not provide any evidence whatsoever regarding whether the quality of higher education increases with increased stratification".

— "Competition under a situation of inequality in information and distorted values has led to undesirable behaviours. For example, the quality of education has a tendency to be measured by students' satisfaction and employability. The quality of research is by publication in international journals and lately by the magnitude of citations. Research results which are not publishable, but are of great local benefit to the country or people, are not given credit".

— "Because of the perceived values in the market and imperfect information, some are seen to try to meet quantitative indicators while losing quality. For instance, teaching universities, with expertise in teaching as their competitive edge, are pursuing research for international publication rather than concentrating their efforts on teaching, or selecting research for the betterment of teaching. Local universities are seen to neglect relevant local problems and go for globally pub-lishable ones. Some try to create doctoral education with limitations and must settle for poor quality. Such unhealthy situations would not be sustainable, but much damage could have happened in the mean time".

— "One drawback of the competitive funding based on calls for proposals is that it focuses creative energy on winning the money rather than on spending it wisely, and tends to absorb the time of the most creative people on competition rather than on research".

In many low-income countries, the facilities or competences of the academic staff are considered so low that a stronger emphasis on incentives and competition is futile. Emphasis on incentives and competition takes for granted that underutilized facilities and competences are there, which could be driven to a higher level of utilization through stimuli.

Evaluation measures are a more direct way of observing the potential or real functioning than incentives or other competitive stimuli. But evaluation measures as such do not safeguard quality enhancement. Knight, for example, observes

> "... the growth in accreditation mills. These organizations are not recognized or legitimate bodies and they more or less 'sell' accreditation status without any independent assessment. They are similar to degree mills that sell certificates and degrees with little or no course work. Different education stakeholders, especially the students, employers and the public need to be aware of these accreditation (and degree) mills which are often no more than a web address and are therefore beyond the jurisdiction of national regulatory systems".

Research funding in higher education is one of the key areas in which a substantial move, from logic of "trust" to logic of incentive and competition, has taken place in many countries.

> "In principle two different principles have been used for funding of research and HE. Traditionally funding has been allocated as block grants based on some estimate of the needs of the institutions... This system has increasingly been replaced by some kind of performance-based, competitive funding, e.g. on incentives putting a premium on output and efficiency as measured in terms of e.g. number of graduates and time to exam, number of scientific publications, as well as the ability to acquire external research funds. The move towards incentive-based funding systems has not been a uniform movement. There are considerable differences across countries as to the portion of funds that are based on incentives, the criteria that are used and their overall system effects. One of the implications of the movement is the establishment of procedures and bureaucratic apparatuses aiming at measuring organizational performance, linked to allocation of funding, as an addition to the traditional evaluation of individual performance tightly linked to the allocation of status and prestige".

We can differentiate the following modes of research funding in higher education:

— Research funding through basic funding of the university without any differentials according to expected output. This holds true, for example, if basic funds are allocated according to number of students and academic staff, possibly only differentiated according to disciplines.

— Research funding through basic funding of the universities whereby the amount of funds provided is differentiated by output criteria, e.g. the number of graduates, research publications etc. Basic funding of research is not viewed as obsolete under conditions of primarily competitive funding of research projects; among others, universities need a certain degree of basic funding of major research areas in order to ensure a certain stability of staff and facilities, which is necessary to apply for competitive funds successfully.

— Incentive-based funding for universities as a whole; e.g. the allocation of resources to ten top German universities in the framework of the so-called "excellence initiative". Actually, incentive-based funding of institutions remained more controversial than the other research funding principle. As a consequence, the Japanese Government transformed its initial plan to support thirty top universities into a support programme for "Centres of Excellence", and the German Government agencies kept in their excellence initiative only one third of the initially envisaged funds for the support of 10 top universities, while two-thirds were transferred to inter-university research "clusters" and graduate schools.

— Allocation of public funds to individual research projects undertaken at institutions of higher education. In selected areas, governments prefer to allocate research funds to research units without any visible competitive selection procedure; this holds true if the expertise for a certain field of study is unique or is best served through long-term cooperation.

— Incentive-based funding for individual scholars or research teams by government agencies, publicly-funded research foundations or private research foundations; in those cases, funds are awarded upon application – mostly for individual research projects—or as prizes for prior achievements.

— Research funding by industry, whereby the criteria and modes of funding might vary substantially.

Certain modes of funding likely follow certain criteria and procedures, but each funding system determines its own criteria and procedures. A detailed look at both criteria and procedures helps to identify the relationships between quality and relevance. In many countries, the proportion of basic funds for research has declined over the years, while in most cases other public funds have increased; these changes were more salient than changes in the money provided from industry. But even in the early years of the twenty-first century, the proportion of basic grants varies substantially by country, namely between almost two-thirds in Germany and about one third in the USA.

Many documents suggest that this shift of research funding was undertaken primarily for the enhancement of research quality. Many experts, though, note a trend towards a growing weight of criteria of relevance over criteria of quality. For example, Sörlin argues that "… the present funding regime for research is the result of an evolution, spurred by massifi-cation and at the same time for differentiation. The background logic is only more apparent and manifest in policy documents, since research is more directly linked to innovation and economic competitiveness... The transformation to a globalizing knowledge-based economy, or at least the perception that this is what is going on at the moment, has been the predominant policy paradigm since the 1990s and explains the focus on innovation systems, the demand on universities for third mission-oriented activities, and the EU Lisbon process. In more general terms, it also explains the growth of research budgets in most nations and the strong tendency of governments to allocate research funds through mission-oriented agencies, with innovation goals, or to formulate the mission orientation of funds directly to the recipient institution".

In an increasing number of research activities, however, researchers are expected to ensure that both quality and relevance will play a major role in their activities. The British expert John Brennan argues that "Pressures for greater accountability and 'performativity' bring with them new types of requirements for relevance and in particular the need to find measures of it. This means that it has become more necessary to talk about relevance, to explicitly make the 'claim' for it and, to varying extents, to find evidence with which to provide justification for the claim. To be more concrete, if you want to obtain a research grant it is probably more important today than in previous periods to be able to make a serious claim for the potential societal relevance of the proposed research".

In many low- and middle-income countries, the establishment of a national research promotion system providing funds for individual research projects on the basis of reviewing and assessing research proposals is viewed as a breakthrough towards quality-driven research funding. The descriptions of these systems often point out more clearly the transparency and fairness of the research promotion system than the weight of quality and relevance criteria. For example, the following "principles of competitive funding" are named for the Indonesian research promotion system:

"1. Competition: the number of grants offered should be smaller than the number of competing units;
2. Specific purpose;
3. Autonomy and decentralization;
4. Consistency in carrying out policies;
5. Tiered competition: a reasonable chance to win. Because the level of variation in development of higher education institutions in Indonesia is quite high, institutions of comparable strength should be placed in one group or tier;
6. Objective selection process: transparency and accountability;
7. Evaluation and monitoring: the winners of the competition should be evaluated and monitored periodically;
8. Incentive and disincentive: an incentive by taking part in more prestigious granting schemes and placement in a higher tier. Punishment should be given if the project does not perform well"..

Quality and Relevance Rationales in Evaluation

Evaluation mechanisms include the following:

— The regular evaluation of research or teaching of a university department.

— The accreditation of study programmes or higher education institutions, and

— The audit of mechanisms established within institutions of higher education to monitor quality internally.

These differ from general incentive mechanisms, efforts to increase competition in various respects, and indicator-based funding by calling, in principle, for clearer assessment criteria. In principle, evaluation can expected to assess the "fitness for purpose" of a unit or programme, i.e. the extent to which the quality- and relevance-oriented goals which were set for the specific unit or programme are achieved. Assessment of quality, in this case, does not follow a general standard. Or evaluation can be expected to assess the "fitness of purpose", i.e. the quality or relevance according to general standards.

Quality and Relevance in Developing Countries

Various contributions in the Forum about expectations of research in low- and middle-income countries emphasize "quality" in teaching and research to the same extent as is customary in economically advanced countries. But this discourse is altogether different in two respects.

First, low- and middle-income countries cannot confine themselves to analyzing the extent to which research as well as teaching and learning in their country are successful according to the prevailing quality standards of the North. Certainly, there is a multitude of publications showing how many (or better: how few) articles deriving from low-income countries are published in international, highly selective academic journals. But many low- and middle-income countries only succeed in encouraging and rewarding research quality according to standards adapted to their current potential.

Also, low- and middle-income countries have had to set their own standards for quality in the evaluation of teaching and learning and in the accreditation of study programmes. For example, Jordanian experts presented the following view in the Forum:

> "In third-world and developing countries, you rarely find academic entities who can readily meet any international accreditation standard for inherent limitations of their own. For these reasons, amongst others, a number of developing countries, in their efforts to attain some minimum standards with their academic systems and preserve their integrity, have developed accreditation bodies of their own, and/or have instituted some assessment and review processes to measure the educational outcomes of their own academic institutions. Jordan, being a developing country with limited financial resources, has instituted an accreditation body of its own, and refers to it as the 'University Accreditation Council'. This local accreditation body operates in pretty much similar ways to their peer organizations around the world by conducting periodic reviews of curricula in the various academic disciplines, assessing the faculty-to-student ratios, reviewing allowable institutional capacity in terms of number of students and equipment that they must avail for student use, etc. Furthermore, Jordan has also required that university graduates, including, those of engineering and IT colleges, sit for what is referred to as the 'University Achievement Exam'. This exam is administered by the Educational Testing Services. These two assessment processes are now helping Jordan to properly review the educational outcomes of its academic institutions, and steer the academic models of the

diversity of academic institutions to meet a bare minimum of global academic standards".

Second, many experts active in the framework of the UNESCO Forum on Higher Education, Research and Knowledge pointed out that research in low- and middle-income countries is driven, and must be more strongly driven, by imperatives of relevance. This does not mean that debates about desirable and acceptable criteria of relevance are less heated and less controversial in low- and middle-income countries. On the contrary, the dominant rhetoric about "quality" of research is less suitable in displacing discourses of relevance. And researchers from developing countries often note that they are expected, by research epistemologically driven by the North, to integrate prevailing themes and paradigms in order to become part of the world-wide accepted community of research "quality".

As already pointed out, there are similar debates in low- and middle-income countries as in economically advanced countries regarding whether research should be more or less independent from the expectations of industry. On the other hand, some "mainstreams" of acceptance of relevant research have emerged in low- and middle-income countries. For example, many experts call for stronger relevance of research to the Millennium Development Goals (MDGs) advocated by the United Nations.

What the tensions between research quality and relevance mean for the developing world was summarized in some sectors of the report *Universities as Centres of Research and Knowledge Creation: An Endangered Species?* produced by the UNESCO Forum:

> "*Rethinking the criteria for research quality*: There has been substantial criticism at the Colloquium of the notion that there can be a one-dimensional set of criteria for assessing the quality of research regardless of where, by whom, and on what subject it was performed. Instead, there appears to be a need dealing with the assessment of research quality in much more differentiated ways, taking into account the research setting, the kinds of research questions asked, the methodological orientation, and the utilization of research findings. This is not to argue for rank relativism in assessing research, but recognizes that research quality is not entirely independent of its relevance and utility".
>
> "*Different Functions and Criteria of Research*: While all societies have a need for knowledge, there are differences in the function that university research can serve. Universities such as Stanford that are much more generously endowed and equipped may be able to serve a broader range of

functions in a global context, even beyond the needs of their particular environment and society; universities like the University of Ghana need to concentrate first and foremost on the present and future knowledge needs of their own communities. This difference in function is to be kept in mind as one looks at global developments in higher education and research, and at league tables and similar rankings. Relevance and utility of research have to be seen and judged with these distinctions in mind, and are not amenable to one-dimensional rankings".

"Rankings, Globalization, and Relevance: The fascination of all universities with league tables and rankings is as understandable as it is problematic. Clearly, the international political economy of higher education is such that certain universities are, by virtue of their location, much more likely to show up on these tables than others. A very important question against this background is thus why such rankings should matter, and whether they are valid instruments for assisting universities in the assessment of their own utility. How can universities, in other words, reconcile the often conflicting mandates of international competitiveness and of meeting its obligations to the knowledge needs of the local community? In case of irreconcilable conflict, which should take precedence: looking to international competitiveness or meeting local knowledge needs? This question is important not only for universities, but also for those agencies that fund university research; it is important that they, as well, recognize this conflict and the need for universities to balance these conflicting expectations. Faced with this dilemma, it is worth considering much more seriously whether there should not and could not be alternative kinds of ranking that take more explicitly into account the degree to which universities and their research programmes serve the knowledge needs of their local communities and societies, without necessarily compromising the standards of what is internationally considered good research".

"Criteria for 'good" research: There is an urgent need for a critical discourse on what we mean by "good" research. The fact that there is no single yardstick for assessing the quality of research across all disciplines, regions, and cultures does not make the question of research quality irrelevant; indeed, it makes it all the more important to place the question of appropriate criteria for assessing the quality of research on the agenda wherever research is being conducted. There certainly are elements that all serious research activities have in common; it is hard to conceive of good research, for example, without decent evidence and without an explicit, transparent set of methodological ground rules. Beyond that, however, different purposes, different kinds, different traditions of research do need to examine critically their own criteria. The process of communicating about these reflections on criteria across the international world of research should be one of the most exciting chapters of future research cooperation".

Questioning Western Cultural Dominance

In search of quality enhancement and modernization of higher education and research, low- and middle-income countries often unconsciously absorb, or consciously follow, presumed success stories from economically advanced countries. This is viewed by many actors and experts as appropriate and desirable given universalistic elements of knowledge, increasing global intercon-nectedness of knowledge, economy and society, and internationally convincing role models for establishing and maintaining efficient and effective organization of higher education and research. Various experts involved in the UNESCO Forum saw a danger in higher education and research in developing countries being too strongly determined by the higher education and research culture of economically advanced countries. In some cases, they noted carry-over of the colonial past, others signs of neo-colonialism, attempts to equal the North with modernization, and other direct current influences from the North. Some quotations might illustrate these concerns:

— "The university is based on foreign models – the areas of study, the departments and faculties, laboratories, diplomas, pedagogy and courses are all usually the same as in the ex-colonial power. The scientific culture of research staff often revolves around references and problems that are foreign to home-country realities. The de-contextualization of knowledge is not a problem *per se*, but it becomes one when the search for conceptual and methodological equivalency is not undertaken".

— "Most developing countries, having inherited the colonisers' education systems, are still facing the challenge of shaping their higher education system to national needs ... i.e. South Pacific islands, like most developing countries, share the experience of European colonialism and its concomitant educational values and practices, including its languages, that has resulted in the evolution of education systems largely Eurocentric in outlook ... Colonialism is argued to have undermined ways of knowing and doing and the next stage of decolonization should be de-hegemonization. This can be done ... 'by finding research and epistemic frameworks that are indigenous', 'by asserting the validity of local ways of knowing' and 'being in resistance to the intensifying hegemony of mainstream epistemology from metropolitan powers' ... Western-based education systems ...

> contribute to the de-legitimization of traditional, indigenous knowledge and a legitimization of the knowledge that enables people to enter the industrial economy".

The Association of African Universities (AAU) argues with reference to Madagascar: "In the public imagination, the education that was brought by European colonialism is a means of freeing oneself from living conditions that are seen as onerous. Education is a passport to the future and you need a reliable passport that has passed the test. It is often forgotten that the elite education of the colonial times cannot be the mass education required by the current objectives of universal education". Moreover, the AAU notes a lack of much-needed research for alternative education. "Problems inherent in the higher education sector are such that in Madagascar, and possibly in French-speaking Africa, there are few structured subjects and teams in the field of alternative education. One possible reason is that university research is relatively dependent on French universities that do not always include it in their disciplines. Moreover, it does not appear as such in the thematic fields of the *Agence Universitaire de la Francophonie* (University Agency of the French-speaking world). Consequently, some academics working in this field do so in non-university settings, but even then they appear to remain lecturers and researchers and their status as 'university staff' follows them everywhere".

Most experts involved in the Forum note an inability or unwillingness to address local issues, the main problem caused by over-reliance on the epistemic and organizational models of the North:

> "For those working in development, whether they seek modernity or greater respect for local people, 'primitive' has been replaced by 'traditional' or, more recently, indigenous and local, and 'civilized' by 'modern'. 'Locals' are problematized, portrayed as deficient in various ways and this deficiency is referred to when legitimizing the intervention of 'expatriates'. This has an impact on local academics which are seen lacking skills and 'it is very difficult to shake off the idea that we know more than them and accept that we might even learn from them'. Some methodologies regard the values, beliefs and practices of communities as 'barriers' to research or as exotic customs with which researchers need to familiarise themselves in order to carry out their research. This attitude is passed on to locals who believe that culture is a barrier to development. ... There is a need to build on local knowledge and encourage young researchers to provide their insights on the role of research in their countries development and to seek local alternatives to studying their cultures and societies".

Some experts point out the diversity of cultures that has emerged in low- and middle-income countries. They vary in the influence of the indigenous past and the impact of the North:

> "Interpreting the academic profession through the lens of culture ... At the risk of oversimplification, would like to outline three models or paradigms of the academic profession in India. The first model emanates from the Hindu tradition. The presence of the preceptor or Guru was essential not only for the transmission of religious tradition but also for the acquisition of knowledge. Therefore, the Guru protected the interests of the disciple who became his family member and respected him as a father ... The second paradigm, introduced in the middle of the nineteenth century when the British established universities... focuses on developments in higher education after independence, i.e. from the 1950s to 1991. After independence, higher education was seen as the engine of industrial and technological growth and also as an agent of modernization and democratization. Merit and objectivity became the criterion for admission of students and recruitment of teachers ... The third phase begins post-1991 when the economy was liberalized. The academic profession is under great stress to perform according to corporate norms, and there is hardly any space for research. Accountability is centre stage in the private for-profit institutions, at the cost of academic freedom and autonomy. Student evaluation of faculty has been introduced in the private sector ... The role and functions of the Guru have influenced the construction of the role of the modern professor. In the process the professionalization of the academic, the dimensions of merit, objectivity, rationality and neutrality along with quality are transformed in the name of tradition. Therefore, it is difficult to talk of the modern academic without reference to the cultural tradition".

Grappling with the past does not only imply responses to colonial and neo-colonial influences of the North or indigenous cultural tradition. The move from an apartheid society towards a new democratic society in South Africa, or the transition from Soviet-style planned systems in Central and Eastern Europe as well as in Central Asian countries, turned out to be difficult. For some period a vacuum was felt between the abolishment of the old regulatory system and the emergence of a new system. This was not only true of new modes or governance, organization and funding, but an absence of "new values and ethical norms" was also felt for some time.

Resistance to Beneficial Modernization

Various experts point out that the argument of neglect of indigenous cultural traditions and local needs is also used to resist desirable modernisation. To quote a few examples:

"Academic freedom and autonomy are misused by a majority of the faculty who do not produce good research or good publications. In addition, merit and objectivity become victims in the recruitment and promotion process. Most professors have also not been motivated to publish because recruitment and selection were not entirely based on merit. Again, if they publish it is not in peer-reviewed national and international journals. Or they will publish in local journals, magazines and newspapers. Some departments start their own journals for in-house publications. In most state universities what counts is quantity, not quality. Most of them do not participate in national and international conferences … There has also been a lack of accountability due to the way the student-teacher relationship has evolved. For instance, there has hardly been any evaluation of professors by students because it fitted in very well with the thinking that the Guru cannot be appraised by the disciple … There has also been no peer evaluation of faculty performance because of the hierarchical nature of Indian society".

"Further, the traditional value in the modernization paradigm is that a scholar and professor is known for his/her scholarship, dedication and reputation and should not have to sell or market his/her knowledge and expertise. In this day and age, when the ability to negotiate for salary and to procure funds for research is an important criterion for recruitment and promotion there are scholars, especially of the older generation, who adhere to the traditional thinking, that is, they do not publicize their work or negotiate for better terms and are reluctant to make themselves visible for consultancy, etc. Those who do not, even if talented, are being left out of the race because the current situation demands repackaging one's expertise and qualifications in the market".

"When nations cannot deploy effectively national institutions' (such as universities) knowledge, incentives and policies, they lack the ability to generate a functioning national system of innovation. Under this context it is often the case that the role of a key component of NSI such as universities that produce the research and knowledge system in a country can be devalued. The key to reverse this negative trend is thus to integrate universities as the premier institutions of knowledge-making and production as a core part of a functioning system of innovation. In many African countries the absence of the analytical framework for building functioning national systems of innovation is at the core of the crises of the universities that is still going on right now. The problem is not simply lack of funding; it is much deeper than that. It lies in the failure to conceptualize the central role of knowledge production and diffusion and utilization for bringing about the structural transformation of economies, societies and polities in poorer and developing economies of Africa, Latin America and Asia … There is a need conceptually to re-centre universities for the making of the national systems of innovation; and conversely to make innovation systems that deploy universities as the key institution for knowledge production".

Various experts active in the Forum discussed obstacles against an inclusion of the perspectives of local needs and indigenous cultures. They often point to a lack of understanding, respect and recognition of "... the value of local knowledge systems" on the one hand. On the other hand, there seems to be a "... lack of confidence of local researchers in conducting research ... and feelings of inferiority related to the perceived superiority of Western knowledge". Other experts name further reasons: "Research results which are not publish-able, but are of great local benefit to the country or people are not given credit. Contracted research from industries and business comes with strings attached. Globally common values and commercial benefits are overshadowing local heritage and public contribution. Some universities are sand dominated. They become subordinated and lose their values and local relevance. Market forces are affecting their basic values. Professionalism is eroded".

Search for New Strategies

Efforts to foster a new research culture in low- and middle-income countries face many challenges. For example, concerning efforts by international organisations to strengthen the local relevance of research in developing countries,

> "Paradoxically, when the most diverse international organisations, from the World Bank to the World Council for Science (ICSU) pose the need that research activity in developing countries attend in a more relevant way to the realities and challenges of their societies, the state of affairs for science in those countries ends up in many cases acting as a significant obstacle precisely to the contribution to sustainable social and environmental development and to the transfer and adaptation of technology in contexts of real application. It is undeniable that the challenges for defeating the problems of underdevelopment are huge, but the single-minded solution adopted by the science institutions in the bulk of countries seems to be neither the most efficacious nor the most efficient".

Some experts argue that as scholars in low- and middle-income countries increasingly become aware of the limited scopes taken over from the North, they move towards a paradigm shift:

> "Along with the ever-increasing dissemination of western education and knowledge through globalization and the internationalization of higher education, there is also an increasing awareness that the western education system and ways of conducting research have their limitations. New

> approaches need to be devised or explored within local contexts. There seems to be a paradigm shift towards integration of local knowledge into education systems albeit slow that calls for a need to adapt research priorities and practices to better reflect local points of view. There are mainly two issues in this problematic situation … the issue of finding appropriate research methods for non-western societies which poses the obvious question of whether different epistemologies require different research approaches … also the issue of finding appropriate research methods for developing countries".

Some authors point out that academics and politicians in low- and middle-income countries have developed views and attitudes which counteract the emergence of a reasonable balance between focus on basic research and the pursuit of knowledge for its own sake on the one hand, and relevance of research on the other:

> "The research undertaken in many developing countries depends on the interest of academics who are generally trained in developed countries and carry the interest back with them. In many countries, imbalance in the areas or problems for research becomes evident … Concentration of research is in some areas, with neglect in other needed fields. Basic research resulting from academics' interest with no immediate use is deemed as waste. Research is thus seen as a luxury with no utility and not relevant to the country's needs. In turn, decision-makers do not depend on evidence from research. Some even want research findings to support their decisions which are already made. At the same time, the public does not know enough to question. Fragmentation also prevails and the research results from small, disconnected projects are not usable. The limited resources are therefore wasted".

Some authors suggest that developing countries have to find their own way in developing research strategies serving their needs:

> "Problems facing developing countries in many regions require reorientation of the way one looks at research relevancy and utility. For instance, there is no satisfactory progress concerning research on ways to overcome problems regarding communication and information distribution over vast areas in the developing world. It is a fact that many recurring natural disasters such as flood, draught, plague and deteriorating farm productivity can improve with proper research … Research capacities to cope with such situations may be in the form of regional or global networks, but the ability to meet the need in the most peripheral areas must be an important criteria. Developing countries can no longer wait for the mercy of the devel-oped world to solve their problems through research. They must develop their own capacity for this purpose".

Other authors suggest that for research planning,"... the starting points for the development of a locality or a region are the economic, institutional, organizational cultures and human resources, which constitute the potential for development ... This local ability to respond to and take care of its own development and mobilize the economic potential is an attribute of the endogenous development action approach".

The Commission on Health Research, in its call for Essential National Health Research, argued among others that:

> "Development efforts and solving local problems through local means must be holistically considered. Technological knowledge alone is not sufficient. Understanding the people and the environment, especially their peculiarities, strengths and weaknesses, is essential. The identification and prioritization of problems in a locality requires adequate understanding of the relevant factors in that specific locality. This can come from essential research. Situation-specific knowledge and site-specific data are also crucial. One of the great mistakes in the past was the adoption of ways to solve local problems by solutions imported from elsewhere. Local peculiarity must be taken into account. For example, soil and water management is important for introducing new crops. Social and cultural beliefs, as well as genetic and environmental conditions, are important for sustainable success and compliance with new health measures. Effectiveness, cost-benefit, safety, feasibility and acceptability must be determined along with how to adapt to local economic, socio-cultural and political conditions".

The same Commission also argues:

> "Public policies ... must take into account not only scientific evidence but also socioeconomic and cultural evidence of local conditions. The answers developed elsewhere may be even harmful if they are applied uncritically in developing countries. Policy and system research are essential for national research and so must be conducted both professionally and holistically. The situation-specific and time-specific information is amalgamated with theoretical or generic knowledge to come up with alternatives or choices, as well as with the information necessary for sound decision-making".

Various experts came to the conclusion that the search for solutions to combine cutting-edge research approaches with awareness and inclusion of local knowledge paradigms in developing countries could be strengthened. Particularly if more "research on research" was undertaken and if its findings were well disseminated, and if the results of this research eventually played an important role in shaping the research activities in a broad range of areas relevant for development. Therefore, the following recommendation was formulated in the Forum:

> "We have very little secure and valid knowledge about the conditions under which research is conducted, the factors that make for good or for bad research, the ways incentives or disincentives work in research, etc. One of the urgent needs for the future ... is, therefore, a more systematic programme of rigorous research on research".

References

Arimoto, A. (2008). "The Competitive Research Environment in the Japanese Context". In: Sala-zar-Clemeña, R. M. and Meek, L. V. (eds.), *Competition, Collaboration and Change in the Academic Profession: Shaping Higher Education's Contribution to Knowledge and Research*. Quezon City: Libro Amigo Publishers, pp. 46-60.

Bleiklie, I. and Kogan, M. (2007). "Organisation and Governance of Universities". *Higher Education Policy* (20) 4, pp. 477-493.

Kelo, M., Teichler, U. and Waechter, B. (eds.) (2006). *EURODATA – Student Mobility in European Higher Education*. Bonn: Lemmens.

Rivža, B. and Teichler, U. (2007). "The Changing Role of Student Mobility". *Higher Education Policy* (20) 4, 457-476.

Teichler, U. (2004). "The Changing Debate on Internationalisation of Higher Education". *Higher Education* (48), 5-26.

UNESCO. (2006. *Global Education Digest 2006: Comparing Education Statistics across the World*. Montreal: UNESCO Institute for Statistics.

Zakri, A. H. (2008). "Research Universities in the 21st Century: Global Challenges and Local Implications". In: Teichler, U. and Vessuri, H. (eds.), *Universities as Centres of Research and Knowledge Creation: An Endangered Species?* Rotterdam: Sense Publishers, pp. 41-46.

8

ICTs and Educational Innovations

Information and communications technology or information and communication technology (ICT), is often used as an extended synonym for information technology (IT), but is a more specific term that stresses the role of unified communications and the integration of telecommunications (telephone lines and wireless signals), computers as well as necessary enterprise software, middleware, storage, and audio-visual systems, which enable users to access, store, transmit, and manipulate information.

The phrase ICT had been used by academic researchers since the 1980s, but it became popular after it was used in a report to the UK government by Dennis Stevenson in 1997 and in the revised National Curriculum for England, Wales and Northern Ireland in 2000.

The term ICT is now also used to refer to the convergence of audio-visual and telephone networks with computer networks through a single cabling or link system. There are large economic incentives (huge cost savings due to elimination of the telephone network) to merge the audio-visual, building management and telephone network with the computer network system using a single unified system of cabling, signal distribution and management.

Nowadays the role of ICT, especially internet in the education sector plays an important role, especially in the process of empowering the technology into the educational activities. Education sector can be the most effective sector to anticipate and eliminate the negative impact of ICT.

Technology (internet) in another side can be the most effective way to increase the student's knowledge.

Being aware of the significant role of ICT (internet) in our life, especially in the educational activities, education authorities should be wise enough in implementing the strategies to empower ICT in supporting the teaching and learning process in the classroom. ICT is not just the bloom of the educational activities, but also it will be the secondary option to improve the effective and meaningful educational process.

There are some unavoidable facts in the modern education; First, the ICT has been developing very rapidly nowadays. Therefore, in order to balance it, the whole educational system should be reformed and ICT should be integrated into educational activities.

Second, the influence of ICT, especially internet (open source tool) cannot be ignored in our student's lives. So, the learning activities should be reoriented and reformulated, from the manual source centered to the open source ones. In this case the widely use of internet access has been an unavoidable policy that should be anticipated by schools authorities.

Third, the presence of multimedia games and online games by internet has been another serious problem that should be wisely handled by the educational institutions. The students cannot be exterminated from this case. They can have and do with it wherever and whenever they want. Schools, as a matter of fact, do not have enough power and time to prevent or stop it after school times. Meanwhile, most parents do not have enough times to accompany and control their children. So, the students have large opportunities to do with multimedia games or online games or browsing the negative and porn sites. Having been addicted, the students will have too little time to study, and even do not want to attend classes.

In such situation, education institutions play an important role to eradicate these problems. One of which is by facilitating the students to do edutainment or educational games. Schools can let their students be familiar with educational games adjusted by their teachers. Besides, they can also support and facilitate their students to have their own blogs in the internet. A lot of WebBlog providers are free to the users, such as WordPress. In their blogs, the students can create and write something, like an article, poem, news, short stories, features, or they can also express their opinion by an online forum provided in the internet. They are able to share experiences throughout their blogs to others from all over the world.

Fourth, the implementation of ICT in education has not been a priority trend of educational reform and the state paid little attention to it. Therefore, there should be an active participation, initiative and good will of the schools and the government institutions to enhance ICT implementation at school.

Fifth, the teachers should be the main motivator and initiator of the ICT implementation at schools. The teachers should be aware of the social change in their teaching activities. They should be the agent of change from the classical method into the modern one. They must also be the part of the global change in learning and teaching modification.

The main aim of ICT in education means implementing of ICT equipment and tools in teaching and learning process as a media and methodology. The purpose of ICT in education is generally to familiarise students with the use and workings of computers, and related social and ethical issues.ICT has also enabled learning through multiple intelligence as ICT has introduced learning through simulation games; this enables active learning through all senses.

During the past 20 years, the use of ICT has fundamentally changed the working of education. In the current environment-conscious world, the importance of education and acceptability of ICT as a social necessity has been increasing. Social acceptability of information and communication tools is necessary to improve the mobility in the society and increase the pitch for equity and social justice. Education as a qualitative development is not confined within the classroom structure. The modern tools of ICT such as eLearning and online practice of learning and getting information are much sought after by the students as well as by the institutions.

The governments are spending a lot of money on ICT. In India, the National Mission on Education is emphasising on the role of ICT in increasing the enrolment ratio in higher education. School education in India has a problem of high dropout rate and we need to work on how to decrease this rate. Similarly, in the field of higher education, we need to increase the number of students. Therefore, if we make our learning more engaging with the use of ICT, it can completely change how our education system works. Also, we should examine the challenges of cost-factor and availability of trained teachers in the process of dissemination of education with the help of ICT.

India is developing as a knowledge economy and it cannot function without the support of ICT. The gap between demand and supply of higher education has necessitated the governments and institutions to formulate the policies for the better use of ICT. And, in order to bridge the gap, it is necessary to evolve the cooperation between the public and private sectors.

The education ICT policy should identify specific ways in which the application of ICT will enhance the educational capacity and the capability of higher education institutions. According to a recent study, innovations such as using Twitter to send messages are really helpful in disseminating education. In a similar fashion, the use of YouTube in sharing video information will go a long way in disseminating education. During the last decade, higher education has gained importance in India's changing policy landscape as the government realises that India's strength lies in education.

Digital Technology in Education

The power of information technology is greatly enhanced by communication technology. This means that connectivity (through wireless, cell phone technology or over cables) is the crucial feature that allows access to the Internet and the World Wide Web. These common platforms have stimulated an explosion of social software and cloud services that have made the Internet a highly interactive medium and created new dynamics in computer use. As computing power and communications have improved, mobile devices play an increasingly important role, notably in the developing world.

Computing power continues to increase in speed while costs are being driven down, thus allowing computer users to run more complex programs and graphic-rich applications. These improvements, coupled with the expansion of broadband Internet connections, are providing for richer entertainment and learning environments, including virtual worlds and an increasing use of Internet telephony and video conferencing. Connectivity that only a few years ago regularly used dial-up connections over hard-wired telephone lines has been rapidly moving over to coaxial cable connections in industrialised countries and to 3G connections via cellular networks in both industrialised and developing countries.

The One-Laptop-Per-Child project, originated by the Massachusetts Institute of Technology with the aim of creating a $100 laptop, stimulated an entirely new market segment that computer manufacturers had not seemed to anticipate. Before this stimulus they preferred to keep the price constant and add more power. Now we see that millions of users are willing to give up processing speed and graphics capacity in the interests of enjoying the benefits of a low-cost, lightweight machine. While these machines gained an initial market share using specialised Linux (open source) installations, they started to "fly off the shelves" once new models were sold with the Windows XP operating system preinstalled.

The constant expansion of the availability of computers and access to the Internet has been driving the availability of cloud computing. Cloud computing, or the provision of services online to computer users, includes services such as folders for data and a host of programs that exist on the Internet that can used by users from any internetconnected computer.

Until recently those wanting to harness ICTs for development have focused on getting personal computers into the hands of learners around the world. However, the cellular phone networks report that nearly half the world's population now either owns a cell phone or has access to one. A growing number of HEIs are experimenting with how to capitalise on this technology, especially in developing countries (e.g. University of Pretoria). Meanwhile, students are using mobile technology liberally for personal purposes (often during lectures!), while their instructors have little idea of how the technology could be applied to improve teaching and learning.

Today's students (digital natives) have a different way of approaching and using technologies like cell phones and computers that their teachers (digital immigrants) still need to come to terms with. Educators need to gain an understanding of the virtual worlds that their learners move in so that they can better understand how to interact with them in ways that make sense to digital natives.

Cloud services have only just started to become truly useful and show potential for freeing users from having to own their own computer. With cloud computing, users are able to save a document on a computer in a computer lab, edit it from their Internet-enabled cell phone, format it on their home computer and publish it to the Internet for public viewing or sharing with their class.

Hand held devices have advanced the potential for making computing truly portable by inventing improved touch-sensitive screens that help to predict what the user is typing on the small screens, communicate wirelessly with the Internet, transmit data wirelessly to printers and other people devices. Synchronising via the cloud and directly with other devices and computers now makes these devices effectively a form of "connective tissue" between computers where they are available.

Often called social networking, this technology has allowed people to meet, interact and share ideas and interests with one another. These applications have become popular and have already found their way into informal learning settings. Now there is considerable interest in the use of social networking in formal education, especially in open and distance learning.

A study on the effective use of social software in further and higher education in the UK to support student learning and engagement has shown that there is growing interest in social dimensions of learning. This has led institutions to adopt virtual learning environments (VLEs), which incorporate collaboration and communication tools such as wikis, blogs, forums and chat. More recently, publicly available web-based social networking tools such as Facebook, GoogleDocs, Delicious, and Flickr have also been adopted in teaching and learning. During its development since 2004 The Virtual University for the Small States of the Commonwealth has been developing course materials using a combination of faceto-face and cloud computing approaches. This allows these small states to engage with each other despite the vast distances between them.

There has been intense competition in some HEIs between Free Open Source Software (FOSS) and proprietary software. Strong interest groups on each side present this as an all-or-nothing choice, but the sensible approach is to use what is appropriate when it is appropriate.

Free software is not free to run (free is used as in 'free speech' rather than 'free beer') and proprietary software may be suitable, but too expensive to buy. A total cost of ownership calculation, including the cost of servers, programming and IT support staff time, needs done when comparing the suitability of software. The ability to integrate data usage between multiple computer programmes without having to re-write the programming is important. Sometimes, proprietary packages that have integration in their design might be most appropriate. The stability of having a programme that works reliably may be paramount while the ability to have programmers rewrite the core program code might be most appropriate in other situations.

ICTs in Research

Applications of ICTs are particularly powerful and uncontroversial in higher education's research function. Four areas are particularly important.

First, the steady increases in bandwidth and computing power available have made it possible to conduct complex calculations on large data sets.

Second, communication links make it possible for research teams to be spread across the world instead of concentrated in a single institution.

Third, the combination of communications and digital libraries is equalising access to academic resources, greatly enriching research possibilities for smaller institutions and those outside the big cities.

Fourth, taking full advantage of these trends to create new dynamics in research requires national policies for ICTs in higher education and the establishment of joint information systems linking all higher education institutions.

For these applications high bandwidth is the key priority since it allows computing power to be aggregated by linking equipment together.

Promoting Better Quality Research

The application of ICTs in academic research has grown steadily in the past 10 to 15 years in both developing and developed countries, although there are wide variations in usage both within and between countries and regions. These variations reflect the vision and commitment of the leadership of HEIs to deploying ICTs in research; the funds and people available to sustain investments in ICT infrastructure and support systems; and the existence of helpful national and institutional ICT policies.

Data Processing

The most straightforward use of ICTs in research is in data processing. The unprecedented growth in bandwidth and computing power provide opportunities for analyzing/processing huge amounts of data and performing complex computations on them in a manner that is extremely fast, accurate and reliable. Computer data processing not only frees researchers from the cumbersome task of manually analyzing data but more importantly facilitates quick and accurate analysis of huge amounts of data from national samples or even multi-national samples covering tens of thousands of respondents.

Analysis and projections of climate change using vast amounts of weather data that would have been impossible even five years ago are now performed routinely. Data from the monitoring of the learning achievement of school children undertaken periodically by Ministries of Education of many countries, some of which have sample sizes in hundreds of thousands, can be processed quickly and accurately only through the use of powerful computers. It would be unthinkable to process data from such huge samples manually without sacrificing accuracy and speed! It is also computing power that permits the speedy and accurate processing of population data generated from periodic national censuses in nearly all parts of the world.

Searching Text

Another important dimension of ICTs in research is the use of online full text databases and online research libraries/virtual libraries which are the direct outcome of the growth in telecommunications networks and technology. These databases and libraries provide researchers with online access to the contents of hundreds of thousands of books from major publishing houses, research reports, and peer- reviewed articles in electric journals. Examples include: the Questia Online library which provides access 24/7 to "the world's largest online collection of books and journals in the humanities and Social Sciences"; EBSCO Publishing's EBSCOhost Online Research databases; and the Online Books Page hosted by the University of Pennsylvania libraries which provides free online access to books and includes an index of thousands of online books and links to directories and archives of online texts.

Use of these online databases and libraries by academic staff has grown rapidly in the higher education systems of many countries. With support from UNESCO, the Hewlett Foundation and other development partners some countries have established their own national virtual libraries. Examples include the National Virtual library of Nigeria which was established by the National Universities Commission to promote access to the most recent publications in nearly all the disciplines offered by Nigerian universities. Apart from making the most current publications available to researchers, they also provide opportunities for the dissemination of research, particularly through on-line electronic journals.

Linking Researchers Globally

ICTs are also being used to transform research from something done by individuals or teams in particular HEIs to an activity involving the instantaneous sharing and the collaborative generation of new knowledge by networks of researchers located around the world. This is facilitated by speedy telecommunications and the emergence of social networking sites, wikis, communication tools and folksonomies (the practice and method of collaboratively creating and managing tags to annotate and categorize content. that catalyze online collaboration and sharing among users).

The major impediments to the effective use of online databases and online research libraries/virtual libraries include: the high cost of bandwidth, particularly in Africa; lack of well conceived national and institutional ICT policies, the high cost of hardware and software and the absence of sustaining services and systems.

Importance of National and Institutional Policy

The examples we have discussed show that use of ICTs for research and teaching by the faculty of HEIs is increasing rapidly. However, ICT infrastructure requires major financial investment, which is best done on the basis of well conceived national and institutional policies. National ICT policies should articulate a vision and a strategic framework for harnessing the potential of ICTs to address a country's development challenges. For the education sector it should provide a sense of focus and direction and spell out clearly how improving the ICT capacity of the education sector can help to address issues of access, equity and quality at all levels. Such a national policy should provide a framework that can be a basis for developing ICT policies by HEIs. An institutional and or sector wide higher education ICT policy that seeks to promote the effective use of ICT in research should *inter alia*:

— Identify the specific ways in which the application of ICTs will significantly enhance the research capabilities of higher education institutions and the sector as a whole;

— Enhance bandwidth/connectivity through the acquisition of suitable hardware, software, and the establishment of LANs, WANs, and Virtual Private Networks for effective coordination and efficient utilization of resources.

— Promote collaboration among higher education institutions in all ICT-related activities. Collaborative strategies such as SURF in the Netherlands and JISC in the UK which are organizations for promoting partnership for ICT and network services in higher education are examples of this. A similar strategy, on a relatively small scale but with potential for further growth, is the Research and Education Network of Uganda, (the consortium of Makerere, Kyambogo and Mukono universities). Such consortia (especially those that cover many institutions), will facilitate the achievement of economies of scale (through large volume procurements) and help reduce the costs of bandwidth which is very high in developing countries, particularly Africa. The ICT policies must also have very clear strategies for sustaining services and systems.

— Build the capacity of faculty and other relevant personnel on ICT including both basic and advanced skills, and the use of ICT in research. Incentive systems that promote the use of ICTs by academic staff should also be implemented.

ICTs in Community Engagement

The economic policies of governments in both the developing and developed world have long been oriented towards growth. Scholars like Huq and Sen have helped to shift their focus from national-income accounting to people-centred policies and development. But development is a complex phenomenon that does not fit into a neat policy and application jacket. Sen helped to create a framework for development through his capability and functioning approach, which provided conceptual clarity and was also amenable to statistical comparisons.

As Sen points out, the objective of development is to enhance the quality of human lives by 'expanding the range of things that a person could be and do (functioning and capabilities to function, such as to be healthy and well nourished, to be knowledgeable, to participate in the life of a community.)' It is important to place of higher education in the context of development and to recognize the scope of ICTs in reinforcing the role of higher education in development process.

Generative Role of HEIs and ICT

The last two decades have seen a critical examination of the role HEIs in economic growth and social development. In addition to teaching and research, contributing to regional economic growth through innovation is now perceived as the third role of universities. The university-industry-government linkage is seen as a triple-helix model through which effective transfer of technologies leads to economic growth.

ICT cannot be the single determining factor influencing the generative and developmental roles of HEIs. It can only play a role once HEIs are geared with appropriate frameworks, so a discourse on the role of ICT requires a broader understanding of the status of HEIs in economic and social development.

Links of HEIs with industries and government vary from region to region. In developed countries linkages are often strong, but HEIs in many developing countries have more limited scope because there is less industry and innovation. The following table indicates the different patterns of university-industry linkages as well as in research and development systems.

Table 1. Different patterns of university-industry linkages as well as in research and development systems

	South Asia	*Africa*	*Latin America*	*Western Europe*	*USA*
University Industry Research Collaboration (in 1-7 Scale)	2.92	2.72	2.84	4.49	5.60
Patents Granted by USPTO (between 2002-2006)	64.84	4.51	15.13	538.24	4216.80
Number of Articles in Scientific Journals (2005)	3093	137	834.08	5704	205320
Total R&D Expenditure as % of GDP (2006)	0.50	0.37	0.28	1.93	2.68
Computer Per 1000 People (2005)	18.00	32.41	84.58	522.67	760.0
Internet Users Per 1000 people (2006)	31.0	39.0	185.83	552.67	690.0
Price Basket for Internet (US$ Per Month) 2005	10.59	45.39	26.92	26.14	14.95
ICT Expenditure as % of GDP, 2005	5.25	5.72	6.06	5.58	8.70

The enormous differences in the R&D systems between various regions are clearly evident in this table. According to the Milken Institute Tech-Pole Index the HEI location has on influence on the technology transfer and HEI intellectual property is absorbed more readily in regions with an existing technology industry base. Most HEIs in developing countries are in regions with an inadequate technology-industry base. Any assessment of the role of ICT in HEIs in influencing technology transfer and economic growth needs to note this context.

In developed countries the universities have acquired a strong foundation in technology transfer. The Bayh-Dole Act in the US helped universities there to strengthen their intellectual property rights and led to a spurt in patenting and technology transfer. Networking institutions such as the Association of University Technology Managers (AUTM) have enabled universities to retain a dominant position in research and development. There is ample evidence that ICTs have played a major role in university-industry partnership and technology transfer. AUTM has strong ICT-based network linking more than 3,000 experts in technology transfer.

ICT has also played a major role in university and industry partnership in Europe. The University of Minnesota's MBBNet (a web portal of the state's virtual biomedical and bioscience community) in collaboration with Zurich MedNet (a web based information source covering 400 universities, companies and institute) offers links to more than 1,300 organizations in the area of technology transfer.

The emergence of Bioinformatics as a separate discipline indicates the symbiotic relationship between academic research and technology transfer using modern ICT. Bioinformatics is an ICT-assisted interface discipline focusing on data management systems of life sciences particularly molecular biology, genomics etc and enables the scientists, industries and development agencies to access data and facilitate technology transfer. Because of their R&D facilities, ICT infrastructure and University-Industry linkages HEIs in North America and Europe have greater strength in bioinformatics than Africa and Latin America.

In an interesting report about the eReadiness of HEIs in Kenya, KENET has come to the following conclusions:

— HEIs are not ready to use ICT for eLearning.
— ICT is not yet a strategic priority for HEIs.
— ICT strategies have not been aligned with educational and development goals of the HEIs.

Among 18 universities in South Africa, only three universities have formal policies, strategic plans and regulatory framework for using ICT for education and development. According to UNESCO:

> The following were identified as weaknesses relating to ICT facilities which adversely affect the use of the technology for research purposes: poor infrastructure; few computers (a low ratio of computers to staff/ research

> students); and the high cost of connectivity which makes high-speed internet service unavailable. Furthermore, staff are unable to access journals online in order to update the knowledge on recent developments in their fields of research. The problems of ICT facilities require strong institutional policy as well as a regional approach for joint negotiations on the cost of bandwidth. With respect to the access to journals online the problem is two fold, the internet connectivity and the cost of the journals. Universities with internet facilities should look for freely available e-journals.

In spite of drawbacks such as poor infrastructure and low levels of industrialization and technology utilization, there are some interesting initiatives in developing countries:

— INOVA in Brazil: The State University of Campinas (UNICAMP) has established a unit for transfer of technology called INOVA. INOVA's patent database is available online. Patents are organized by market sector and can be searched by key word. This structure has helped to simplify the localization of the available technologies by sector, which is useful for INOVA's commercial team and also for external customers (industry or investors). With the help of INOVA the university has successfully transferred many technologies and is expected to operate at the same level of technology transfer as many successful universities in USA and Europe.

— SunSpace in South Africa: The SunSat satellite programme of Stellenbosch University developed SunSpace, South Africa's first satellite. Nearly 100 students were involved in the project and over 50 Masters and PhD degrees were awarded. In February 1999 SunSat was launched by the American space agency, NASA, and the satellite successfully operated in space, fulfilling all mission objectives. The University has established a company which manages the operation of the SunSat. The initiative has the potential to provide a Geographical Information System for strengthening the sustainable development of Africa.

— Technology Parks in India: In addition to the Indian Institutes of Technology and Deemed Universities, India has 1346 Engineering Colleges and 1244 polytechnics approved by All India Council of Technical Education (AICTE). ICT infrastructure is one of the parameters on the basis of which the engineering colleges are approved. These institutions, in addition to other colleges of science and technology, are playing a major role in the development and management of technology parks.

The HEIs have good linkages with Technology Parks through ICT networks. The government and industries are providing ICT connectivity, infrastructure and tax concessions.

Developmental Role of HEIs and ICT

The developmental role of an HEI can be seen from its initiatives and impacts in addressing social issues such as poverty, inequality, gender, environment and empowering the poor and marginalized sections of the society to play a major role in the developmental process.

In addition to contributing to social and economic policies and planning through theoretical perspectives, policy research and evaluation studies, HEIs have also played a role in directly reaching communities and society. Extension as a discipline has given agricultural colleges and universities a long tradition of reaching farming communities The State Agricultural Universities in India were modelled after the Land Grant colleges and these institutions played major role in green revolution. Similarly medical colleges and universities, through their community health programmes, reach large number of people in the communities. Over a period of time, HEIs along with civil society have questioned the conventional transfer of technology models in the developmental process and have begun to emphasise indigenous knowledge and interactive learning empowerment of the communities.

In many countries programmes like National Social Service (NSS) and youth programmes are raising students' awareness of the social dimensions of development. Unlike University-Industry linkages and technology transfer, which are continuously monitored, the linkages between HEIs and community have yet to be tracked in a systematic manner.

Agricultural and medical institutions have exploited the potentials of radios in their community outreach programmes. With the spurt in ICTs, HEIs—particularly universities—are involved in ICTs for Development (ICT4D) through projects and programmes. This has also led to the emergence of a specific discipline called Community Informatics.

In addition to above there are many other initiatives all over the developing and developed world which have strengthened the role of HEIs in ICT4D. While there are limits to the lessons we can learn from all the projects because of different levels of monitoring and evaluation, the specific challenges of universities in ICT4D has been well brought by the study of Colle in Africa. Based on survey among faculties and staff in 13 universities, Colle found that while there is an interest in ICT4D there are doubts about the support universities will provide in terms of policies and eReadiness.

Skills development is another important area in which ICT could be used effectively. Attempts are being made to strengthen the ICT framework for Technical and Vocational Education (TVET). The emerging discourse on the role of skill development in addressing poverty and developmental issues indicates the potential role of ICT4D. King and Palmer argue that skill systems, particularly TVET, left to the market will tend to favour non-poor and more-educated: 'Worldwide it seems to be the case that the more educated are the ones who get most access to further training. Those with minimum education levels do not get access to skills training.'

ICT can play a major role in integrating skill development as a component of a poverty alleviation strategy. GTZ has recommended Nine Generic Building Blocks for a VET Intervention Aimed at Pro-Poor Growthh. The role of ICT4D in TVET and skill development could be perceived vis-à-vis these building blocks. There is a need for understanding the framework in which the ICT4D by HEIs operate. Operationalizing development using ICT requires clear perspectives and well-defined roadmap.

The following matrix puts forward three basic elements of development: Accessing Development Infrastructure, Knowledge Management, and Empowerment. There are three stages of process in operationalizing the elements: They are: inform, interact and transact.

Process Through ICT Elements	Inform	Inform	Transact
Accessing Development Infrastructure			
Knowledge Management			
Empowerment			

Figure 1. Basic elements of development

Accessing Development Infrastructure: This refers the role of ICT in helping target communities and groups in linking with various development institutions, schemes, programmes and projects etc. Initiatives such as e-governance, egovernment, telemedicine, technology, connectivity etc would fall under this element.

Knowledge Management: This refers to the institutional process by which communities identify, create, represent, distribute, enable adoption and internalize as norms and values of insights and experiences which flow through vertical and horizontal sources. Learning, extension, training, etc. would fall under this element.

Empowerment: This is the process of increasing the capacity of individuals or groups to make choices and to transform those choices into desired actions and outcomes. The target community's ability to negotiate with various stakeholders and initiate selfsustaining development activities for sustainable livelihood is the important dimension of empowerment.

ICT could act at three levels vis-à-vis these three elements. In the first stage of the process, *inform*, information is provided about the three elements. In the second stage of the process, interact, two-way communication systems between the target communities and the developmental organizations including HEIs are established using modern ICT. Transact refers to the process of accessing development infrastructure and knowledge institutions through ICT and transforming this access into desired actions.

In the absence of a comparative database, it would be difficult to arrive at an understanding regarding the status of ICT4D in HEIs. However based on the reports and various case studies, following hypothetical conclusions could be arrived at:

— A large number of projects of HEIs operate within a limited framework on ICT4D.

— Most of them are in the area of informing about access to development institutions and knowledge management. Some projects enable the target communities to interact with various agencies using ICT4D.

— Very few projects are involved in the process of transacting and providing opportunity for achieving empowerment.

Education, ICTs and society: Next Steps

Many HEIs do not have well-defined policies and action plans regarding their generative and developmental roles in the society. Most of their policies are inward looking, focusing activities within institutions and giving little emphasis to linkages with external stakeholders. Though HEIs in developed countries have policies on the generative role, there are controversies about balancing longterm academic research with short-term technology transfer projects. There is a need to strengthen HEIs in policy development strategies vis-à-vis generative and developmental role.

In the absence of strong policy framework, ICT is seen more as an infrastructure and not as a tool for strengthening these generative and developmental roles. Hence, in addition to a general policy framework, specific policies and plans for integrating ICT for generative and developmental roles should be defined. Most of the ICT4D initiatives are *project-based* and mostly supported by external development agencies. These projects are initiated through the interests of particular individuals. In many developed countries, patents and royalties have encouraged faculties to get involved in the generative role. Very few HEIs have taken steps to recognize the contribution of faculties and staff in the developmental role. If ICT4D is to be internalised, recognition of developmental role is crucial and appropriate policies are required for internalising it.

The capacity HEIs to perceive and operationalize ICT4D is vital. The approach is still based on a beneficiary-benefactor relationship.Most of the discussions on ICT4D by HEIs are oriented towards connectivity and technology issues. Digitising and populating ICT with contents are some of the areas on which HEIs could concentrate. In particular, issues such as standards in content creation and management in many local languages should be addressed. For example, FAO has evolved AGROVOC, a structured multilingual thesaurus for agriculture. Its main role is to standardise the indexing process in order to make searching simpler and more efficient, and to provide the user with the most relevant resources. At present it is available in 23 languages.

Other Applications of ICTs in Community Service

Finally, ICTs can facilitate action research in communities and make it possible to involve the general public in research, for instance by collecting data or pooling the power of hundreds of personal computers. The expansion of multi-media centres, ICT kiosks and cyber cafés into rural areas creates new possibilities for extension services and the application of university research. Higher education has also been instrumental in the development of community informatics. Emerging technologies like Second Life, Facebook, YouTube, Flickr, Blogger, Twitter and LinkedIn, which at first seemed to be entertainment devices or toys, are proving useful in the relationships between the academic world and its community stakeholders. Such developments have created the new role of knowledge 'infomediaries', who take advantage of ICTs to facilitate linkages between universities and communities.

ICTs in Teaching

Academics have taken to the use of computer in teaching much more readily than they adopted earlier audio-visual media. This is because the strength of computers is their power to manipulate words and symbols—which is at the heart of the academic endeavour. There is a trend to introduce eLearning or online learning both in courses taught on campus and in distance learning. Distance education and eLearning are not necessarily the same thing and can have very different cost structures. Whether eLearning improves quality or reduce cost depends on the particular circumstances. ICTs in general and eLearning in particular have reduced the barriers to entry to the higher education business. Countries and those aspiring to create new HEIs can learn from the failures of a number of virtual universities. They reveal that ICTs should be introduced in a systematic manner that brings clarity to the business model through cost-benefit analyses.

Emerging Context

With many developing countries envisioning a future in which they hope to become learning societies built on knowledge economies, higher education has a signal role to play in development strategies in the pursuit of such aspirations.

The accounting firm KPMG recently released research which estimates, conservatively, that the real rate of return on investments in the education and research functions of universities yields 15% or more for university training and 20%-40% for public university research. This finding should give countries confidence to increase their investments in higher education.

No knowledge economy can function without ICTs. Therefore, it is imperative that higher education institutions afford their graduates the literacy and competencies that their future work environments are likely to demand of them. Furthermore, being ICT-rich gives an HEI a competitive advantage in recruiting students.

In many countries, demand for higher education far outstrips supply and Governments and institutions are turning more and more to the use of ICTs to bridge the access gap. It is too early to say whether the role of ICTs in the teaching function of higher education is truly transformative, or whether it is simply a repackaging of previous pedagogy.

Benefits and Challenges of ICTs

Learning and course management systems are useful in generating and managing a variety of student support services and products, such as course outlines, digitallyrecorded classroom material, discussion groups, laboratory manuals and lab assignments, lecture notes, live lectures for later viewing and re-viewing, links to course specific websites, online tutorials, supplementary readings, and virtual office hours for teacher-student consultations. Virtual libraries, where they exist, are a particular boon to students as they cut down on costs of acquiring expensive textbooks, journals and reference material.

Tools are also now available on the Internet to assist both teachers and students to manage writing assignments to detect and avoid the pitfalls of plagiarism and copyright violations.

One of the great benefits of ICTs in teaching is that they can improve the quality and the quantity of educational provision. For this to happen however, they must be used appropriately.

While using ICTs in teaching has some obvious benefits, ICTs also bring challenges. First is the high cost of acquiring, installing, operating, maintaining and replacing ICTs. While potentially of great importance, the integration of ICTs into teaching is still in its infancy. Introducing ICT systems for teaching in developing countries has a particularly high opportunity cost because installing them is usually more expensive in absolute terms than in industrialized countries whereas, in contrast, alternative investments (e.g., buildings) are relatively less costly.

Inexperience in procuring institution-wide hardware and software and attendant services may cost institutions dearly as they may end up with wares that are outdated and subject to unworkable but binding supplier contracts. Using unlicensed software can be very problematic, not only legally but in the costs of maintenance, particularly if the pirated software varies in standard formats. Even under ideal circumstances of licensed hardware and software acquisition, lack of capacity in equipment maintenance can pose serious implementation problems. Clear policies and procedures for procuring computer hardware and software are necessary to prevent such problems.

Even though students can benefit immensely from well-produced learning resources, online teaching has its own unique challenges as not all faculty are ICT literate and can teach using ICT tools. Even those who are may not be keen on teaching online because of the extra time and effort involved.

A related issue is the readiness of students to learn online. Limited ICT resources may cause institutions to put their energies into making their students ICT literate as a foundation step but the lack of enhanced teaching methods (using multimedia resources, for example) may lead to inferior learning outcomes for students.

e-Learning

The introduction of eLearning in education engendered high expectations that it would transform the organization and delivery of higher education. It prompted significant investments in starting up new virtual universities by universities in Europe and the United States including New York, Columbia and Cornell Universities and the US Open University. Numerous Virtual Universities such as the UK e-University, the Digital University in the Netherlands, the Bavarian Virtual University, the Virtual University in Finland, the Net-University in Sweden and the African Virtual University were launched.

However, in most cases these virtual universities and eLearning experiences have failed to achieve the desired levels of sustainability and would not survive without massive government support. The OECD's 2001 Report contended that despite the investment of up to $16 billion made in eLearning by the OECD countries, there was no evidence that it led to any significant improvement in teachers' performance and or students' learning outcomes nor had it enhanced quality and access to education on the scale predicted initially. In its 2005 report, the OECD concluded that ICT in higher education had more impact on administrative services than on teaching. The reports attributed the failure of eLearning to its inability to be relevant to local needs and cultures.

This does not imply a complete retreat from eLearning/online education but requires a re-conceptualisation of eLearning so that it achieves a difficult balance. On the one hand it must recognize the importance of the effective interaction of students with content, fellow students and teachers/tutors during the learning process. On the other hand, if it is not to increase institutional costs there must be some substitution of capital for labour, as occurs in traditional open and distance learning (ODL). For this reason HEIs that already operate through ODL (e.g. open universities) can more easily introduce eLearning cost-effectively than those that try to graft it onto classroom teaching.

The instructional success of eLearning is dependent on the development of appropriate pedagogies and an integrated use of ICT based on students' prior learning experiences. Its failure can be traced to its conception of learning as the transfer of knowledge instead of seeing learning as an active process of knowledge creation. Therefore, there must be a paradigm shift from an emphasis on stand-alone courses and resource-based learning to a process that promotes interaction, communication, collaboration and construction.

However, the economic success of eLearning must be based on some substitution of technology for labour and the development of a learning system that cuts costs through specialisation and division of labour. The 'lone-ranger' approach to eLearning, where each instructor tries to convert their own course into an online format is not likely to be effective, economic or sustainable. Introducing eLearning without increasing institutional costs is a serious challenge, particularly for public institutions.

Strategies for Introducing ICTs

The importance of overarching and guiding telecommunications and ICT policies at the national level, particularly as they relate to ICTs in education, cannot be overemphasized. Not only do such policies enable institutions and networks of institutions to generate their own internal ICT policies, strategies and plans, they also foster an appropriate allocation of resources. In institutions, they determine staffing issues and faculty roles and how these can be made sustainable.

In response to increased demand for higher education, many countries are witnessing the mushrooming of higher education institutions, both private and public. Bricks and mortar may be a necessary part of the accommodating infrastructure for this expansion but they are not sufficient to meet and address all the access issues in the sub-sector satisfactorily. Nationally, where the infrastructure exists, many institutions working together could tap into an ICT network to facilitate collaboration and sharing to cut down on costs and optimize the returns gained in the use of ICTs. ICT networks are critical for the successful implementation of ICTs in education; wellarticulated policies will ensure that such access is possible.

UNESCO Bangkok has developed an *ICT-in-Education Toolkit* that Governments can use in drafting ICT policies in education.

Apart from having enabling telecommunications and ICT policies, governments and higher education institutions will need to develop strategies for effective ICT and media deployment and sustainability. A relatively less costly medium that has not been fully exploited in some jurisdictions for educational purposes is the radio. Recognizing the potential reach of this medium, 27 tertiary education institutions in Nigeria have received government licences to operate *campus radios* for teaching, research and entertainment.

Where capacity is lacking for the proper assessment of ICTs and their benefits, institutions would do well to, first, mount training workshops in the areas of ICT procurement, contracting and the total cost of owning particular systems, which includes acquisition, installation, power supply, maintenance, allied material and equipment, replacement, training, recycling, etc.

Such training should be undertaken within the context of a technology plan that includes long term budgeting or funding scenarios, acquisition, maintenance, replacement and possible sharing, at least coordination, of ICT usage with other institutions. For governments, it is important for an education ministry to liaise and coordinate efforts with other departments in the country, e.g., Finance, Telecommunications, Industry & Commerce and Economic Development.

In developing internal capacity in the use of ICT in teaching, learning, and research, teachers need to be involved in designing particular ICT initiatives to ensure their relevance and effectiveness. Rather than introducing ICT wares across the institution all at once, it is prudent to test the efficacy of a technology at, say, the departmental level before deploying it institution-wide. Such piloting, if successful, will reassure institutional policymakers of the soundness of the technology in facilitating improved teaching and, on the part of students, more and better learning outcomes. On the other hand, this must not lead to each department adopting its own IT solutions. Students appreciate having some consistency in the platforms (say for eLearning) that they will find in different parts of the HEI.

Pitfalls

The four most common mistakes in introducing ICTs into teaching are:

i) installing learning technology without reviewing student needs and content availability;

ii) imposing technological systems from the top down without involving faculty and students;

iii) using inappropriate content from other regions of the world without customizing it appropriately; and

iv) producing low quality content that has poor instructional design and is not adapted to the technology in use.

Technology is of little use if the pedagogical skills needed to effectively and optimally use it are lacking. It is important, therefore, that serious consideration be given to content preparation before deciding on the most appropriate way to deliver it to students. When this is accomplished, teaching is likely to improve in ways that foster more and better learning. Institutional policies and procedures for adopting and adapting technology must be in place and faculty and students involved in at least assessing content vis-à-vis the technological mode to deliver it. Where expertise is lacking in conducting such assessments, training should be introduced to ensure that the implications of technology adoption and use are clearly understood and accounted for in short and long-term planning.

It is essential more generally to provide prior training for faculty when introducing ICTs since students are often more familiar with these technologies than they are. A new dynamic is that institutions are adopting cloud services which are of three basic kinds: 1) free social software; 2) free online services (Facebook, Blogger, etc); and, 3) subscription online services. Subscription services may sometimes represent good value because users can buy only what they need without having to run and maintain their own servers. Note that the business model for some online services is still evolving and may lead to user fees for services that are now free.

Promise of Open Educational Resources (OERs)

OERs are educational materials and resources offered freely and openly for anyone to use and under some licenses to re-mix, improve and redistribute. They are the expression of an Internet empowered worldwide community effort to create a global intellectual and educational commons. In Africa, for example, one of the most successful collections of OERs are those developed and. Disseminated by the Teacher Education in Sub-Saharan Africa (TESSA) Consortium. It has 18 memberinstitutions in nine African countries. TESSA has developed a wide variety of audio and text materials (online and print) that provide support to primary school teachers and teacher educators in Africa. MIT's Open Courseware project and the UK Open University's OpenLearn site are the best known examples of open content in higher education in the industrialised world.

OERs have great potential for improving the cost-effectiveness of eLearning, since the creation of high quality courses ab initio is a costly process. However, institutions that specialise in eLearning, such as the Asian e-University, now find that most of the quality content that they need is already available as an OER somewhere, and all they need do is find it and adapt it to their own context and needs. However, Institutions should develop appropriate policies and train their staff about the related technical, pedagogical and legal (copyright) issues if they are to take full advantage of OERs.

Another network that is creating and taking advantage of OERs is the Virtual University for Small States of the Commonwealth (VUSSC), a collaborative initiative of the Ministers of Education of 32 small states. They share training events and collaborate on the creation of eLearning courses that all can use. This is facilitated by a Transnational Qualifications Framework that has also been developed by the VUSSC. The VUSSC is an interesting example of south-south cooperation at the leading edge of the applications of ICTs in teaching.

ICTs in Educational Administration

HEIs have engaged ICTs in administration since the early seventies. This early uptake of ICTs included systems for: student admission and records, examination results and transcripts, finance database, human resources database and management information.

The rapidly increasing student population in higher education accelerated the need for ICTs to process, store and retrieve data in a fast, systemic and accurate fashion. In the 2008 edition of *Education at a Glance*, OECD revealed that, on average, 57% of school-leavers in OECD countries went on to university in 2006, compared with 37% in 1995. The need to manage this increasing student intake and monitor students' progression through the education system required HEI administrators to turn to ICTs for solutions. Similarly, the growing power, effectiveness and potential of ICTs also meant that technology could provide possibilities that did not exist three decades ago. Some examples of new ICT applications that became available to administrators include: eGovernance, online registration by students, online access to course outlines and materials, online assignment submissions, online examinations and online discussion forums with students and instructors. As a result of applying ICTs in university administration, a dynamic new shift occurred in higher education.

Using ICTS in higher education administration is fundamentally about harnessing technology for better planning, setting standards, effecting change and monitoring results of the core functions of universities. More and more universities are looking into developing ICTs applications that will:

— improve on the quality and capacity of management information systems to support strategic decision-making and policy implementation;

— stimulate and facilitate free flow of information throughout the higher education system; and

— respond to the needs and demands of the younger generation for better and increased access to university services and information through the web.

There are multiple benefits of ICT application for the university administration, students and instructors.

First, ICT technology can process voluminous records quickly, meticulously and impeccably.

Second, technology can generate reliable and consistent records.

Third, records and data produced are searchable and quickly retrievable. Fourth, digital records save space, a premium cost to institutions. Fifth, technology saves human resources for data entry and servicing student admission and registration. With advanced scanning technology, completed application forms can be read into the databases in a matter of seconds.

Other software like Learning Management Systems (LMS) (e.g. the open source Moodle used by Athabasca University and many other institutions, including those in the VUSSC network mentioned earlier) allow students to register for courses directly online, pay online and get course information online. Sixth, technology can expand the geographical boundary for student intake and facilitate cross-border higher education.

There are many benefits for students in terms of increased flexibility in registering for courses/classes online, accessing course outlines and content online, interacting with students and instructors online through chats or online discussions, submitting assignments and writing examinations.

The mushrooming capabilities of LMS are allowing institutions and instructors to create and maintain comprehensive, searchable, retrievable and reusable records of content development and content dissemination. More effective class management can be done through the use of virtual space in interacting with students, supporting learning needs, monitoring student progress and maintaining an account of student performance and results.

While the potential benefits of ICTs for administration are substantial, there are associated challenges that decision makers should be aware of before introducing technology changes.

As the goal is for seamless transfer of data from the point of student registration to registry, finance, student services, human resources and so forth, the respective systems or databases involved in the process must be able to communicate with each other intelligently. Reliability and security are of the essence. As access to registration and course content are web-based, this leads to the debate about security over the net. The difficult question to grapple with is how to widen access without giving away internal security to possibilities of hacking and virus attack? How strong a firewall and a back up are required in order that the "cardiovascular function" of institutions can be foolproof?

Another important consideration is how can the services provided by universities through ICTs be accessed by all the students they serve? In

Africa, where the penetration of the Internet stands at 5.6% compared to the world's 26.6%, any technology deployment for learning and academic services will need to address the issue of connectivity by students and instructors. Fortunately, the IT landscape of countries is improving continuously which also requires that institutions need to monitor the situation regularly to keep up with the pace of technology changes.

Other challenges are people related. The wide adoption of ICTs calls for mindsets and skill sets that are adaptive to change. An attitude of resistance to change attitude is often caused by the lack of appreciation of the benefits brought by ICTs and by the fear that technology will replace jobs, which it should if it is to be cost-effective. Institutions investing in ICTs will need to underpin changes with a training and capacity building plan for a workforce that is heads on, hearts on and hands on with ICTs.

The purpose of using ICTs in administration is to support the business strategies and processes of the HEI. Thus a perquisite for any application is absolute clarity about the steps in each business process and how they related to each other. This sounds simple but it is not—and is the reason that so many administrative software projects experience time and cost overruns. IT algorithms are not very forgiving of fudges in the process and programming is held up while they are clarified and turf battles within the administration are resolved.

A new challenge in merging business processes is to link existing student record systems, which usually employ proprietary software, to the learning management systems for eLearning, which are often based on open source software such as Moodle. This is essential if eLearning is to have any hope of achieving cost-efficiency gains.

Another key to the successful use of IT in HEI administration is extensive user consultation, which should be a facet of clarifying business processes. Clerks and others who provide the interface with students will be understandably nervous at the prospect of a change in the IT systems that they use all day long. If the new system delivers well on their wishes implementation will proceed very smoothly. Transparent and inclusive system development processes take time, but reap bountiful results in the long run.

While not always possible, a pilot phase or dummy runs to iron out any likely bugs and glitches will contribute greatly to results and success.

Phased roll-out is easier for managing results if the change is wide-ranging and far-reaching. There should be a clear time table for change and for each milestone to be underpinned by sufficient preparation, training and help desk/ hotline support. An integrated monitoring and evaluation plan will ensure timely collection of user and stakeholder feedback, and any needs for further system/software adjustment and enhancement.

REFERENCES

Edquist, C. (1997). *Systems of Innovation: Technologies, Institutions and Organisations.* Paperback. London: Pinter.

KENET. (2007). *E-Readiness Survey of Higher Education Institutions in Kenya* 2006, Kenya Education Network, Nairobi, Kenya.

McKeown, R. (2006). Reorienting Colleges and Universities to Address Sustainability. *Globalization and Education for Sustainable Development: Sustaining the Future.* International Conference, Nagoya, Japan, 28-29.

McMahon, W. (2002). *Education and development: Measuring the social benefits.* Oxford: Oxford University Press.

Remoe, S.O. (2005).*Governance of Innovation Systems*, Vol. 1. Synthesis Report, Paris: OECD.

UNESCO. (2006). *Revitalizing science and technology training institutions in Africa : the way forward.* UNESCO, Nairobi.

9

Establishing World-class Education Institutions

Governments are becoming increasingly aware of the important contribution that high performance, world-class universities make to global competitiveness and economic growth. There is growing recognition, in both industrial and developing countries, of the need to establish one or more world-class universities that can compete effectively with the best of the best around the world.

Preoccupations about university rankings reflect the general recognition that economic growth and global competitiveness are increasingly driven by knowledge, and that universities can play a key role in that context. Indeed, rapid advances in science and technology across a wide range of areas from information and communication technologies (ICTs) to biotechnology to new materials provide great potential for countries to accelerate and strengthen their economic development. The application of knowledge results in more efficient ways of producing goods and services and delivering them more effectively and at lower costs to a greater number of people.

The 1999 *World Development Report on the Knowledge Economy* (World Bank) proposed an analytical framework emphasizing the complementary role of four key strategic dimensions to guide countries in the transition to a knowledge-based economy: an appropriate economic and institutional regime, a strong human capital base, a dynamic information infrastructure and an efficient national innovation system.

Tertiary education is central to all four pillars of this framework, but its role is particularly crucial in support of building a strong human capital base and contributing to an efficient national innovation system. Tertiary education helps countries build globally competitive economies by developing a skilled, productive and flexible labor force and by creating, applying and spreading new ideas and technologies. A recent global study of patent generation has shown, for example, that universities and research institutes, rather than firms, drive scientific advances in biotechnology. Tertiary education institutions can also play a vital role in their local and regional economy.

Within the tertiary education system, research universities play a critical role in training the professionals, scientists and researchers needed by the economy and generating new knowledge in support of the national innovation system. In this context, an increasingly pressing priority of many governments is to make sure that their top universities are actually operating at the cutting edge of intellectual and scientific development.

World-class University

In the past decade, the term "world-class university" has become a catch phrase for not simply improving the quality of learning and research in tertiary education but more importantly for developing the capacity to compete in the global tertiary education marketplace through the acquisition and creation of advanced knowledge. With students looking to attend the best possible institution they can afford, often regardless of national borders, and governments keen on maximizing the returns on their investments on universities, global standing is becoming an increasingly important concern for institutions around the world. The paradox of the world- class university, however, as Altbach has succinctly and accurately observed, is that "everyone wants one, no one knows what it is, and no one knows how to get one".

To become a member of the exclusive group of world-class university is not something that one achieves by self-declaration. This is an elite status conferred by the outside world on the basis of international recognition. Until recently, the process involved a subjective qualification based mostly on reputation. For example, Ivy League universities in the United States, such as Harvard, Yale or Cornell, Oxford and Cambridge in the United Kingdom, and Tokyo University have traditionally been counted among the exclusive group cf elite universities. But no direct and rigorous measure was available to substantiate their superior status in terms of training of graduates, research output, and technology transfer. Even the higher salaries captured by their graduates could be interpreted as a signaling proxy as much as the true value of their education.

With the proliferation of league tables in the past few years, however, more systematic ways of identifying and classifying world-class universities have appeared. Although most of the best-known rankings purport to categorise universities within a given country, there have also been attempts to establish international rankings. The two most comprehensive international rankings, allowing for broad benchmark comparisons of institutions across national borders, are those prepared by:

— The times Higher Education Supplement (THES), produced by AS Quacquarelli Symonds Ltd.

— Shanghai Jiao Tong University (SITU).

A third international ranking compiled by Web matrix, produced by the Cyber matrix Lab (a unit of the National Research Council, the main public research body in Spain), compares 4,000 world tertiary education institutions and marks them on scales from 1 to 5 across several areas that purport to measure visibility on the Internet as a proxy of the importance of the concerned institution.

To compare the international stature of institutions, these league tables are constructed by using objective or subjective data (or both) obtained from the universities themselves or from the public domain. The THES ranking selects the top 200 universities in the world. First presented in 2004, the methodology for this ranking focuses most heavily on international reputation, combining subjective inputs (such as peer reviews and employer recruiting surveys), quantitative data (including the numbers of international students and faculty), and the influence of the faculty (as represented by research citations).

Operating since 2003, SJTU uses a methodology that focuses on seemingly more objective indicators, such as the academic and research performance of faculty, aluminium, and staff. The measures evaluated include publications, citations, and exclusive international awards (such as Nobel Prizes and Fields Medals). Shanghai's ranking is also presented slightly differently:

The top 100 institutions are listed in ranked ordinal. The remaining 400 institutions are listed by clusters of approximately 50 and 100 and alphabetically within those clusters.

Table 1. Top 20 Universities in THES and SJTU World Rankings, 2006

Rank	THES
1	Harvard University
2	University of Cambridge
3	University of Oxford
4	Massachusetts Institute of Technology
5	Yale University
6	Stanford University
7	California Institute of Technology
8	University of California, Berkeley
9	Imperial College London
10	Princeton University
11	University of Chicago
12	Columbia University
13	Duke University
14	Beijing University
15	Cornell University
16	Australian National University
17	London School of Economics and Political.Science
18	Ecole Normale Supérieure (Paris)
19	National University of Singapore
20	Tokyo University
Rank	*SJTU*
1	Harvard University
2	University of Cambridge
3	Stanford University
4	University of California - Berkeley
5	Massachusetts Institute of Technology
6	California Institute of Technology
7	Columbia University
8	Princeton University
9	University of Chicago
10	University of Oxford

11	Yale University
12	Cornell University
13	University of California - San Diego
14	University of California - Los Angeles
15	University of Pennsylvania
16	University of Wisconsin - Madison
17	University of Washington - Seattle
18	University of California – San Francisco
19	Johns Hopkins University
20	Tokyo University

Notwithstanding the serious methodological limitations of any ranking exercise, world-class universities are recognised in part for their superior outputs. They produce well-qualified graduates who are in high demand on the labour market; they conduct leading edge research published in top scientific journals; and in the case of science and-technology oriented institutions, they contribute to technical innovations through patents and licenses.

Most universities recognised as world-class originate from a very small number of countries, mostly Western. In fact, the University of Tokyo is the only non-U.S., non-U.K. University among the top 20 in the SITU ranking. If one considers that there are only between 30 and 50 world-class universities in total, according to the SITU ranking all come from a small group of eight North American and Western European countries, Japan being again the only exception. THES has a slightly wider range of countries of origin among the top 50 universities, including Hong Kong (China), New Zealand, and Singapore besides the usual North American and Western European nations. The broad geographical distribution of the countries whose universities appear among the top 50 in the world rankings.

The few scholars who have attempted to define what world-class universities have that regular universities do not possess have identified a number of basic features, such as highly qualified faculty; excellence in research; quality teaching; high levels of government and non-government sources of funding; international and highly talented students; academic freedom; well-defined autonomous governance structures; and well-equipped facilities for teaching, research, administration, and (often) student life. Recent collaborative research on this theme between U.K. and Chinese universities has resulted in an even longer list of key attributes, ranging from the international reputation of the university to more abstract concepts such as the university's contribution to society, both very difficult to measure in an objective manner.

In an attempt to propose a more manageable definition of world-class universities, this chapter makes the case that the superior results of these institutions (highly sought graduates, leading-edge research, and technology transfer) can essentially be attributed to three complementary sets of factors at play in top universities:

— A high concentration of talent (faculty and students).

— Abundant resources to offer a rich learning.

Concentration of Talent

The first and perhaps foremost determinant of excellence is the presence of a critical mass of top students and outstanding faculty. World-class universities are able to select the best students and attract the most qualified professors and researchers. In the sciences, being at the right university the one where the most state of-the-art research is being done in the best-equipped labs by the most visible scientists is extremely important. George Stigler describes this as a snowballing process, where an outstanding scientist gets funded to do exciting research, attracts other faculty, then the best students until a critical mass is formed that has an irresistible appeal to any young person entering the field.

This has always been the hallmark of the Ivy League universities in the United States or the Universities of Oxford and Cambridge in the United Kingdom. And it is also a feature of the newer world-class universities, such as the National University of Singapore (NUS) or Tsinghua University in China. Beijing's Tsinghua University said last month it would increase the number of awards this year. Students with high scores, such as champions of each province and winners of international student academic competitions, will be entitled to scholarships of up to 40,000 yawn, more than double that of last year.

Important factors in that respect are the ability and the privilege of these universities to select the most academically qualified students. For example, Beijing University, China's top institution of higher learning, admits the 50 best students of each province every year. Harvard University, the California

Institute of Technology, the Massachusetts Institute of Technology (MIT), and Yale University are the most selective universities in the United States, as measured by the average Scholastic Assessment Test (SAT) scores of their incoming undergraduate students.

One corollary of this observation is that tertiary education institutions in countries where there is little internal mobility of students and faculty are at risk of academic inbreeding. Indeed, universities that rely principally on their own undergraduates to continue into graduate programs or that hire principally their own graduates to join the teaching staff are not likely to be at the leading edge of intellectual development. A 2007 survey of European universities found an inverse correlation between endogamy in faculty hiring and research performance: the universities with the highest degree of endogamy had the lowest research results.

It is also difficult to maintain high selectivity in institutions with rapidly growing student enrolment and fairly open admission policies. The huge size of the leading universities of Latin American countries such as Mexico or Argentina the University National Autonomy de Mexico (Autonomous University of Mexico, or UNAM) has 190,418 students, and the University of Buenos Aires (UBA) has 279,306 is certainly a major factor in explaining why these universities have failed to enter the top league, despite having a few excellent departments and research centres that are undoubtedly world-class. At the other extreme, Beijing University maintained its overall enrolment at less than 20,000 until the early 2000s and even today has no more than 30,000 students. World-class universities also tend to have a high proportion of carefully selected graduate students, reflecting their strength in research and the fact that graduate students are closely involved in the research activities of these institutions.

The international dimension is becoming increasingly important in determining the configuration of these elite institutions . Both the THES world ranking of universities and the News week 2006 ranking of global universities weighted their rankings to favour institutions with strong international components. In most cases, world-class universities have students and faculty who are not exclusively from the country where the university operates.

This enables them to attract the most talented people, no matter where they come from, and open themselves to new ideas and approaches. Harvard

University, for instance, has a student population that is 19 percent international; Stanford University has 21 percent; and Columbia University, 23 percent. At the University of Cambridge, 18 percent of the students are from outside the U.K. or European Union (EU) countries. The U.S. Universities ranked at the top of the global surveys also show sizable proportions of foreign academic staff. For example, the proportion of international faculty at Harvard University, including medical academic staff, is approximately 30 percent. Similarly, the proportion of foreign academics at the Universities of Oxford and Cambridge is 36 and 33 percent, respectively. By contrast, only 7 percent of all researchers in France are foreign academics. Unquestionably, the world's best universities enrol and employ large numbers of foreign students and faculty in their search for the most talented.

The new patterns of knowledge generation and sharing, documented by Gibbons in their ground breaking work on the shift toward a problem-based mode of production of knowledge, are characterised by the growing importance of international knowledge networks. In this respect, the fact that world-class universities succeed in mobilising a broadly diverse national and international academic staff is likely to maximise these institutions' knowledge-networking capacity.

Abundant Resources

Abundance of resources is the second element that characterises most world-class universities, in response to the huge costs involved in running a complex, research-intensive university. These universities have four main sources of financing: government budget funding for operational expenditures and research, contract research from public organisations and private firms, the financial returns generated by endowments and gifts, and tuition fees.

In Western Europe, public funding is by far the principal source of finance for teaching and research, although the top U.K. universities have some endowment funds, and "top-up fees" have been introduced in recent years. In Asia, the National University of Singapore, which became a private corporation in 2006, has been the most successful institution in terms of substantial endowment funding. It has managed to build up a sizable portfolio of US$774 million through effective fund-raising, making it richer than any British university after Cambridge and Oxford. The United States and (to a lesser extent) Japan have thriving private research universities.

The sound financial base of the top U.S. Universities is the result of two factors. First, they have large endowments, which provide budget security, comfort, and the ability to focus on medium- and long-term institutional priorities. On average, per student, the richest U.S. Private universities receive more than US$40,000 in endowment income every year, compared with a mere US$1,000 for Canadian universities. Unlike many universities in Europe, these U.S. Universities are not at the short-term mercy of government funding. Second, U.S. Universities benefit from the success of their faculty in competing for government research funding. At least two-thirds of the research funding captured by the top U.S. Research universities comes from public sources. The top-ranking Canadian universities in international league tables are also the top universities in research income. A comparative analysis of the SJTU rankings of U.S. And Western European universities confirms that level of expenditures is one of the key determinants of performance.

Total spending on tertiary education (public and private) represents 3.3 percent of gross domestic product (GDP) in the United States versus only 1.3 percent in the EU 25 countries. Per student spending is about US$ 54,000 in the United States, compared with US$ 54,000 in the European Union. Similarly, there are large spending variations among European universities that are correlated with the rankings results of the respective countries. The United Kingdom and Switzerland have relatively well-funded universities and achieve the highest country scores in terms of rankings, while universities from the Southern European countries, including France and Germany, have lower ranking scores associated with low levels of funding.

The availability of abundant resources creates a virtuous circle that allows the concerned institutions to attract even more top professors and researchers, as is often the case among elite universities in the United States. Annual surveys of salaries indicate that private universities in research income. United States pay their professors 30 percent more than public universities do, on average.

The salary gap between public and private universities has increased in the past 25 years. In 1980, the average salary of full professors at doctor-of-philosophy (PhD) granting public universities amounted to 91 percent of that at private universities. Today, the US$ 106,500 average annual salary at public universities represents 78 percent of the salary at private universities. It is not surprising, then, that not one U.S. Public institution ranks nationally in the top 20, private universities reward excellent faculty with higher salaries, so the best academics tend to seek employment there. The Challenge of Establishing World-Class Universities documented how years of scarce funding led to the loss of significant numbers of top faculty "raided" by other institutions and a drop in its national rankings.

Salaries in countries with the highest numbers of institutions on the world rankings of tertiary education are the highest, while countries with little or no global tertiary education presence have the lowest salaries. It must not be mistaken as a coincidence that the best-quality research appears to be coming out of the best-paid researcher pools. In academic, the adage "you get what you pay for" appears accurate regarding better-quality work being done where salaries are relatively highest.In the United States, an even larger remuneration gap between private and public institutions is prevalent when it comes to the pay packages of university presidents.

The resource gap affects, in turn, the financial capacity of countries to put in place the kind of digital infrastructure enjoyed by top universities in North America and East Asia. A recent report on French universities, for example, underscores the need to catch up with more-advanced tertiary education systems, which explains the poor showing of French universities in the Web matrix rankings. In the words of the Minister of Education, In the context of globalisation of higher education, it appears that France shows a certain delay compared with other Western countries in the access it provides to on-line courses and in offering distance education. At the very time when mastering information and communication technologies seems increasingly to be an element of a nation's competitiveness, this delay in the digitilisation of higher studies risks impeding France's development in coming years.

Appropriate Governance

The third dimension concerns the overall regulatory framework, the competitive environment, and the degree of academic and managerial autonomy that universities enjoy. The Economist referred to the tertiary education system in the United States as "the best in the world" and attributed this success not only to its wealth but also to its relative independence from the state, the competitive spirit that encompasses. The corrective coefficients in those countries are the purchasing power parity (PPP) published by the World Bank. PPP is expressed as the local currency unit to the international dollar.

The Challenge of Establishing World-Class Universities every aspect of it, and its ability to make academic work and production relevant and useful to society. The report observed that the environment in which universities operate fosters competitiveness, unrestrained scientific inquiry, critical thinking, innovation, and creativity. Moreover, institutions that have complete autonomy are also more flexible because they are not bound by cumbersome bureaucracies and externally imposed standards, even in light of the legitimate accountability mechanisms that do bind them. As a result, they can manage their resources with agility and quickly respond to the demands of a rapidly changing global market.

The comparative study of European and U.S. Universities mentioned earlier also found that governance was, along with funding, the other main determinant of rankings. "European universities suffer from poor governance, insufficient autonomy and often perverse incentives". A subsequent paper reporting on a survey of European universities found that research performance was positively linked to the degree of autonomy of the universities in the sample, especially with regard to budget management, the ability to hire faculty and staff, and the freedom to set salaries.

With respect to the composition of university boards, the report concludes that "having significant outside representation on the board may be a necessary condition to ensure that dynamic reforms taking into account long-term institutional interests can be decided upon without undue delay." The autonomy elements outlined above are necessary, though not sufficient, to establish and maintain world-class universities. Other crucial governance features are needed, such as inspiring and persistent leaders; a strong strategic vision of where the institution is going; a philosophy of success and excellence; and a culture of constant reflection, organisational learning, and change.

The cases of Germany and France are interesting to discuss in this context. Despite having economies that are among the strongest in the world, their universities are hardly recognised as elite institutions. In 2003, when the first SJTU ranking was published, the best French university (the

University of Paris VI) was ranked 66th, and the first German university (the University of Munich) was ranked 49th. In 2008, the best French and German universities were placed 42nd and 55th, respectively.

Benchmark them against the three sets of criteria proposed above shows clearly why universities of these two countries do not shine in international rankings. To begin with, there is very little screening of students entering tertiary education. By law, French universities are not allowed to be selective. In most programs, having graduated from secondary school is the only prerequisite to admission, with the exception of the highly selective French engineering and professional grenades écoles, which have a separate status.

Another important factor is the absolute lack of competition among universities. All universities are treated equally in terms of budget and assignment of personnel, making it quite difficult, if not impossible, to mobilise the necessary resources to set up centres of excellence with a large concentration of top researchers. For both Germany and France, per student public expenditures on tertiary education are slightly below the Organisation for Economic Co-operation and Development (OECD) average and are half the level of U.S. Universities.

When the first SJTU ranking was published at the end of 2003, the daily paper Le Monde ran an article on January 24, 2004, entitled "The Great Misery of French Universities." The university presidents and union leaders interviewed for that article argued that the lack of budgetary resources and the rigidities associated with their utilisation were the main explanations for the demise of the French university system. Finally, in both countries, universities are government entities constrained by civil service employment rules and rigid management controls.

This means, in particular, that it is not possible to pay higher salaries to reward the more productive academics or to attract world-class researchers or to invest in leading-edge research facilities. For example, the salaries of French business administration professors are 20 percent lower than those of their U.S. Counterparts.

Commenting on the 2005 initiative of the European Union to create a European Institute of Innovation and Technology (EIT) after the MIT model, the scientific magazine Nature noted in a March 2008 editorial that the very existence of the EIT concept and its survival through the rough seas of EU politics is an indictment of Europe's suffocating national bureaucracies, which have made it impossible for universities and publicly funded research institutes to evolve into MITs on their own. "Elite" has too often been treated as a dirty word, and interactions with industry considered a betrayal of academic purity. In many countries, including France, Germany and Italy, it is still generally impossible to offer internationally competitive packages for top researchers.

The EIT may yet surprise its critics. Either way, national efforts to boost universities are by far the best way to address the problems that the EIT is intended to solve. In the case of France, two additional structural features complicate the situation further. First, according to Orivel , one of the main reasons why French universities are not internationally competitive is the dual structure of the tertiary education system.

The top engineering and professional schools (grenades Eccles) recruit the best students through very competitive national examinations, while the universities receive the bulk of secondary school graduates who have automatic access. Bccause the grenades écoles are predominantly elite, professionally oriented schools, they conduct very little research; as a result, most doctoral students in the research universities do not come from the most academically qualified student groups. This is quite unlike the practice in more competitive university systems in the United States, the United Kingdom, or Japan. Second, the strict separation between the research institutes affiliated with the Centre National de la Recherche Scientific (the National Centre for Scientific Research, or CNRS) and the research departments of the universities results in the dispersion of human and financial resources. The strength of world-class universities is that research is usually integrated at all levels.

Alignment of Success Factors

Finally, it is important to stress that it is the combination of these three sets of features concentration of talent, abundant funding, and appropriate governance that makes the difference. The dynamic interaction among these three groups of factors is the distinguishing characteristic of high-ranking universities.

The results of the recent survey of European universities confirm that funding and governance influence performance together. They indicate clearly that the higher-ranked universities tend to enjoy increased management autonomy, which, in turn, increases the efficiency of spending and results in higher research productivity.

Having an appropriate governance framework without sufficient resources or the ability to attract top talent does not work either. Similarly, just investing money in an institution or making it very selective in terms of student admission is not sufficient to build a world-class university, as illustrated by the case of Brazil's top university, the University of Sao Paul (USP). Brazil is the 5th most populated nation and the 10th largest economy on the planet, it is among the six largest producers of cars in the world, it has world-class companies such as Embers and Aracruz Cellulose, but there is no Brazilian university among the 100 top-ranked universities in the world.

How is it that USP, the country's foremost university, does not make it into the top group in the international rankings, despite having some of the features of world-class universities? When it was created in 1934, the USP founders and first leaders made it a point to hire only prominent professors from all over Europe.

Today, it is the most selective institution in Brazil, it has the highest number of top-rated graduate programs, and every year it produces more PhD graduates than any U.S. University.At the same time, USP's ability to manage its resources is constrained by rigid civil service regulations, even though it is the richest university in the country. Added to this is the fact that, at USP as in other Brazilian universities, the spirit of democracy has translated into multiple representative bodies (assemblies) which complicates decision making and the implementation of any forward-looking reform. USP has very few linkages with the international research community, and only 3 percent of its graduate students are from outside Brazil.

The university is very inward looking: most students come from the state of São Paul, and the majority of professors are USP graduates (this latter feature of endogamy being a typical feature of European universities, as discussed earlier). Foreign students are forbidden to write a doctoral dissertation in a language other than Portuguese. According to Schwartzman , the key missing element is the absence of a vision of excellence to challenge the status quo and transform the university. The lack of ambitious strategic vision can be observed as much at the national and state government levels as among the university leadership.

The Role of Government

In the past, the role of government in nurturing the growth of world-class universities was not a critical factor. The history of the Ivy League universities in the United States reveals that, by and large, they grew to prominence as a result of incremental progress, rather than by deliberate government intervention. Similarly, the Universities of Oxford and Cambridge evolved over the centuries of their own volition, with variable levels of public funding, but with considerable autonomy in terms of governance, definition of mission, and direction.

Today, however, it is unlikely that a world-class university can be rapidly created without a favourable policy environment and direct public initiative and support, if only because of the high costs involved in setting up advanced research facilities and capacities. At Bach reports a late 19th century conversation between John D. Rockefeller and the then-President of Harvard University, Charles W. Eliot, in which Rockefeller asked Eliot what would be the cost of establishing a world-class university. Eliot's answer was "50 million dollars and 200 years." However, the University of Chicago was able, at the beginning of the 20th century, to achieve this goal within only 20 years, although the price tag at that time was already more than US$ 100 million.

Professor At Bach estimates the cost of creating a world-class university today to be around US$ 100 million, and, indeed, the actual cost would very likely be much higher. The School of Medicine established by Cornell University in Qatar in 2002 cost alone US$750 million. The government of Pakistan is planning to spend US$700 million for each of the new Universities of Engineering, Science, and Technology that it is planning to create in the next few years.

In that respect, some of the key questions that national authorities need to ponder is how many if any world-class universities their country can afford and how to make sure that investment for that purpose will not come at the expense of investing in other priority areas in the tertiary education sector. Adopting the goal of building world-class universities does not imply, however, that all universities in a given country can be or should aspire to be of international standing.

A more attainable and appropriate goal would be, rather, to develop an integrated system of teaching, research, and technology-oriented institutions that feed into and support a few centres of excellence that focus on value-added fields and chosen areas of comparative advantage and that can eventually evolve into world-class institutions.

The California higher-education master plan, formulated in the early 1960s, is a good example of strategic vision translated into a highly diversified system. The California system of higher education integrates and supports a broad array of tertiary education institutions, which are connected through administrative and academic bridges and clear recognition rules. Today, California boasts 474 tertiary education institutions: 145 public universities, 109 private universities, and the remaining institutions divided between community colleges and vocational oriented institutes. Out of these, two private universities (Stanford University and the California Institute of Technology) and four public universities (the Universities of California at Berkeley, Los Angeles, San Diego, and San Francisco) are among the top 20 universities in the SJTU ranking.

Higher education is increasingly a tale of two worlds, with elite schools getting richer and buying up all the talent. It's only fitting that Watchman College, Princeton's new student residence, is named for bay CEO Meg Whitman, because it's a billionaire's mansion in the form of a dram. After Whitman pledged $30 million, administrators tore up their budget and gave architect Diametric Paraphrase virtual carte blanche. Each student room has triple-glazed mahogany casement windows made of leaded glass. The dining hall boasts a 35-foot ceiling gabled in oak and a "state of the art servers." By the time the building complex in the Collegiate Gothic style opened in August, it had cost Princeton $136 million, or $272,000 for each of the 500 undergraduates who will live there. Whitman College's extravagance epitomises the fabulous prosperity of America's top tier of private universities.

The next relevant set of questions is about the most effective approach to achieve the proposed goal of becoming world-class. International experience shows that three basic strategies can be followed to establish world-class universities:

— Governments could consider upgrading a small number of existing universities that have the potential of excelling (picking winners).

— Governments could encourage a number of existing institutions to merge and transform into a new university that would achieve the type of synergist corresponding to a world-class institution (hybrid formula).

— Governments could create new world-class universities from scratch (clean-slate approach).
— Each one of these approaches presents advantages and drawbacks that are now explored.

Upgrading Existing Institutions

One of the main benefits of this first approach is that the costs can be significantly less than those of building new institutions from scratch. This is the strategy followed by China since the early 1980s, with a sequence of carefully targeted reforms and investment programs. Indeed, Beijing University and Tsinghua University, China's top two universities, have been granted special privileges by the national authorities, allowing them to select the best students from every province before any other university, much to the consternation of the other leading universities around the country.

But this approach is unlikely to succeed in countries where the governance structure and arrangements that have historically prevented the emergence of world-class universities are not drastically revised. A comparison of the experiences of Malaysia and Singapore can serve to illustrate this point. Because Singapore was initially one of the provinces of the Malaysian Kingdom during the first few years following independence from the British, the contrasting stories of the University of Malaya and of the National University of Singapore (NUS) can be quite instructive, given their common cultural and colonial origins.

At independence, the University of Malaya operated as a two-campus university, one in Kuala Lumpier and the other in Singapore. The former evolved into the flagship University of Malaya from the very beginning, and the other became the University of Singapore, which merged with Nanyang University in 1980 to create NUS. By all global ranking measures, NUS today functions as a true world-class university, while the University of Malaya struggles as a seconder research university. In examining the different evolutionary paths of these two institutions, several factors appear to be constraining the University of Malaya's capacity to improve and innovate as effectively as NUS: affirmative action and restrictive admission policies, lower levels of financial support, and tightly controlled immigration regulations regarding foreign faculty.

The affirmative action policy implemented by the Malaysian government in favour of the children of the Malaya majority population

(Bumiputras) has significantly opened up opportunities for that segment of the population. The proportion of Malaya students the Malaya population represents 52 percent of the total Malaysian population went from about 30 percent to two-thirds of the total student population between the early 1970s and the late 1980s. The proportion of Chinese students decreased from 56 to 29 percent over the same period.

The downstage of these equity policies was that they prevented the university from being very selective in its student admissions to target the best and brightest in the country. Large numbers of academically qualified Chinese and Indian students, in particular, were unable to attend Malaysia's best universities and had to seek tertiary education abroad, thereby removing important talent from Malaysia In addition to restrictions among its own population, the Malaysian Ministry of Higher Education places a 5 percent cap on the number of foreign undergraduate students that public universities can enrol.

By contrast, the proportion of foreign students at NUS is 20 percent at the undergraduate level and 43 percent at the graduate level. The cost of their studies is highly subsidised by NUS. The primary consideration for attracting these foreign students is not to generate income, as often happens in U.K. and Australian universities, but to bring in highly qualified individuals who will enrich the pool of students.

NUS is also able to mobilise nearly twice as many financial resources as the University of Malaya (US$ 205 million annual budget versus US$118 million, respectively) through a combination of cost sharing, investment revenue, fund-raising, and government resources. The success of NUS's fund-raising efforts is largely the result of the generous matching-grant program set up by the government in the late 1990s as part of the Thinking Schools, Learning Nation Initiative, which provided a three-to one matching at the beginning and is now down to one-to-one. As a result, the annual per student expenditures at NUS and the University of Malaya were US$ 6,300 and US$4,053, respectively, in 2006.

Finally, in Malaysia, on one hand, civil service regulations and a rigid financial framework make it difficult, if not impossible, to provide competitive compensation packages to attract the most competent professors and researchers, particularly foreign faculty. NUS, on the other hand, is not bound by similar legal constraints. The PS21 public service reform project in the early 2000s aimed at promoting a culture of excellence and innovation in all public institutions, including the two universities. NUS is therefore able to bring in top researchers and professors from all over the world, pay a global market rate for them, and provide performance incentives to stimulate competition and to retain the best and the brightest. Indeed, a good number of Malaysia's top researchers have been recruited by NUS.

Governments need, therefore, to construct a supportive external policy environment and create the financing and regulatory conditions that enable and encourage their universities to compete at an international level on a host of indicators on which the quality and relevance of university education are commonly assessed, including reputation and awards, foreign students and faculty, and research grants. One way to facilitate this is to grant management autonomy to the universities. Another is to provide performance-based financing, and a third is to put in place favourable taxation systems that allow companies and philanthropists to make tax-free donations to universities. The United States and India provide good examples of this practice.

Merging Existing Institutions

The second possible approach to building up a world-class university consists of promoting mergers among existing institutions. France and Denmark are two countries that have diligently embarked on this path in recent years. In France, individual universities and grenades écoles are exploring the feasibility of merging on a regional basis. In Denmark, the government has set up an Innovation Fund that would reward, among other things, the combination of similar institutions. In China, too, a number of mergers have taken place to consolidate existing institutions.

For example, Beijing Medical University merged with Beijing University in 2000; similarly, in Shanghai, Fudan University merged with a medical university, and Zhejiang University was created out of the merger of five universities. In 2004, in the United Kingdom, the Victoria University of Manchester (VUM) and the University of Manchester Institute of Science and Technology (UMIST) merged, creating the largest university in the United Kingdom, with the purposefully stated goal. Also in the United Kingdom recently, Cardiff University and the South Wales School of Medicine have merged as a deliberate step to establish a world-class university in Wales. These mergers, in most cases between already strong institutions, have often the explicit or implicit goal of creating larger and more comprehensive research universities in clear response to the fact that international rankings compare the number of publications and faculty awards of institutions independently from the size of their student enrolment.

The government of the Russian Federation is also relying on amalgamation as a key policy within its overall strategy of developing elite research universities. In 2007, two pilot federal universities were set up by merging existing institutions in Rostovon-Don in southern Russia and in the Siberian city of Krasnoyarsk. The two new institutions will also receive additional funding to support efforts to allow them to recruit highly qualified researchers and equip state of-the-art laboratories.

The great advantage of mergers is that they can result in stronger institutions able to capitalise on the new asynergies that their combined human and financial resources may generate. But mergers can also be risky, potentially aggravating problems instead of resolving them. In the case of France, for example, mergers would augment the critical mass of researchers and bring about a higher place in the SJTU ranking that favours research output, but they would not address the fundamental limitations of French universities, including inflexible admission policies, a weak financial basis, rigid governance arrangements, and outdated management practices. The Danish case, however, has greater chances of success because the push for mergers is taking place within the context of an overall governance reform aimed at transforming all universities in the country into more flexible and dynamic institutions.

Another danger associated with mergers is that the newly consolidated institution could suffer because of clashing institutional cultures. It has become clear, for example, that the previously mentioned merger between VUM and UMIST has not been as successful as expected or originally perceived. Currently acknowledging a £30 million budget deficit and the likelihood of up to 400 jobs lost on the campus, the University of Manchester has had immediate experience with the complexities of merging.

Among the main problems encountered are duplication of staff and curricular offerings, the political challenges of engendering support for the merger by making promises that have proven detrimental to keep (for example, committing to no compulsory redundancy at the time of merger and at present foreseeing a need to cut positions as rapidly as possible), and the short-term absorption of labour contracts and institutional debt. In addition, the newly formed institution, with its commitment to achieving world-class status, invested heavily in hiring "superstar" academic staff and supplying them with correspondingly superstar facilities.

This exacerbated further the staffing debt that the institution inherited with the merging of the distinct and separate institutional staffs and their individual cultures, norms, and labour contracts into the one university. It remains to be seen how Manchester will address these financial, cultural, and interpersonal obstacles while simultaneously maintaining its quest for world-class status.

Thus, one of the main challenges when undertaking a merger is to create a shared academic culture and transformation vision among all constituting units (faculties, schools, departments) and bring internal coherence to the newly established institution. In many cases, the leaders of merged universities are severely constrained by the high level of independence Paths to Transformation 45 claimed by constituting units. The new university established by merging existing universities may carry the legacy of the old brands, which in some cases may actually be an obstacle in attracting excellent students and staff. The leadership of the new, consolidated institution requires the political savvy to manage the various needs of conflicting constituents.

Creating New Institutions

In countries where institutional habits, cumbersome governance structures, and bureaucratic management practices prevent traditional universities from being innovative, creating new institutions may be the best approach, provided that it is possible to staff them with people not influenced by the culture of traditional universities and provided that financial resources are not a constraint. New institutions can emerge from the private sector, or governments can allow new public institutions to operate under a more favourable regulatory framework. Kazakhstan is a country intent on following this path as it seeks to make its economy less dependent on oil and more competitive overall.

The government of Kazakhstan has decided to set up a new international university in Astana. The plan is that this university will follow a highly innovative multi-disciplinary curriculum in cooperation with leading international universities. In the same vein, the government of Saudi Arabia announced in late 2007 its plans for a US$ 3 billion graduate research university, King Abdullah University of Science and Technology, which would operate outside the purview of the Ministry of Higher Education to allow for greater management autonomy and academic freedom than the regular universities of the kingdom enjoy. One of the earlier success stories in that respect was the establishment of the Indian Institutes of Technology, which, in the past decades, have gradually risen to world-class status.

A third promising example is the creation of the Paris School of Economics (PSE) in February 2007, modelled after the London School of Economics and Political Science (LSE). This initiative combines elements of mergers with the creation of a brand new type of institution in the French context. Co-sponsors by four grenades écoles, the University of Paris I (the Serbian), and CNRS, PSE will operate as a private foundation re-grouping the best economics departments from the participating institutions. Its initial funding comes not only from the state and the region but also from private companies and a U.S. Foundation. Unlike traditional French universities, PSE will be highly selective in terms of incoming students. Many of the core professors will come from the most prestigious universities in the world.

The creation of new institutions may also have the side benefit of stimulating existing ones into becoming more responsive to a more competitive environment. Examples from many parts of the world showing the emergence of high-quality private universities in countries with a predominantly public tertiary education sector have provoked the public universities into becoming more strategically focused. In Uruguay, the venerable University of the Republic which had exercised a monopoly over tertiary education in the country for 150 years started a strategic planning process and considered establishing postgraduate programs for the first time only after being confronted in the mid-1990s with competition from newly established private universities. Similarly, in Russia, the creation of the Higher School of Economics and of the Moscow School of Social and Economic Sciences in the 1990s pressured the Department of Economics at the State University of Moscow to revamp its curriculum and get more actively involved in international exchanges.

Maintaining the favourable conditions that are instrumental for the establishment of a new world-class institution requires constant vigilance, as the growing faculty shortage faced by the IITs illustrates. India's economic success has translated into a much larger income gap between the Institutes and industry than existed in the past. As a result, fewer promising graduates seek an academic career. It is estimated that the IITs are already suffering from a shortage of at least 900 qualified faculty. At the Delhi IIT alone, 29 percent of faculty

positions are unfilled. Without the autonomy to raise salaries and offer more competitive employment packages, the IITs are at risk of losing their competitive edge. The younger Indian Institutes of Management face the same hurdle in their quest for world-class status. The IITs and the Institutes of Management are also concerned about the recent decision of the Federal Ministry of Human Resource Development requiring them to implement a 49.5 percent quota ("reserved places") for various minority groups (Scheduled Castes, Scheduled Tribes, and Other Backward Classes) in the faculty. The institutions are asking the government to grant them the same exemption from reservation as the one given to the Data Institute of Fundamental Research, the Bhabha Atomic Research Centre, and the Hari-Chandra Research Institute because of their status as "institutes of national importance".

Finally, one of the major risks with implementing this third strategy in developing countries is that emulation by other institutions in the national tertiary education system may not be possible if most of the scarce public funds are concentrated in a few universities. Similarly, the good practices applied in the new institutions could simply not be applicable within the tight governance environment that usually binds public tertiary education institutions. This could lead to a highly dual system beyond what would be generally expected from a reasonably tiered system.

Evaluating the Approaches

Governments need to assess the degree to which they want to manage the process in a centralised way, cherry-picking institutions where centres of excellence could be established or boosted, or whether it would be preferable to steer the tertiary education system at a distance, relying on broad strategic orientations and financial incentives to entice the most dynamic universities to transform themselves.

International experience suggests that in medium to large countries, the latter approach, which encourages competitive behaviours among tertiary education institutions, could be more effective in the long run. The China 211 and 985 projects, the Brain 21 program in South Korea, the German Initiative for Excellence, and the Millennium Institutes recently established in Chile are examples of how countries stimulate the creation or consolidation of research centres of excellence.

In smaller states, where the capacity for mobilising and combining public and private resources is constrained, greater selectivity in investment funding may be a more appropriate approach to optimising the deployment and utilisation of public resources. In New Zealand, for instance, the country's premier tertiary education institution, the University of Auckland, has been calling for targeted government efforts to help transform the university into a leading research university:

The Government's acknowledgement (through the reforms) that not all institutions are, or should be, the same is a critical and ultimately enabling first step towards the positioning of one or more New Zealand research universities as institutions of international quality and status. The challenge New Zealand must address is that the most successful tertiary institutions in the world, those against which the best universities ought to be benchmark themselves, operate with levels of public investment in New Zealand struggle to comprehend. To cite just one example, federal and state funding in the United States public universities is estimated at US$12,000 per student approximately twice that of New Zealand in equivalent purchasing terms. And that doesn't take into account the additional impact of the substantial endowments that many US universities enjoy.

A critical mass of leading staff and outstanding students in a university, enabled by adequate investment and an international reputation for teaching and research, produces research outputs, an atmosphere of intellectual excitement, and productive relationships with industry that cannot be replicated elsewhere. To cite just one example of what is possible, a November 2006 study by the Ministry of Research, Science and Technology found that of 16 New Zealand-developed drugs currently in clinical trials approved by the US Food and Drug Administration, 13 had been developed by the universities and 12 of them by The University of Auckland!

To reach this goal, and achieve the characteristics shared by world-class research universities, vision, commitment, and a desire for change are required. These will assist New Zealand's leading universities to provide a learning environment of the highest quality, to lead the advancement of knowledge creation, intellectual discovery, and innovation within New Zealand, and to take our place with world-class research universities on the global stage. Vision, commitment, and a desire for change will, however, not be sufficient.

Increased levels of public and private investment will also be required, along with a particular commitment to the stated aim of the current reforms differentiation. Both Australia and the US concentrate research excellence (and investment) in those institutions most likely to produce results for economic and social development.

The Role of Private Sector

It is important to stress that national governments are not the only major player when it comes to facilitating the establishment of world class institutions. In large countries and federal systems, regional or provincial authorities often play a critical role, as illustrated by the active role played by the Californian authorities in designing and establishing an integrated system of tertiary education in the 1960s or more recently in establishing special Innovation Funds to strengthen linkages between the research universities and the regional economy.

Similarly, in the past 10 years, the Shanghai municipality has given active support to its leading universities, especially Fudan University, as part of its accelerated development policies. In the State of Novae Leon in Mexico, the business community has also contributed substantially to the success of the Institute Technological by de Studios Superiors de Monterrey (the Monterrey Institute of Technology and Higher Education, or ITESM).

The complementary role of the private sector in supporting the development of world-class universities should not be overlooked either. Private industry can make important financial contributions to help increase the endowment of top institutions, as happened in Singapore and Hong Kong, China. In some cases, philanthropists have even taken the initiative to launch a new institution with aspirations of excellence, as demonstrated by the examples of Olein College of Engineering in Massachusetts or Quest University Canada in British Columbia. An Indian billionaire, Anil Agarwal, gave US$1 billion to establish a multi-disciplinary research institution in Orissa, India. In Germany, Klaus Jacobs donated 200 million euros to the new private International University Barmen. Besides potential funding, the active participation of private sector leaders on the board of the new institutions is important to steer its development.

The contribution of the private sector can also take the form of close linkages to ensure inputs into the choice of relevant programs, the design of appropriate curricula, and full alignment of the new institution's applied research agenda with the needs of the local economy.

Strategic Dimensions at the Institutional Level

The first and perhaps most important aspect at this level is the quality of leadership and the strategic vision developed by the would-be world-class university. The second element is the proper sequences of plans and activities envisaged to reach the proposed goal. Finally, particular attention needs to be given to the internationalisation strategy of the university.

Leadership and Strategic Vision

The establishment of a world-class university requires, above all, strong leadership, a bold vision of the institution's mission and goals, and a clearly articulated strategic plan to translate the vision into concrete programs and targets.

Universities that aspire to better results engage in an objective assessment of their strengths and areas for improvement, set new stretch goals, and design and implement a renewal plan that can lead to improved performance. By contrast, as illustrated by the earlier discussion of the University of São Paul, many institutions are complacent in their outlook, lack an ambitious vision of a better future, and continue to operate as they have in the past, ending up with a growing performance gap compared with that of their national or international competitors.

Recent research on university leadership suggests that in the case of top research universities, the best-performing institutions have leaders who combine good managerial skills and a successful research career. To be able to develop an appropriate vision for the future of the university and to implement this vision in an effective manner, the university president, vice-chancellor, or rector needs to fully understand the core agenda of the institution and to be able to apply the vision with the necessary operational skills.

A case study of the University of Leeds in the United Kingdom illustrates how the arrival of a new leader in 2003 marked the beginning of a conscious effort to reverse a downward trend through carefully planned and implemented strategic change. Rapid growth in student numbers (the second-largest university in the United Kingdom) had led to tensions between the teaching and research missions of the university, resulting in diminishing research income and results. Among the main challenges faced by the new vice-chancellor was the need to create a sense of urgency among the entire university community and to convince everyone of the importance of achieving a better alignment between corporate goals and the contribution of individual faculties and departments with a long tradition of autonomy.

Institutions aspiring to become world-class universities do not need to replicate what the current top universities do; they can innovate in many different ways. One possible path is to adopt a radically different approach to organising the curriculum and pedagogy of the institution, as the newly established Olein College of Engineering in Massachusetts in the United States and the Linkage wing University of Creative Technology in Malaysia have attempted in the field of engineering and technology.

The Franking W. Olein College of Engineering was founded in 1999 with a US$400 million endowment from the Olein Foundation and the mandate to implement an innovative engineering curriculum. Olein College seeks to produce graduates trained in the new skills identified in a 2005 report, Educating the Engineer of 2020, such as competency in teamwork, communication, entrepreneurial thinking, creativity and design, and cross-disciplinary thinking. Most of the learning at Olein takes place through design-build team projects.

All students are required to complete a program in the fundamentals of business and entrepreneurship, as well as a special project in the arts, humanities, or social sciences. To foster its philosophy of interdisciplinary work, the college does not have any academic departments. To encourage a culture of continuous innovation and risk taking among professors, there is also no tenure system at Olein. All students receive merit scholarships to cover the cost of tuition and living expenses in Olein's residential environment.

Even though it is too early to draw definitive conclusions the first batch of graduates completed their degrees in May 2006 there are clear indications that the Olein College of Engineering has managed to attract talented students and excellent faculty, to put in place an innovative and stimulating curriculum, and to develop a culture of intellectual empowerment. Its graduates appear to be successful in finding appealing jobs or accessing top graduate schools.

Similarly, the Limkok wing University of Creative Technology in Malaysia has established itself as an innovative private institution emphasising the acquisition of creativity and design competencies relevant to a wide array of activities in industry and services. The rapid development of its new campuses in Botswana, Lesotho, and London attests to the success of its model.

Another innovative approach links the transformation of the institution to shifting regional or local development opportunities, as illustrated by the example of Clemson University in South Carolina, United States. Sometimes, going through a crisis can energise an institution into changing its culture and revitalising itself, as happened with the Catholic University of Leuven (Belgium) in the late 1960s after it faced a large financial deficit. Today, it ranks among the top European universities.

The Pontifical Catholic University of Peru (in Lima) went through a similar positive transformation in the late 1990s after a drastic reduction in student enrolment that led the university to undertake a thorough strategic planning exercise. Concerned that student demand was diminishing because of the location of the university in an area of the capital city that had lost its appeal over the years, the leadership thought briefly about moving to a new site, close to where the middle classes were now living. But extensive consultations with stockholders during the strategic planning period made the university aware that the fundamental issue was one of deteriorating quality and relevance. Drastic renewal measures were taken, including course redesign and a strong emphasis on continuous quality monitoring and improvement, resulting in higher student demand and successful fund-raising.

The subjective nature of world class status means that institutions will attempt to address those dimensions that are considered in assessing reputations and that are visible. In this respect, research activity, publications, citations, and major faculty awards are highly visible and measurable while the quality of the educational process is not. Thus, it is not surprising to see a focus on research criteria in the surveys and in the efforts of institutions to promote their importance and little or no attempt to measure and assess teaching quality or educational activities. Indeed, there is a tacit assumption that if an institution is highly competitive in its admissions that the educational quality is also very high, even without measuring that quality. Yet, student competition for admission may be based upon a prestigious reputation that is largely due to the research visibility of a university rather than its educational virtues.

Sequencing

Time is an important dimension that also needs to be factored into the strategic plan of the aspiring world-class university. Developing a culture of excellence does not happen from one day to the next. Proper sequencing of interventions and careful balance among the various quantitative objectives are required to avoid experiencing the kinds of growing pains that some of the Chinese universities have encountered. It is important to stress that vision development and strategic planning are not one-time exercises. In a highly competitive environment, the more successful organisations in both business and academy are those that are relentless in challenging themselves in the pursuit of better and more effective ways of responding to client needs. With constant replenishment of intellectual capital, performance is never static in the best universities. The most successful institutions are not content with relying on past accomplishments, but always aspire to be among the best in the world. They are successful in creating, internally, a supportive atmosphere that encourages everyone to define and pursue stretch goals.

This is one of the characteristics of the Olein College of Engineering, whose president defined the challenge of continuous improvement in the following terms: Innovation and continuous improvement require certain cultural attitudes and commitments. First, an implicit humility is required to embrace the notion that improvement is always possible, and that we can always learn from others outside our community. Listening to those outside academy has not always been the strong suit of American higher education. In addition, continuous improvement is only possible if continuous assessment is employed to guide the process.

Not even the most famous universities are immune from the necessity of evolving and adapting to changing circumstances, as the University of Oxford's failed attempt at financial reform illustrates. In the current increasingly competitive market for academics, central authorities at the university face the need for additional resources to continue hiring internationally renowned professors and researchers.

They have been constrained, however, by centuries-old governance arrangements and authority structures that give the control of a large share of the university's wealth to its individual colleges. The colleges have no desire to share their resources coming from traditional endowments and a large intake of foreign postgraduate students whose fees are more than three times higher than those paid by domestic students.

One aspect of the reform proposals submitted in 2006 by Vice-Chancellor John Hood, who had been recruited from New Zealand to lead Oxford in attempting to redress the balance, was to give more power over these resources to the university's central leadership, while also allowing for increased financial oversight by outsiders. The reform was ultimately rejected by Oxford's academic community, leading to Hood's decision to step down at the end of his five-year term in 2009. A number of allium have expressed concern about the potentially negative consequences of these arrangements, which may have resulted in academic overload and lack of proper supervision of postgraduate students.

Internationalisation Dimension

One way of accelerating the transformation into a world-class university is to use internationalisation strategies effectively. An influx of top foreign students can be instrumental in upgrading the academic level of the student population and enriching the quality of the learning experience through the multi-cultural dimension. In this regard, the capacity to offer programs in a foreign language, especially English, can be a powerful attraction factor. Among the 100 top universities according to the SJTU ranking, 11 come from non-native-English-speaking countries where some graduate programs are offered in English.

The ability to attract foreign professors and researchers is also an important determinant or characteristic of excellence. Universities need to be able to offer incentives, including flexible remuneration and employment conditions, to recruit top academics from other countries. These talented individuals can help upgrade existing departments or establish graduate programs and research centres in new areas of competitive advantage. In the United Kingdom, for example, 27 percent of all academic staff appointed in 2005/06 were foreign nationals. In cases in which it is difficult to attract foreign faculty on a full-time basis, the university can start by bringing in leading foreign scholars on a temporary basis.

To facilitate the contribution of foreign scholars, a number of aspiring world-class universities have formed fruitful partnerships with top universities in industrial countries. This was the case with the Indian Institutes of Technology in the early years of their establishment. More recently, one emerging world-class university, the National University of Singapore, has relied extensively on strategic alliances with the Australian National University, Duke University, Eindhoven University of Technology in the Netherlands, Harvard University, Johns Hopkins University, MIT, and Tsinghua University in China, to mention only the better-known partner institutions. These partnerships have not always functioned smoothly, however, as shown by the recent rupture with Johns Hopkins University in Singapore because of dissatisfaction with the quality of faculty and outputs offered by the foreign partner.

Attracting leading scholars from the disappear is another internationalisation strategy that a few universities in India and China have implemented with success. Beijing University, for example, has hired hundreds of academics of Chinese origin. As part of its human resource strategy, the university closely monitors good Chinese scholars abroad and creates favourable conditions for their return. Mexico, Scotland, and South Africa have also started to implement interesting strategies to harness the contribution of talented nationals living outside the country.

Related to this internationalisation dimension of improving an institution's global reputation is the extent to which national researchers have the linguistic competence to publish in English. One way in which institutions and academics advance their reputation is by their presence in scientific publications. Because citation indexes compile data primarily from journals published in English, the facility with which academics. Attracting the best students, scholars, and research partners from anywhere they can be found has become the modus operandi of the world's best institutions. As borders become softer, the competition for the best has become more intense.

In the case of science-and technology oriented universities, the ability to attract research contracts from foreign firms and multinational corporations is a good measure of the scientific standing of rising universities. In recent years, a few Chinese and Indian universities have received important research contracts from North American and European firms, sometimes at the expense of universities in the countries of origin of these companies.

At the National Level

- Why does the country need a world-class university?
- What are the economic rationale and the expected added value compared with the contribution of existing institutions?
- What is the vision for this university?
- What niche will it occupy?
- What would be the investment and recurrent costs of a world-class university?
- How many world-class universities are desirable and affordable as a public sector investment?
- What strategy would work best in the country context:
    - Upgrading existing institutions.
    - Merging existing institutions.
    - Creating new institutions.
- What should be the selection process among existing institutions if the first or second approach is chosen?
- What will be the relationship and articulation between the new institutions and existing tertiary education institutions?
- How will the transformation be financed?
- What share should fall under the public budget?
- What share should be borne by the private sector?
- What incentives should be offered (for example, land grants and tax exemptions)?
- What are the governance arrangements that must be put in place to facilitate this transformation and support suitable management practices?
- What level of autonomy and forms of accountability will be appropriate?
- What will the government's role be in this process?

At the Institutional Level

- How can the institution build the best leadership team?
- What are the vision and mission statements?

- What are the specific goals that the university is seeking to achieve?
- In what niches will it pursue excellence in teaching and research?
- What is the target student population?
- Should the university be set up in partnership with a foreign institution?
- What type of partnership should be sought?
- What are the internationalisation goals that the university needs to achieve (with regard to faculty, students, programs, and so forth)?
- What is the likely cost of the proposed qualitative leap, and how is it going to be funded?
- How will success be measured? What monitoring systems, outcome indicators, and accountability mechanisms will be used?

In the tertiary education sector, the World Bank's work with governments in developing and transition countries has focused essentially on system wide issues and reforms. World Bank assistance has combined policy advice, analytical work, capacity-building activities, and financial support through loans and credits to facilitate and accompany the design and implementation of major tertiary education reforms.

In recent years, however, a growing number of countries have asked the World Bank to help them identify the main obstacles preventing their universities from becoming world-class universities and map out ways of transforming them toward this goal. To accommodate these requests, the World Bank has found that it needs to consider how to align support for individual institutions with its traditional emphasis on system wide innovations and reforms. Experiences to date suggest that this goal can be achieved through three types of complementary interventions that would be combined in a variety of configurations under different country circumstances: Technical assistance and guidance to assist countries in:

- Identifying possible options and afford ability.
- Deciding the number of elite universities that they need and can fund in a sustainable way.

Role of World Bank

In the tertiary education sector, the World Bank's work with governments in developing and transition countries has focused essentially on system wide issues and reforms. World Bank assistance has combined policy advice, analytical work, capacity-building activities, and financial support through loans and credits to facilitate and accompany the design and implementation of major tertiary education reforms.

In recent years, however, a growing number of countries have asked the World Bank to help them identify the main obstacles preventing their universities from becoming world-class universities and map out ways of transforming them toward this goal. To accommodate these requests, the World Bank has found that it needs to consider how to align support for individual institutions with its traditional emphasis on system wide innovations and reforms. Experiences to date suggest that this goal can be achieved through three types of complementary interventions that would be combined in a variety of configurations under different country circumstances:

— Facilitation and brokering to help new elite institutions get exposure to relevant international experience through workshops and study tours. This can involve linking up with foreign partner institutions that can provide capacity-building support during the start-up years of the new institution or the transformation period of an existing institution aspiring to become world-class. The World Bank can also facilitate policy dialogue by bringing different stockholders and partners together to agree on the vision and to garner support for the new institutions.

— Financial support to fund pre-investment studies for the design of the project and investment costs for the actual establishment of the planned institution.

In countries that have established a positive regulatory and incentive framework to promote the development of private tertiary education, International Finance Corporation (IFC) loans and guarantees can also be used to complement or replace World Bank Group financial support if the target university or universities are set up or transformed as public private partnerships.

It is, of course, important to tailor these options to specific country situations. Upper-middle-income countries are unlikely to be seeking financial aid as such, but are definitely looking for advice reflecting the World Bank's comparative advantage as both a knowledge broker and an observer of international experience. This advice could be provided on a fee-for-service basis.

Middle-income countries may be interested in receiving both technical and financial assistance. Based on the World Bank's experience with Innovation Funds in a large number of countries, using a competitive approach could be envisaged to ensure that funding goes to those institutions that have formulated the most innovative strategic visions and developed well-thought-out implementation plans. Low-income countries, especially those of relatively small size (fewer than 5 million inhabitants), confront a unique set of challenges in their efforts to establish a flagship institution that could address critical human skills requirements and advanced research needs.

Issues and Concerns

The highest ranked universities are the ones that make significant contributions to the advancement of knowledge through research, teach with the most innovative curricula and pedagogical methods under most conducive circumstances, make research an integral component of undergraduate teaching, and produce graduates who stand out because of their success in intensely competitive arenas during their education and, more importantly, after graduation. It is these concrete accomplishments and the international reputation associated with these sustained achievements that make these institutions world class. There is no universal recipe or magic formula for "making" a world-class university.

National contexts and institutional set-ups vary widely. Countries must therefore choose, among the various possible pathways, a strategy that plays to its former strengths and present resources. But international experience provides a few lessons regarding the key features of such universities (high concentration of talent, abundance of resources, and flexible governance arrangements) and successful approaches to move in that direction, from upgrading or merging existing institutions to creating new institutions altogether. Under any scenario, building a world-class university does not happen overnight. No matter how much money can be thrown at the endeavor, it is unrealistic to expect instant results. Creating a culture of excellence and achieving high quality outputs take many years.

Furthermore, the transformation of the university system cannot take place in isolation. The long term vision for creating world class universities, and its implementation, should be closely articulated with

(i) the country's overall economic and social development strategy,

(ii) ongoing changes and planned reforms at the lower levels of the education system, and

(iii) plans for the development of other types of tertiary education institutions in order to build an integrated system of teaching, research, and technology-oriented institutions.

In that respect, it is worth observing that, while world-class institutions are commonly equated with top research universities, there are also world-class tertiary education institutions which are neither research-focused nor operate as universities *strictu sensu*. The UK Open University, for example, is widely recognized as the premier distance education institution in the world, and yet it does not make the international rankings. Conestoga College in Ontario is ranked as the best community college in Canada, and in Germany the Fachhochschulen of Mannheim and Bremen have an outstanding reputation. Two European countries that have achieved remarkable progress as emerging knowledge economies, Finland and Ireland, do not boast any university among the top 50 in the world, but they have excellent technology-focused institutions. Even among universities, international rankings clearly favor research-intensive universities at the cost of excluding first-rate institutions that enroll primarily undergraduate students. As countries embark on the task of establishing world-class universities, they may also want to consider the desirability of creating, besides research universities, excellent alternative institutions to meet the wide range of education and training needs that the tertiary education system is expected to satisfy.

References

Alden, J. and G. Lin (2004). "Benchmarking the Characteristics of a World-Class University: Developing an International Strategy at University Level". London: The UK Higher Education Leadership Foundation. May 2004.

Altbach, Philip.G. (Summer 2005). A World-Class Country without World-Class Higher Education: India's 21st Century Dilemma. *International Higher Education.* Retrieved April 10, 2007.

Khoon, K.A. (2005). Hallmark of a World-Class University. *College Student Journal.* Retrieved April 10, 2007.

Kuznetsov, Y. (2006). *Diaspora Networks and the International Migration of Skills: How Countries Can Draw on their Talent Abroad.* Washington, DC: World Bank Institute Development Studies.

Yusuf, S. and K. Nabeshima (2007). *How Universities Promote Economic Growth.* Washington D.C., The World Bank.

Bibliography

Aho, E., Pitkanen, K. & Sahlberg, P. *Policy Development and Reform Principles in Finland since 1968.* Washington, DC: World Bank.

Åkerblom, M. (2007). "Study on Policies and Models for Research Funding". Report for Sida/ SAREC, Stockholm: Sida.

Alden, J. and G. Lin (2004). "Benchmarking the Characteristics of a World-Class University: Developing an International Strategy at University Level". London: The UK Higher Education Leadership Foundation. May 2004.

Altbach, Philip.G. (Summer 2005). A World-Class Country without World-Class Higher Education: India's 21st Century Dilemma. *International Higher Education.* Retrieved April 10, 2007.

Anon,. 55 *Policy Recommendations for Raising Croatia's Competitiveness.* Zagreb, Croatia: National Competitiveness Council.

Arimoto, A. (2008). "The Competitive Research Environment in the Japanese Context". In: Sala-zar-Clemeña, R. M. and Meek, L. V. (eds.), *Competition, Collaboration and Change in the Academic Profession: Shaping Higher Education's Contribution to Knowledge and Research.* Quezon City: Libro Amigo Publishers, pp. 46-60.

Arrow, K. (1962). The Economic Implications of Learning by Doing, The *Review of Economic Studies*, Vol. 29, No. 3, pp. 155-173.

Askling, B. and Henkel, M. (2000). "Higher Education Institutions". In: Kogan, M., Bauer, M., Bleiklie, I. and Henkel, M. (eds.), *Transforming Higher Education: A Comparative Study.* London: Jessica Kingsley, pp. 109-130.

Bell, D. *The Coming of the Post-Industrial Society: A Venture in Social Forecasting*, Middlesex: Penguin.

Bienenstock, A. (2006). "The Global Forum on International Quality Assurance and Accreditation". Papers presented at the UNESCO Forum's Global Colloquium on Research and Higher Education Policy. UNESCO Forum on Higher Education, Research and Knowledge, 29 November to 1 December 2006.

Bleiklie, I. and Kogan, M. (2007). "Organisation and Governance of Universities". *Higher Education Policy* (20) 4, pp. 477-493.

Braudel, F.(1979). *The Wheels of Commerce, Volume II of Civilization and Capitalism.* New York: Harper and Row.

Brooks, J. & Brooks, M.. *In Search of Understanding: The Case for Constructivist Classrooms.* Alexandria, VA: Association for Supervision and Curriculum Development.

Carnoy, M. (2000). *Sustaining Flexibility: Work, Family, and Community in the Information Age*. Cambridge, MA: Harvard University Press and New York: Russell Sage.

____, Castells, M., Cohen, S., and Cardoso, F.H. (1993). *The New Global Economy in the Information Age*. University Park. PA: Pennsylvania State University Press.

____. *Globalization and Educational Reform. What planners need to know?*. Paris: Unesco and IIEP.

Castells, M.(1996). *The Rise of the Network Society*. London: Blackwell.

Drucker P. *The Age of Discontinuity: Guidelines to our Changing Society*. London: Heinemann.

Edquist, C. (1997). *Systems of Innovation: Technologies, Institutions and Organisations*. Paperback. London: Pinter.

____. (2006). "Universities as Centres of Research and Knowledge Creation: An Endangered Species?" UNESCO Forum Global Colloquium, Centre for Innovation Research and Competence in the Learning Economy (CIRCLE), 20 November to 1 December. Lund, Sweden: Lund University.

Eduards, K. (2006). *Review of Sida's Research Cooperation: A Synthesis Report*. Swedish International Development Cooperation Agency (Sida). Stockholm.

El Kaffass, I. (2007). "Funding of Higher Education and Scientific Research in the Arab World". Presentation at the UNESCO Forum Regional Research Seminar for Arab States ("The Impact of Globalization on Higher Education and Research in the Arab States"), Rabat, Morocco, 24 and 25 May 2007.

Hazelkorn, E. (2009). "The Impact of Global Rankings on Higher Education Research and the Production of Knowledge". Occasional Paper. UNESCO Forum on Higher Education, Research and Knowledge. Paris: UNESCO.

International Association of Universities (IAU). (1987). 6th Round Table Harare Statement, Harare, Zimbabwe, 1987, in response to the World Bank's *Financing Education in Developing Countries: An Exploration of Policy Options*.

Kelo, M., Teichler, U. and Waechter, B. (eds.) (2006). *EURODATA – Student Mobility in European Higher Education*. Bonn: Lemmens.

KENET. (2007). *E-Readiness Survey of Higher Education Institutions in Kenya* 2006, Kenya Education Network, Nairobi, Kenya.

Khoon, K.A. (2005). Hallmark of a World-Class University. *College Student Journal*. Retrieved April 10, 2007.

King, Banking on Knowledge: the new knowledge projects of the World Bank *Compare*, 32 (3), pp. 312-326.

Kuznetsov, Y. (2006). *Diaspora Networks and the International Migration of Skills: How Countries Can Draw on their Talent Abroad*. Washington, DC: World Bank Institute Development Studies.

Lundvall, B-A. *National Innovation Systems: Toward a Theory of Interactive Learning*, London: Pinter Publishers.

Lyotard, J.F. (1984). *The Post-modern Condition: A Report on Knowledge*. Minneapolis: University of Minnesota Press.

McKeown, R. (2006). Reorienting Colleges and Universities to Address Sustainability. *Globalization and Education for Sustainable Development: Sustaining the Future*. International Conference, Nagoya, Japan, 28-29.

McMahon, W. (2002). *Education and development: Measuring the social benefits*. Oxford: Oxford University Press.

Mouton, J. (2007). "UNESCO Forum Special Initiative: Study on National Research Systems. Regional Report on Asian Countries". Paris: UNESCO (mimeo).

OECD. (1996). *The Knowledge-based Economy*. Paris: Organisation for Economic Cooperation and Development.

____. (2008). *Reporting Directives for the Creditor Reporting System: Corrigendum on Programme-Based Approaches*. DCD/DAC(2007)39 FINAL/Corr2. Paris: OECD.

Perkin, H. (1991). "History of Universities". In: Altbach, P. (ed.), *International Higher Education: An Encyclopaedia*. Garland: New York, pp. 169-204.

Psacharopoulos, G. (1989). Time trends of the returns to education: Cross-national evidence, *Economics of Education Review,* vol. 8, no. 3:225-39.

____. and Patrinos, H. A. (2002). *Returns to Investment in Education: A Further Update*. Policy Research Working Paper Series, World Bank.

Reichert, S. *The Rise of Knowledge Regions: Emerging Opportunites and Challenges for Universities*, Brussels: EUA.

Remoe, S.O. (2005).*Governance of Innovation Systems*, Vol. 1. Synthesis Report, Paris: OECD.

Rivža, B. and Teichler, U. (2007). "The Changing Role of Student Mobility". *Higher Education Policy* (20) 4, 457-476.

Sarason, S.. *The Unpredictable Failure of Educational Reform. Can we Change the Course Before it's Too Late?*. San Francisco, CA: Jossey-Bass.

Stadtman, V.A. (1980). *Academic Adaptations: Higher Education Prepares for the 1980s and 1990s*. San Francisco: Jossey Bass.

Steiner-Khamsi, G. (ed.). *The Global Politics of Educational Borrowing and Lending*. New York, NY: Teachers College Press.

Teichler, U. (2004). "The Changing Debate on Internationalisation of Higher Education". *Higher Education* (48), 5-26.

UNESCO. (2005). *Towards Knowledge Societies*. First UNESCO World Report, with preface by Koïchiro Matsuura, Director-General of UNESCO. Paris: UNESCO Publishing.

____. (2006). *Revitalizing science and technology training institutions in Africa : the way forward.* UNESCO, Nairobi.

____. (2006. *Global Education Digest 2006: Comparing Education Statistics across the World*. Montreal: UNESCO Institute for Statistics.

____. (2007). *Summary Reports of the 2007 Regional Research Seminars: Main Findings & Conclusions*. Paris: UNESCO.

World Bank *Lifelong Learning for a Global Knowledge Economy*, Washington, DC:

____. *Expanding Opportunities and Building Competences of Young People*. A New Agenda for Secondary Education. World Bank, DC: Washington.

Yusuf, S. and K. Nabeshima (2007). *How Universities Promote Economic Growth*. Washington D.C., The World Bank.

Zakri, A. H. (2008). "Research Universities in the 21st Century: Global Challenges and Local Implications". In: Teichler, U. and Vessuri, H. (eds.), *Universities as Centres of Research and Knowledge Creation: An Endangered Species?* Rotterdam: Sense Publishers, pp. 41-46.

Index